JOURNEYS IN
FAMILY HISTORY

JOURNEYS IN FAMILY HISTORY

Exploring your Past ● *Finding your Ancestors*

David Hey

the national archives

First published in 2004 by

The National Archives
Kew, Richmond
Surrey, TW9 4DU, UK

www.nationalarchives.gov.uk/

The National Archives was formed when the Public
Record Office and Historical Manuscripts
Commission combined in April 2003.

A catalogue record for this book is available
from the British Library.

ISBN 1 903365 61 9

Jacket illustrations
Front: Richard Marles (see also p. 17), proprietor of a
carriage business in Exeter, escorting a family party in
the early twentieth century
Back: Upper Works at Coalbrookdale, 1758;
late-Victorian family photograph of an unknown
subject (see also pp. 41 and 186)

Pages designed and typeset by
Carnegie Publishing, Lancaster, Lancashire

Printed in the UK by
CPI Colour Books, Blantyre, Glasgow

Contents

Preface   ix

Acknowledgements   xii

Introduction

    Getting started   2

    The internet   8

1 Into Recent Memory (1900–)

Exploring your Past

Introduction   14

Families   16

Houses   18

Work   22

Poverty   28

Stability and mobility   32

The First World War   34

Finding your Ancestors

Gravestones   36

Photographs   41

Newspapers   44

Land surveys   46

First World War records   49

2 Through the Nineteenth Century (1800–1900)

Exploring your Past

Introduction   56
Urban and rural   58
Farming   62
Industry   66
Families   72
Stability and mobility   76
Emigrants and immigrants   79
Houses   83
Progress   88

Finding your Ancestors

Civil registration   92
Census returns   106
Trade and commercial directories   116
Military records   120
Education records   131
Enclosure and tithe awards   133
The New Poor Law, 1834–1930   138
Working men   142
Prison records   144
Protestant Nonconformity   146
Roman Catholicism   150
Jewish records   152

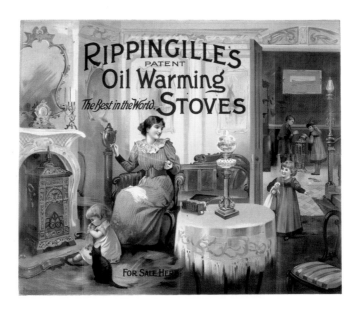

3 Making Early Connections (1550–1800)

Exploring your Past

Introduction 156

Urban and rural 158

Families 161

Houses 166

Rich and poor 169

Core families and 'country' 173

Kinship and inheritance 178

Servants and apprentices 180

Migration 182

Work 185

Finding your Ancestors

Parish registers 190

The Old Poor Law 204

Wills and other probate records 211

Apprenticeship and freemen records 222

Land tax assessments 227

Hearth tax returns 229

Protestation returns, 1641–2 234

Muster rolls and militia lists 236

Courts of Chancery, Exchequer, Star Chamber, and Requests 239

The legal profession 241

Title deeds 242

4 Back to the Middle Ages (–1550)

Exploring your Past

Introduction   246
The Black Death   248
Families   252
Houses   254
The countryside   256
Towns   258
Stability and mobility   262
The origins of surnames   266

Finding your Ancestors

Manor court records   272
Subsidies and poll taxes   280
Other medieval records in print   284
Heraldry   286

Resource Bank
    Useful addresses and websites   290
    Further reading   297

Picture sources   300
Index   302

Preface

The last few years have seen remarkable developments in information technology. In the comfort of our homes we can use a personal computer to browse through a census return on a CD-ROM or on the internet, we can turn to a microfiche reader to search local parish registers that have been transcribed by members of a family history society, and we can click on to websites to see which taxation returns for our area are held by the National Archives. Several websites offer basic guidance or put us in touch with fellow searchers. If we don't own our own machine, we can learn how to use one at a record office or reference library and it is still possible (though more time-consuming) to trace a family tree in the ways that we did twenty or thirty years ago. Even the most skilled computer buff still has to book a place at the local record office and search through the archives. We still have to know which records to look at, to learn how to read various styles of old handwriting, and to understand what the documents are telling us. The compensation for all the toil is the joy of discovery – the sudden appearance of the name that we have long been looking for. We have all been in search rooms when a neighbour has suddenly punched the air with his fist or jumped up with excitement. Record offices these days do not have the calm, restrained air that they possessed

when I was a young man, too well-mannered (or perhaps just scared of the dragon archivists) to speak louder than a whisper.

The techniques of the genealogist remain the traditional ones that have been refined over the years. We have to proceed backwards in time, from the known to the unknown, proving firm links in the chain. All too often we meet others who do not use such rigorous methods and who loudly assert their descent from a famous or infamous family in the past, preferably someone who is named in the Domesday Book. Such people have never seen a copy of the Domesday Book and would be bewildered by it if they did. Believing in a fictitious family tree is an ancient vice and one that is shared by people from all over the world. I have come across a surprising number of Australians who claim to be descendants of Ned Kelly and I have never met an American who claims that his ancestor was a transported convict or an indentured servant rather than a passenger on the Mayflower. Their English equivalents have a fondness for supposed Huguenot ancestors or for an aristocratic connection 'on the wrong side of the blanket'. But the truth of the matter is that in the Middle Ages most people were peasants and in recent centuries they were industrial workers. They are the ones from whom most of us are descended.

The methods of genealogy are well established, but a new technique is helping us to discover our origins. A spin-off from the remarkable advances in molecular biology and medicine after the discovery of the structure of DNA has been the genetic tests that have proved whether or not people with the same surnames share a common ancestry. After the initial excitement, it has gradually dawned on us that funded laboratories that will do all these tests nationwide are not going to be built in the foreseeable future. But the technique of determining the structure of the male Y-chromosome, which is passed down from father to son, has offered dramatic support to those who have long argued that very many surnames have a single-family origin. It has also shown that we must not make simple assumptions that all surnames of an unusual form are connected even if they are found in different parts of the country. We must always examine the local circumstances under which family names were formed.

Following the male line down the centuries is the most obvious option for the family historian, but it is by no means the only one. We get a far better sense of our genetic inheritance from tracing all 16 of our great-great-grandparents. I have ancestors from all three Ridings of Yorkshire, but a quarter of me comes from Somerset people

who migrated to Yorkshire in search of work during the great agricultural depression of late Victorian times. My wife's family were Londoners, but only half of her great-great-grandparents were born there. The rest came from the New Forest, Lincolnshire, Essex and Sussex. London has always drawn people from all over the country. Fitting the movements of our ancestors into the larger picture of national social history is an essential part of the fascination of family history. We should not be satisfied with a list of names and dates.

We have to be prepared to accept what we find, even if it is very different from what we had been led to believe from older members of the family. A friend from Barnsley, proud of his Yorkshire background, said to me, 'It's a funny business, this family history. I was prepared to find illegitimacy, as we all know it was common, but what I've found is far worse. I've proved beyond doubt that we come from Lancashire'.

Our illusions may be shattered by our discoveries, but ultimately the truth is more satisfying. We cannot choose our ancestors. The journey is one of personal discovery. Tracing the lives of our forebears is the best way of studying the past that I know. We are pursuing paths that no-one has followed before, learning as we go along about the shared human experience in distant times.

We enter worlds that in many ways were very different from our own, but find that human nature has not altered. We rejoice at the triumphs of our ancestors and sympathize with their despair. An interest in family history is not triggered by a desire to find firm roots in an insecure world, as some glib 'commentators' suggest. The people who use the resources of the Family Records Centre or of record offices up and down the land look secure and sensible enough to me. The remarkable surge in the popularity of family history is the result of better facilities and more leisure time to pursue this interest. People have always been interested in their ancestors, in every part of the world and at all periods of time. Nowadays, the rich resources of the National Archives and local record offices are readily available to anyone. Tracing a family tree has never been easier. This book offers a guide to the major collections of records and explains how to proceed on the journey.

A group of boys outside the shops of W. S. Stanley, Bagshot, Surrey, in 1904.

Acknowledgements

I give my warm thanks to all the team who have worked on the production of this book, starting with Sheila Knight for her editorial advice and encouragement through every stage of the process. I much appreciate the contributions of Amanda Bevan of the National Archives and Dave Annal of the Family Records Centre, who commented on the entire text, saving me from errors, and bringing me up to date with the rapid changes in cataloguing. The attractive appearance of the book is largely due to the picture researchers, Peter Leek, Deborah Pownall and Julia Harris-Voss; the jacket designers, Penny Jones and Michael Morris; and the text designer, Alistair Hodge of Carnegie Publishing.

Special thanks are due to Jane Parker for the loan of photographs from her album.

For the production and marketing processes I would like to thank Rosemary Amos, Charlotte Hulse, Sian Morris, Lisa Kenwright, Helen Turner and Nora Talty-Nangle.

Then there are a large number of staff at the National Archives whom I thank for their time and expertise in helping in numerous different ways: Adrian Ailes, Hugh Alexander, Brian Carter, Phaedra Casey, Elaine Collins, Lynne Cookson, David Crook, Karen Grannum, Alistair Hanson, Paul Johnson, Roger Kershaw, Rose Mitchell, Stephen O'Connor, Bruno Pappalardo, Michael Parker, William Spencer, Nigel Taylor and Helen Watts.

For Pat

Introduction

Getting started   2
The internet   8

Getting started

'Old lady reading',
1902.

The obvious way to start tracing your family tree is to collect and write down what you already know, or think you know, about your family history and then see what your relations have to contribute. Interviewing the oldest of your close relatives is a task that should never be delayed. You must give this occasion some thought, prepare some questions, and take along any old photographs or other mementoes that you might have, for they are a wonderful aid to memory and conversation. Make your relatives feel part of the adventure by

providing information as well as receiving it and by keeping them up to date with your findings. Above all, write everything down and note where you have got the information. This practice will stand you in good stead when you start your enquiries in record offices.

Of course, what you are told by an aged relative may turn out to be untrue. Many a family has a romantic story, such as being descended illegitimately from someone rich and important, which has no basis in fact.

The truth of the matter is that most of us had working-class ancestors who led fairly humdrum lives. But although family memories are not always accurate, they often suggest lines of enquiry and sometimes explain matters that are not dealt with in the records, such as when and why a move was made to a distant place. Your relatives may well have photographs, certificates, funeral cards, newspaper obituaries and other memorabilia that can be copied, if they are willing. Some people might be uncomfortable about aspects of their family history, but most are only too ready to talk about their ancestors and any scandals that they got into. Women usually know far more about the history of their wider family than do the men and throughout the ages some have taken on the role of custodian of this knowledge. My mother was the person whom all our relatives turned to for information and humorous stories about great-aunts and uncles and distant cousins. I could not fail to be interested in family history from an early age.

Which line?

You soon have to decide which particular line to pursue. This is a matter of personal choice, but most people begin with their father's line so as to follow the history of the surname. It is much more difficult to trace a direct female line. I have been able to follow the Heys back over ten generations, but have managed to trace the female line over only five, through the surnames Batty,

Webster, Kell, Dean, and (possibly) Pickering. Once you have got stuck with a name, it is natural to turn to another line. A more balanced view of your family history is obtained once you have traced your 16 great-great-grandparents. Easier said than done, of course, but well worth the effort. Beyond that, the genetic connections with your ancestors become increasingly diluted, though it is still of great interest to try to identify the original home of your surname back in the Middle Ages. The recent advances in the study of the DNA structure of the male Y-chromosome that help

'Family register' template, 1898.

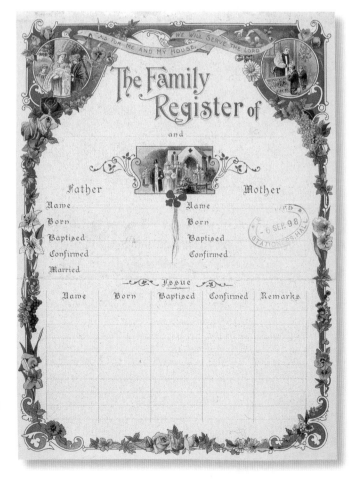

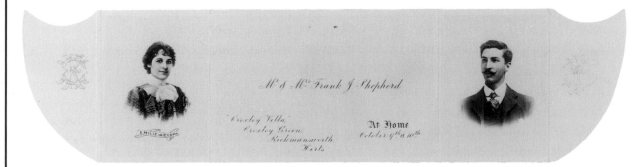

Mr and Mrs Frank J. Shepherd 'At Home', Croxley Villa, Croxley Green, Rickmansworth, Herts, 9/10 October 1901.

determine whether or not everyone with the same surname shares a common ancestor are an enormous stimulus to this line of enquiry. The other direction for research, once a basic family tree has been compiled, is to put flesh on the bare bones of our nineteenth- and twentieth-century ancestors, by discovering as much as we can about their lives and the local communities in which they lived. In this way, we shall learn a great deal, not only about family and local history but about the social and economic history of our country.

Getting organized

🖝 A golden rule is to work backwards in time, starting with yourself. I once knew someone who began with a famous person in the past and proved a descent to himself, but this method rarely works.

🖝 It is good practice to make a careful record of your information and its source, for you may need to check it later and some of the clues that it provides may not be obvious at first sight.

🖝 Keeping systematic records helps us to

succeed in our research. We each have our own ways of doing things and it is pointless recommending a single approach, but the use of separate notebooks or files for each branch of the family is obviously desirable.

🖝 Some excellent computer software programs are available: Reunion for Macs, and Brother's Keeper, Family Historian, Family Origins, Family Tree Maker and Generations for PCs.

🖝 It is also sensible to sketch family trees at regular intervals, even if they are tentative, for they highlight gaps in your knowledge and suggest possible connections.

🖝 Some trees need to display only the basic information, so that we can see a clear line of descent. Others may include everyone on a particular branch within a certain period of time. Adopt methods that suit your own findings, for the number of children varies so much from one family to another and over time that what might suit one researcher may not be the best method for you.

🖝 The standard genealogical abbreviations that are used on family trees are:

b.	born
bapt.	baptized
d.	died
d.unm.	died unmarried
d.s.p.	(from the Latin *decessit sine prole*) died without children
dau.	daughter
s.	son
div.	divorced
unm.	unmarried
=	married
l.	left descendants.

Societies

Joining your local family history society (and, in time, others in those parts of the country where your ancestors lived), and perhaps attending an adult education class, will bring you into contact with fellow enthusiasts who will share information and useful tips. Societies have regular meetings and their own journals and many have published editions of local records, such as indexes of parish registers, census returns, and monumental inscriptions. You can usually find their address at your local library or on the website <www.genuki. org.uk/Societies>.

☛ The national Federation of Family History Societies publishes cheap and useful guides to records and a magazine, *Family History News and Digest*.

☛ The Society of Genealogists (founded 1911) is based at 14 Charterhouse Buildings, Goswell Road, London EC1M 7BA. It organizes courses, lectures and visits, promotes two annual family history fairs, and publishes *Genealogists' Magazine* and the journal *Computers in Genealogy*, as well as the *My Ancestor was … * series of guides. Its extensive collection of material is particularly valuable for the long period before civil registration started in 1837.

Visiting a record office or library

Soon, the decision has to be made to visit a local record office, the National Archives or the Family Records Centre to search the enormous amount of material that is available. All the English and Welsh counties and most of the metropolitan districts have their own record offices. They are listed at the end of this book. Local material can also be found in a variety of other locations such as museums, heritage centres, and local history collections at county libraries. In most cases admission is free and professional archivists will advise you on which records to search.

☛ Arrive prepared with as much information as you have already gathered and the questions which you hope to answer.

The National Archives.

› It is advisable to check opening hours and to find out whether you need to book a microfilm or microfiche reader or a computer terminal.

› You will need to obtain a reader's ticket, so take a driving licence or some other means of identification.

› Bring a notebook and pencil (for pens are not allowed) and note all the document reference numbers from which you have obtained information or have searched to no avail.

› Photocopies of documents and print-outs of microfiche or computer records may usually be purchased.

› Much of your first visit will be taken up with finding your way around the catalogues and indexes and with familiarizing yourself with the practical arrangements, such as filling in request slips or remembering the times that documents are brought out of storage.

› In some parts of the country it may be practical to visit one of the Latter-day Saints (LDS) Church's Family History Centres. These welcome family historians, whether or not they are members of the Mormon Church, and make available any records that have been microfilmed, including census returns and parish registers, as well as the International Genealogical Index (IGI).

Making progress

We must proceed as carefully as if we were proving a case before a court of law. It is not enough to find a baptism with the right name, in about the right place at the right time, and assume we have found our ancestor. We must look at all the other records that are available, to see if the same name crops up elsewhere and to check that the person whom we found did not die as an infant or child. If our information comes from a transcription, either in printed form or on the internet, we must check it against the original document. To prove a line of descent, we may have to search through many different types of records. It takes time to work out where to look and how to link different types of records: this is the craft of genealogy. Sometimes, we are defeated by the impossibility of deciding between two rival candidates.

How far might we realistically expect to get back in time? Many lines will be difficult, if not impossible, to prove beyond the late eighteenth or nineteenth century, simply because of the gaps in the records. We will do well to get back to the sixteenth or seventeenth centuries and exceptionally well to prove a line, step by step, back into the Middle Ages. Many will claim a descent from someone recorded in the distant past, but to claim is not the same as to prove.

The Enquiry Desk at the Family Records Centre.

The internet

The most radical change in the field of family history during the past few years has been the enormous growth in the use of the internet. It is now easier than ever to find information or to contact others who share your interests. Most local family history societies have websites, over 20,000 mailing lists are devoted to genealogy, and numerous newsgroups can be contacted. The essential book of guidance is P. Christian, *The Genealogist's Internet* (The National Archives, 2003).

Peter Christian makes the point that if you are only just beginning to trace your family tree, you will have plenty to do offline before you take full advantage of what is available online. You won't find much information online about ancestors who were born in the twentieth century. It is only when you get back 100 years, and privacy restrictions on records are lifted, that significant amounts of source material become available on the internet. Of course, it is still perfectly possible to do everything without switching on a computer. The chief attraction of the internet is that, while it may not as yet display many original records, it offers a great deal of help, advice and contacts. Family historians who live a long way from the homes of their ancestors will be particularly grateful for its services.

The amount of genealogical material on the internet is growing so rapidly that any information in a printed publication is in danger of quickly becoming out of date. Web pages come and go, but some are now well established. The best starting point is <www.genuki.org.uk>, which has the most

comprehensive collection of online information about family history for the British Isles. GENUKI is run by volunteers and is a non-commercial site. A number of pages are devoted to general information, beginning with Frequently Asked Questions and how to get started. These are followed by pages devoted to individual general topics, e.g. military records. The county pages provide links to the websites of county record offices, local family history societies, county surname interest lists, etc. National genealogical organizations and all relevant mailing lists are also noted and GENUKI provides the main newsletter for British family historians. If your genealogical interests extend beyond the British Isles, the most comprehensive site is Cyndi's List at <www.cyndislist.com>.

The leading national organizations also have websites that include guidance for the beginner:

- ☞ The Family Records Centre has a website at <www.familyrecords. gov.uk/frc> which gives advice.

- ☞ The National Archives, at <www.nationalarchives.gov.uk>, has a link to 'Pathways to the Past', which has a family history section.

introductory material on <www.familysearch.org> under 'Search', then 'Research Guidance'.

- ☞ The Society of Genealogists has a number of leaflets online at <www.sog.org.uk/leaflets/>, but these are not designed as a coherent introduction.

We must not think that the internet will solve all our problems. It provides help and guidance, but at the moment relatively few original sources can be seen online. Digitizing the records does not pose great technical problems, but images take up a lot of disk space and they are of limited use if they are not transcribed and indexed, tasks that take an enormous amount of time. Within a few years, however, a large

http://www.nationalarchives.gov.uk/default-content.htm

- ☞ The Federation of Family History Societies provides a number of leaflets at <www.ffhs.org.uk/General/Help>, including one on 'First Steps in Family History'.

- ☞ The Church of Jesus Christ of Latter-day Saints (LDS) has extensive

proportion of the indexes of civil registration records and the census enumerators' books that are over 100 years old, together with an increasing number of other genealogical sources, will become available. For most of us it will be cheaper and more convenient to use an online service than to travel to a record office.

Like all transcripts and indexes that are prepared by knowledgeable amateurs or by clerical workers, most of whom do not have specialist skills in palaeography, those available online are subject to errors. The internet is like a library that is stocked with information on where to find original sources and with transcriptions of some of them. It is not a substitute for seeing the original sources in a record office.

Record offices and libraries

Record offices and libraries usually have good online facilities. If you use the online finding aids before visiting a record office you will be able to use your time there more profitably.

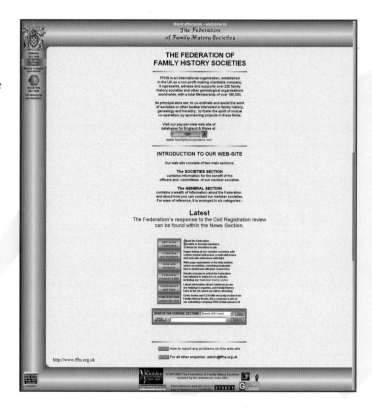

☞ Welsh archives are listed at <www.llgc.org.uk/cac/>. The Scottish archives are listed at <www.scotlandspeople.gov.uk>.

☞ One of the most important facilities provided by the National Archives is the Catalogues page at <www.nationalarchives.gov.uk>, which has 9 million entries that can be browsed or searched, but although the online catalogue is straightforward to use, it cannot simplify the organization of records, which has been developed by different government departments since the Middle Ages. Research Information Leaflets are available online for all the most popular research area (indexed in the catalogue under Guided Search), and A. Bevan, *Tracing Your Ancestors in the Public Record Office*

(Public Record Office, 2002) is a helpful guide to the thousands of sources for family history in the National Archives. As well as publishing research advice, the National Archives has an enquiry desk to help you progress in your research there.

☞ The simplest way to find information about local record offices is to visit the GENUKI site or that at <www.hmc.gov.uk/archon>.

☞ The national project, Access to Archives (A2A) at <www.a2a.org.uk>, names catalogues of archives in England, other than those at the National Archives. Typing in the place-name 'Derbyshire', for example, produces a list of 723 catalogues.

☞ The website for public libraries is at <www.familia.org.uk>, a comprehensive guide to genealogical holdings, with a page for every local authority.

 Searches by surname or place can be made at <www.familysearch.org/Eng/Search/frameset_search.asp>. It is also worth trying <www.one-name.org/> to see whether any member of the Guild of One-Name Studies has researched your surname.

Family historians who are looking for ancestors in places with which they are not familiar will need to turn to the definitive gazetteer provided by the Ordnance Survey at <www.ordnancesurvey.co.uk/products/50kgazetter>, which has a database of all the places that are listed on the Landranger series of maps. The site's Get-a-map facility at <www.ordnancesurvey.co.uk/

oswebsite/getamap> enables you to find a map from the 1:50,000 and 1:250,00 series that is centred on a particular place. You can search by place-name, postcode, or O.S. grid reference. The maps are free for personal use. The complete collection of six-inch O.S. maps for the whole of England, Wales and Scotland, dating from 1846 to 1899, is available on <www.old-maps.co.uk>. The best starting point for street maps of cities is the relevant GENUKI county page.

The internet can provide only some of the information that you need to trace a family tree. It is tempting to assume descent from a source that is available online, but you need to check this against the original record and to search other possibilities in the archives. Nor should you take on trust pedigrees that others have put online. They may be accurate, but equally they may not.

A2A | Access to Archives | The English strand of the UK archives network | Search the Database ► Search

Home | Search A2A | About A2A | New A2A Users | Family History | Research Interests | Useful Links | Contact Us

Troubleshooting | Site Map

Welcome to A2A

The A2A database contains catalogues describing archives held throughout England and dating from the 900s to the present day. Click the Search button to search these catalogues.

A2A does not yet offer a full description of *all* the archives in England, but it is regularly updated, so **revisit often** for newly-included catalogues.

A2A has a new URL! Please use www.a2a.org.uk next time you visit!

A2A usage since launch: **2.7 million** searches / **5.6 million** catalogue downloads

What's New?

The A2A database was last updated on **12 November 2003** and currently contains more than **5.7 million** catalogue entries from 335 record offices and other repositories.

For more details see the list of catalogues which are new this month or the latest news from the Central Team: A2A Update

For information on what to look out for in the future, see A2A Projects in Progress

  the national archives

BRITISH LIBRARY | the national archives | Supported by the **Heritage Lottery Fund** | ISB

Copyright © 2001-2004, The National Archives - Legal Disclaimer - About cookies

right: *William Harrison Ainsworth; Engraving by E. Finden, 1844*
Birmingham City Archives, ref: MS 168/114

ENGLAND & IRELAND
· VIA HOLYHEAD ·

1 Into Recent Memory (1900–)

For we are the people of England, that never have spoken yet.

G. K. Chesterton, *The Secret People* (1915)

EXPLORING YOUR PAST

Introduction	14
Families	16
Houses	18
Work	22
Poverty	28
Stability and mobility	32
The First World War	34

FINDING YOUR ANCESTORS

Gravestones	36
Photographs	41
Newspapers	44
Land surveys	46
First World War records	49

Introduction

Images of our children and grandchildren have been captured on hundreds of occasions in colour photographs or, nowadays, on video. By contrast, our immediate ancestors in the early years of the twentieth century were rarely caught on camera, and when they were, the occasions were usually formal and the images stilted. We gaze at them as they appeared at only one or two moments in time. Yet these elusive images are precious to us. In the age before photography, all we usually have – unless we are lucky enough to possess a portrait – are names and dates and some information about where our ancestors dwelt and the ways in which they earned their living. We have no way of knowing what they looked like.

George Hey, aged two, in 1906.

This photograph, taken in 1906, is one of the few that I have of my father before he was married. When I was young we laughed at the photographs of our parents and grandparents, for fashions of dress change so quickly. Now my children laugh at mine. No boy would nowadays be dressed like my father was at the age of two, nor would they clutch a toy parrot, but my father's appearance was not unusual at the time. His father was a tall man with a beard and a stern frown, who farmed a 15-acre

smallholding and worked as a waggoner at the local corn mill. His mother was the daughter of a Somerset farm labourer who had migrated north to work at a coke oven attached to a coal mine. They were typical of the respectable working classes who formed 75–80 per cent of the population of England and Wales in late-Victorian and Edwardian times. Most of us have ancestors who shared the same standard of living and who lived intensely local lives within a neighbourhood that extended as far as the nearest towns. Many of them spoke of this neighbourhood as their 'country', just as their ancestors had since time immemorial. They knew little of the England or Wales that stretched beyond.

These local lives have to be set in the wider context of British social and economic history if we are to understand them fully.

IN BRIEF

- Most of us have working-class ancestors, for at this time they formed 75–80 per cent of the population.

- They lived intensely local lives and most people stayed in the neighbourhood that they knew.

- Standards of living rose from the 1870s onwards.

- We need to place these ancestors in the wider context of British social and economic history if we are to understand their lives.

My father grew up to earn his living as a coal miner and in later life he moved two or three miles to the nearest market town to live in a council house, a type that was almost unheard of when he was born. The British economy was based on coal and by the First World War over 1 million men were employed in the mines. Coal mining was by far the largest single occupation in England and Wales, so many of us have miners on our family trees. The industry had grown enormously since the mid-nineteenth century and the pit village had become a special type of new community in northern and midland England and south Wales. Mining remained a sweat and muscle job with picks and shovels and the miners prided themselves as the leaders of the working class. But industries come and go and by the end of the twentieth century only a few thousand miners were still employed in the pits. Most of the greatest coalfields of the nineteenth century are no longer worked. The pit villages lasted for only three or four generations in their original form.

Studio photographs show our ancestors in their best clothes. Only when they were caught unawares in street scenes or as children playing in the countryside do we see them in their everyday attire. The young were often dressed in ill-fitting hand-me-downs or clothes bought cheaply at a jumble sale, the adults in drab uniformity. The working classes were instantly recognizable from their clothes. By today's standards, they appear overdressed. The men rarely took off their waistcoats and hats; the women wore long dresses and aprons, shawls, and stiff underwear to keep out the cold. But standards of living had been rising since the 1870s and most families could afford a new set of clothes and footwear when required. In northern England the annual Whitsuntide Sunday school procession had become the occasion to parade in one's best outfit. Multiple chain stores and the 'co-operative' in the local market town offered the latest fashions at affordable prices. In the photographer's studio men sat stiffly in their suits, displaying the watch chain that hung from their waistcoats, while the women prided themselves on their embroidery and frills. This is how they wanted the world to view them.

A formal family group in the 1920s. Mrs W. H. Bulley (1886–1976) is shown with her three children: William Richard (1908–86), Reginald (1912–86) and Beatrice Jane (b. 1915). This photograph, and the one on p. 17, are from a family album.

Families

As the Victorian age drew to a close in 1901, large families were becoming a thing of the past. People were marrying later or not at all, and birth control was practised more widely. By 1911 the median average age at first marriage for women was 24.5, compared with 23.2 in 1881 and the proportion of English women who never married had reached 16 per cent. The national population was still rising, but the pace was slowing down. In 1901 the population of England and Wales stood at 32.5 million, by 1911 it had reached 36.1 million. After the First World War, the rise was less dramatic and cities stopped growing at the intense rate that they had achieved during the reign of Queen Victoria.

The 1911 census was the first to record fertility by social class. By then, the average number of children in an aristocratic family had fallen to 2.5 and in a middle-class one to 2.8. Working-class families were larger, though they too had fallen in size over the previous generation. By 1911 textile workers had 3.19 children on average, unskilled workers 3.92, farm labourers 3.99 and miners 4.33. Average figures mask the range of family size within occupational groups, but they are nevertheless revealing. Families also varied in size from one place to another, for the general practice of the neighbour-hood was often a more important influence

than the father's job. Working-class men and women often chose their marriage partners from the same occupational groups and the upper and middle classes expected their children to marry only with their social equals. Many of us find that our ancestors were working-class on all sides of the family.

Families would have been larger had it not been for the considerable number of those

IN BRIEF

☞ Family sizes fell noticeably towards the end of the Victorian era, and after the First World War population growth slowed down.

☞ Infant mortality rates remained high, especially in the towns and industrial districts.

☞ Medical discoveries, public health measures, better diet and more spacious living conditions all helped to prolong life.

☞ Present-day society is far more elderly than it was before the First World War.

Leicestershire (144) and significantly lower in Wiltshire (91), Hertfordshire (92), Dorset (92), Westmorland (97) and Surrey (105). A change for the better occurred during the same decade when infant mortality rates across the country fell by nearly a quarter, but the large industrial cities remained black-spots. Children in the countryside tended to live longer and so on the whole rural families were larger than those in the towns. Medical advances, public health reforms, better diet and less crowded houses all played a part in extending the expectancy of life. Between 1901 and 1951 the proportion of the population of England and Wales aged 65 and over more than doubled, from 4.7 per cent to 11 per cent. Society today is far more elderly in its composition than it was in the world familiar to our immediate ancestors in the years before the First World War.

who died as infants or young children. Between 1901 and 1905 the infant mortality rate in England and Wales remained stubbornly high at 138 deaths for every 1,000 births. The rates were much higher than average in Lancashire (163), Durham (157), the East Riding of Yorkshire (152), Warwickshire (152), Staffordshire (151) and

This photograph of the wedding of William Henry Bulley (1879–1952) and Beatrice Jane Marles (1886–1976) in Exeter on 17 September 1907 shows the groom in the centre of the back row behind his wife. The bride's father stands next to the groom and her mother is seated at the right-hand end of the front row. The men are hatless, in marked contrast to the ladies.

Houses

RIGHT
An advertisement for one of the cookers that came onto the market once gas was laid on and slot meters were widely installed in homes from the 1890s.

Each town still had its dreadful slums, the legacy of cheap and speculative building in the early Victorian era. Even the newest houses were packed together in brick or stone terraces that formed monotonous streets in working-class districts. In 1911 Lady Florence Bell's investigators reported that most houses in Middlesbrough had a kitchen or living room that opened straight from the street, a parlour or bedroom behind, and a little scullery at the back, with two bedrooms above. She thought that the space was sufficient for parents with two or three children but not for the larger families that were often found there. On the eve of the First World War Birmingham had more than 40,000 back-to-backs, over 40,000 houses without any drainage or water tap, and nearly 60,000 without a separate lavatory. Their condition was typical of the houses in towns and cities that had mushroomed in the industrial districts of England and Wales during the reign of Victoria.

Park Road, Port Sunlight, in 1913. William Hesketh Lever (later Lord Leverhulme) had completed his model community by 1900. The 400 houses had three or four bedrooms and outside water closets. Influenced by the Arts and Crafts movement, they set new standards for working-class housing.

This photograph from the James Ramsay MacDonald collection was taken between 1906 and 1909 and entitled 'The Worst Street in London'. The street led off Grays Inn Road and was disowned by the two parishes of Clerkenwell and Holborn. In his Life and Labour of the People in London *(1903) Charles Booth wrote about the 'roughness and drunkenness', the dirty children and the 'towzled haired women', standing at open doors, bare-armed' that he saw there.*

But housing conditions were better than they had been a generation or two earlier. By 1911 most families, except those who lived in the remote countryside, had their own supply of piped water and the majority of houses in 85 of the 95 English towns that had a population of over 50,000 had their own water closets. The north-eastern towns of Darlington, Gateshead, South Shields and Stockton were the only ones where over half the houses still had privies in the backyard. The rate of conversion had accelerated between 1907 and 1911, during which time 9,785 privies had been demolished in Sheffield, 7,758 in Bradford, and 6,894 in Oldham. Meanwhile, gas lighting and gas cookers had replaced paraffin lamps and open fires, especially in the towns, though many homes were still without these conveniences. Electric lighting did not become widely used at home or work until the 1930s.

The model by-laws that had been issued by the Local Government Board in 1877 were generally adopted. They insisted on wider streets and more space at the rear of houses. The working-class suburbs that developed when men and women were able to travel to work cheaply on the trams were more spacious than their Victorian predecessors. A small number of model housing schemes by paternalist employers – at Port Sunlight and Bournville and at New Earswick and Woodlands in Yorkshire – were influential in setting standards, with lower-density housing, varied architectural styles, and curving streets instead of unimaginative grid patterns of uniform buildings. Three-bedroomed cottages were now built for working-class people in pleasant environments. These schemes were the forerunners of the Garden City Movement: Letchworth (1903), Hampstead Garden Suburb (1907),

IN BRIEF

- Housing conditions were improved by piped water, water closets, and gas lighting and cookers.
- But every town still had its slums and the condition of rural cottages was often lamentable.
- Model housing schemes pointed the way to a better future, but few council estates were built before the 1920s.
- Transport improvements encouraged suburban growth, and London expanded at a tremendous rate.

Anchor site housing scheme, Darwen, Lancashire. The plan of an estate that was built between 1920 and 1926, drawn up by the borough engineer. Such schemes were made possible by the Housing Act (1919), which provided state subsidies for the first time.

and Welwyn Garden City (1920). Meanwhile, the Housing of the Working Classes Act (1890) authorized local councils to buy and demolish slum properties and to replace them with houses built by public subsidies. By 1914, however, even the most active authorities like London and Liverpool had managed to re-house less than two per cent of their populations. Over Britain as a whole, the 24,000 houses owned by local authorities in 1914 accounted for less than 0.5 per cent of the total housing stock.

In the countryside, cottages were not packed together but their condition was often

lamentable. The estate villages built by enlightened squires stood in marked contrast to the mud-and-thatch dwellings that were found in neighbouring parishes. In 1911 Francis Heath revisited the places that he had seen on a tour of the West Country in 1873 and concluded that many improvements had been made. He attributed these benefits to the sharp drop in the rural population that had eased the old problem of overcrowding and to better sanitation. The Royal Commission on the Housing of the Population (1917) nevertheless found unsatisfactory conditions in every part of the countryside. Many farmhouses and

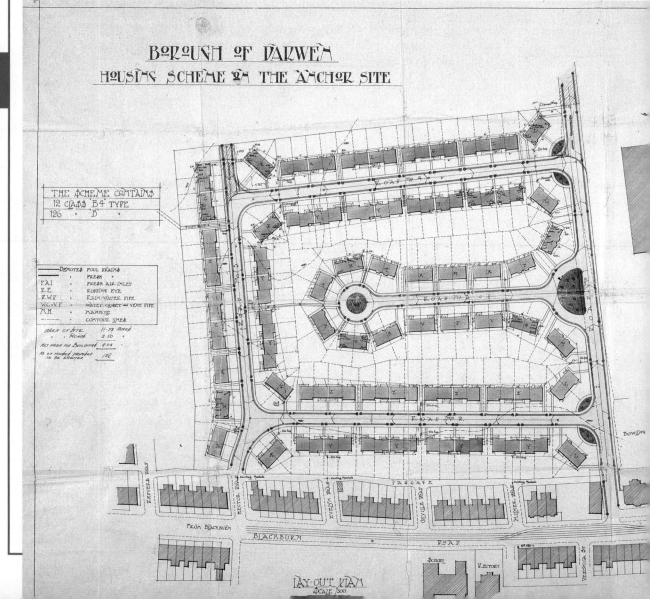

The London Underground rail system opened in 1865. Deep-tunnelling methods extended the network in the 1890s, so people were able to travel quickly and cheaply from the suburbs to their places of work, and at weekends they had the opportunity to explore attractive places on the outskirts.

cottages were without piped water, flush toilets or gas lights and cooking was still done over an open fire. Some rural dwellings had to wait until the 1960s for such facilities.

Although the the transformation of much of England and Wales to an urban, industrial society was almost complete by 1900, the division between town and countryside was much sharper than it is today. After the First World War a succession of Housing Acts led to the creation of large 'council estates' on the edges of towns and the building of smaller estates in villages. The houses were built to low densities, with front and rear gardens, like the new garden cities. The Housing Act (1919), which introduced state subsidies both for private and council houses, was followed by further Acts in 1923 and 1924. Nottingham Corporation, for example, took advantage of the new powers to build 20 municipal estates during the 1920s and 1930s, mainly on the northern and western fringes of the city, often on slum clearance sites. Together with the private suburban houses which were built in sprawling new suburbs or in 'ribbon development' along main roads in the inter-war period, the council estates transformed the appearance of both urban and rural settlements in many parts of the country.

After 1918 London expanded at an even faster rate than before. Between the two world wars the size of London's conurbation doubled as it accounted for more than one-third of the population increase of the whole of England and

TOO MUCH OF A GOOD THING

EVERY VARIETY OF PLEASURE RESORT.
PARKS & PLAYGROUNDS
RIVER-SIDE
COUNTRY-SIDE
SEASIDE
PALACES & GARDENS.

Wales. Most of the growth was in the outer suburbs through the creation of London County Council housing estates and the spread of semi-detached private housing. The electrification of the railways and improvements in road transport (from electric trams to motor buses) encouraged the spread of commuting. At the same time, the coastal fringe of the south-east was being covered with new homes, but away from the lure of the capital, most of the smaller market towns scarcely grew at all, or even declined in population between 1911 and 1931. The motor car had not yet turned village houses into commuter residences. Horses and carts on dusty lanes remained more typical than tarmacadamed roads for cars and lorries. Most country dwellings still had no electricity, mains drainage, or piped water.

Work

At the beginning of the twentieth century, Britain was the leading industrial nation in the world. Company towns and industrial villages in northern and midland England and south Wales were dominated by a mine, a quarry, an ironworks or a textile factory, which were often the only places of employment, while the workers' houses and the few public buildings were usually company-owned. Cotton was still king and Lancashire experienced a boom in mill building between 1904 and 1907. On the eve of the First World War total annual exports rose to a record of over 7 billion yards of cotton cloth. The 1901 census had shown that no less than 85.1 per cent of the workforce in the cotton mills in England and Wales lived in Lancashire, and that the rest were found mainly in neighbouring parts of the West Riding of Yorkshire, Cheshire and Derbyshire. Many other parts of England and Wales were noted for particular products. The woollen and worsted branches of the textile trades in the

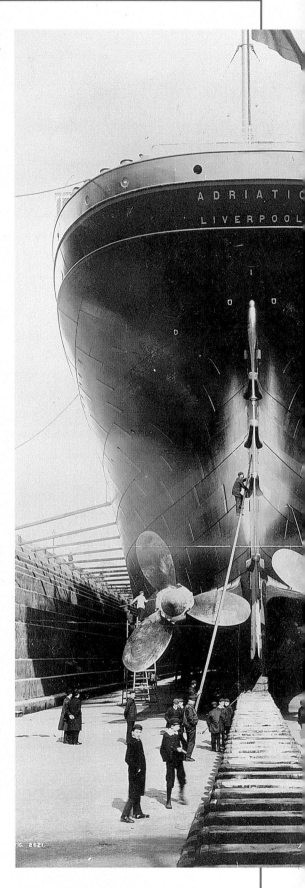

The shiny new Royal Mail Steamer Adriatic *in dry dock, 1907. The building of liners for transatlantic journeys enabled Liverpool to challenge London for the title of Britain's major port.*

West Riding of Yorkshire and the hosiery trade in the East Midlands, for instance, remained buoyant in the years leading up to the First World War.

Other districts were centres of heavy industry. Northumberland and Durham, for example, had been transformed during the previous two generations by coal mining, the manufacture of iron and steel, and ship building. By 1900 more than half of the world's new tonnage was built in British shipyards and more than half of Britain's share was built on Wearside and Tyneside. In the boom years of 1905–7, Sunderland's shipyards alone built 1 million tons of new shipping. At that time, 23,000 men were directly employed by the various Armstrong enterprises on Tyneside and many more relied indirectly upon the company for their employment. The wages earned by Tynesiders were high by contemporary standards, especially in the skilled trades. Meanwhile, the tonnage of shipping that passed through Liverpool's docks doubled between 1890 and 1914. Britain was still ahead of its competitors in most branches of heavy industry. In 1914 its share of world trade in manufacturing amounted to 31 per cent.

The standard of living of most working men and their families in the late-Victorian

A weaving shed, Burnley, 1907. The Lancashire cotton industry had just enjoyed four boom years when many new mills were built. Cotton was Britain's most important manufacturing industry and its products were sold all over the world. The industry was highly mechanized and strict work discipline was enforced. The noise of the machines was unbelievable when they were all at work.

and Edwardian era was markedly higher than it had been in the mid-nineteenth century, especially for the 'labour aristocracy' of skilled workers who earned higher wages than the semi-skilled and unskilled workforce, many of whom were dependent on casual employment. Not only did wages rise, but the price of food and raw materials from abroad fell as Britain benefited from its expanding empire. This rise in working-class standards of living was matched by increased leisure time. Normal weekly working hours fell from 60 or 70 per week in the mid-nineteenth century to 53 by 1910, though in certain occupations they remained much longer. The reduced hours of working, Saturday half-holidays and bank holidays had encouraged the growth of mass entertainments such as spectator sports, while annual holidays, lasting a week or even a fortnight when firms shut down, allowed families to spend time at the new seaside resorts.

The service sector of the economy grew in response to this increased wealth and the needs of the rising population. Old photographs show urban workers in their uniforms: policemen, post office employees, railwaymen, and bus drivers. In 1901 the transport and postal services employed 1,267,825 people in England and Wales, of whom only 18,825 were females. Half a million people were employed in road traffic, a quarter of a million in postal services and the delivery of messages, and over a third of a million on the railways. Uniformed railwaymen had regular wages, jobs for life, company houses, pensions and the prospect of

promotion to keep them at their jobs. The years leading up to the First World War heralded the end for the horse-drawn society that had characterized towns and cities throughout the land, as omnibuses were replaced by electric trams and motor buses and later by private motor cars. Whereas in 1898 English cities had just over 1,000 miles of tramways for horse-drawn trams, by 1914 the network was three times as large and electric trams offered cheaper services. Suburbs for both the middle classes and the working classes now began to spread beyond the old limits of the towns.

Domestic service remained the most common occupation for working-class women. The 1901 census enumerated 1,330,783 female domestic indoor servants, a number that was even larger than that for coal miners. It has been estimated that one

Henry Turton forging a saw file at the Suffolk Works, Sheffield, about 1902. The hand-cutting of files had largely disappeared because of competition from machines, so photographers were keen to record the rapidly dwindling number of old craftsmen.

in three women in Victorian England was a domestic servant at some stage in her life, mostly between the ages of 15 and 25. The hours were long and irregular and the segregated life could be lonely, but it was preferable to taking in washing or factory work. Other young women worked as shop assistants in the new department stores or perhaps as dressmakers. The great change to office work was yet to come.

In the Edwardian era, while heavy industry was booming, many old hand-crafts were disappearing. We must not be misled by old photographs into thinking that what we see

was still a normal way of life. Photographers were keen to capture the 'quaint survivals' of vanishing domestic trades, such as handloom weaving, framework knitting, lace making and the manufacture of straw bonnets. About 1902 old Henry Martin was photographed using a distinctively-shaped filemaker's hammer to forge a saw file at Thomas Turton's Suffolk Works, Sheffield. File making had become a specialist hand-craft in Sheffield in the mid-seventeenth century and in Birmingham soon afterwards. It started as an urban trade but ended three centuries later as a depressed craft in the outlying

IN BRIEF

- At the beginning of the twentieth century Britain was the leading industrial nation in the world.

- Heavy industry was booming, but many old hand crafts disappeared. Photographers recorded them just in time.

- The standard of living of working-class families was much higher than it had been at the beginning of Victoria's reign.

- Suburbs grew as cheap fares on trams meant that people no longer needed to live close to their place of work.

villages, long after machines had taken over in the town. In its heyday the Sheffield tool-making industry supplied all the world with its products, including tools to make tools, and its craftsmen took a justified pride in the quality of their work; but new technology does not need files, and in the 1990s the last Sheffield file works were closed.

The way of life of the inshore fishermen lasted much longer. They worked in small groups, sharing the profit of the catch, and they had to find other ways to make ends meet, for the weather made it impossible for them to rely on a regular income. The seasonal pattern of work started in the second week of October, when fishing by line occupied the winter months. Potting and crabbing supplemented this activity in the spring, then the men followed the herring shoals in the summer season until October came round again. Fishermen were regarded as unskilled manual workers when they worked at other jobs, but at sea they acquired a variety of craft skills and a considerable body of knowledge and lore

relating to winds and tides, the behaviour of the sea, habits of fish, the contours of the seabed, and the landmarks which enabled them to navigate to and from the fishing grounds. Frank Sutcliffe's famous photographs show fishermen and their wives in their distinctive dress, with their gear and traditional sailing ships, or 'cobles'. Like most occupational groups, fishermen had their own specialized language and vocabulary which were virtually incomprehensible to the outsider or even to non-fisherfolk in the same community. The women made a substantial contribution to the family economy. Not only were they in charge of the household economy, they had the wearying, repetitive task of gathering limpets and mussels in wicker baskets. On returning home, they removed the soft part with knives for the men to use as bait. For most of the year, this task dominated the daily routine. A woman might have to 'skane' several thousand mussels each day. Cleaning the lines of putrefying bait, mending nets and hauling cobles on the shore were women's jobs, but only the men experienced the danger and hardship of the actual fishing.

This pride in skilled craftsmanship was also evident in the countryside and was immortalised in George Bourne, *The Wheelwright's Shop* (1923). The first half of the twentieth century saw the end of the age-old tradition of working the land with hand tools and animal power. Farm tractors first appeared during the First World War, though they did not become widespread until after the Second. The 1911 census revealed that the agricultural labour force was still the second largest male occupational group in England and Wales, but the number of farm workers was far lower than it had been in the peak years of the middle decades of the nineteenth century. Farming had come through the worst times of the late Victorian era but it remained depressed in the 1920s and 1930s. On the eve of the First World War, Britain's agriculture produced but a fraction of the nation's food. Imports accounted for 80 per cent of the wheat that was consumed, 60 per cent of the butter, 80 per cent of the lard, 75 per cent of the cheese and 67 per cent of the ham and bacon. Nevertheless, many English and Welsh counties retained their rural nature and most of their inhabitants earned their living directly from the land. By 1914 it was evident that many large estates were

Whitby harbour, 1895. One of Frank Meadow Sutcliffe's many evocative photographs of the Yorkshire port and its community of fishermen and their families.

changing hands as aristocratic families were hit by falling rents and the introduction of Estate Duty in 1894. After the First World War estates across the country were put up for sale to sitting tenants or institutions. The Forestry Commission (created in 1919) eventually became the largest private landlord in Britain with about 3 million acres, and later in the twentieth century vast acres were bought by the Ministry of Defence, the National Trust, the electricity, water, and other utility companies, pension funds and other investment groups. The political power of the aristocracy declined sharply during the half-century after the First World War.

Poverty

In 1901 Seebohm Rowntree published *Poverty: A Study of Town Life*, which showed that the poorest inhabitants of the ancient cathedral city of York had the same dismal standard of living as the wretched poor in the East End of London. He and his assistants obtained personal details from 11,560 families who were living in 388 of the city's streets. They concluded that 27.84 per cent of the inhabitants could not afford the nutritional standard that was necessary to maintain physical health. This underclass was divided between the 9.91 per cent who lived in continuous poverty and the 17.93 per cent who descended below the poverty line in times of hardship caused by unemployment or illness. As York was a typical English town, with heavy (railways) and light (confectionery) industry, the implications were that the rest of the country shared the same problem. Although London's slums were more extensive, they were no worse than those in other large towns in England and Wales.

Rowntree showed that families descended into poverty at various stages of the life-cycle, particularly when young married couples had their children and in old age. Old photographs show children from the poorest families dressed in ill-fitting clothes. They often went barefoot in summer and wore boots supplied by charities to go to school during the rest of the year. At the other end of the life-cycle, one in five people who reached the age of 70 during the reign of Edward VII became paupers; by the age of 75 the proportion was one in three. About one in ten old people ended their days in a workhouse. The greatest reforms of the Liberal Government that was elected in 1906 were the introduction of old age pensions and a national insurance scheme. From 1 January 1909 people over 70 received a pension of five shillings a week if their annual income was less than £31.10s. and provided they had no criminal convictions and had never received support from the Poor Law guardians; the rest of the destitute still went to the workhouse. Some workhouses continued to operate until the introduction of the National Health Service in 1948, when many were converted into hospitals. Almost half a million people qualified and in 1925 the pensionable age was lowered to 65. Meanwhile, the National Insurance Act (Health and Unemployment) of 1911 had introduced sickness and unemployment benefits that were paid for by contributions from both employers and employees.

Some of the wretched poor were Jewish immigrants from the Russian Empire, who had fled Tsar Alexander III's pogroms in the 1880s and 1890s. By 1911 68,420 of them

*Dustmen and women at work in a yard off Vauxhall,
south London, 1900–09, from the collection of James
Ramsay MacDonald, the future Labour Prime
Minister.*

had settled in the poorest districts of the East End of London (especially the borough of Stepney), about 30,000 lived in Manchester and another 20,000 were found in Leeds. They followed the age-old tendency of immigrant groups to cluster together in well-defined quarters for mutual support and protection. Most people never met a foreigner, but all shades of political opinion supported the Aliens Act (1905), which restricted further entry of Jews from the Russian Empire. During the reign of Victoria the number of immigrants into England and Wales had been slightly less

than the number of those who had left for a new life across the seas. The steady flow of emigrants leaving these shores continued until the First World War and resumed at a lesser pace in the 1920s until the Wall Street Crash and the subsequent depression reduced it to a trickle.

The poorest sections of society were the ones most likely to turn to crime. All the industrial towns had their notorious criminal gangs, but the level of crime was much lower than it is today. In 1902 about 170,000 people were sent to prison, including 52,000

females, and over 40,000 were sentenced to hard labour in default of paying a fine. In 1908 over 27,000 people were imprisoned for begging and 'sleeping out'. Far fewer people were sent to prison than in the first half of Victoria's reign, and from the 1870s the punishment of criminals had gradually become less severe. The treadmill was abolished in 1902, young offenders were put on probation from 1907, and flogging ceased in 1917.

Poverty was also tackled through the education service. The Education (Provision of Meals) Act (1906) established school canteens and provided free meals from the rates. In 1907 local authorities were given responsibility for the health of schoolchildren. They appointed doctors and nurses to look for vermin infestation, ringworm, impetigo, scabies and defects of vision, hearing and speech. They soon reported that one in every six pupils in England and Wales could not benefit from their schooling because they were underfed, verminous or suffering from bad teeth, faulty vision or skin complaints. Nearly one-quarter of the elementary schoolchildren of Gloucestershire who were examined in 1908 suffered from head infestation. Throughout England and Wales nose and throat problems were common and teeth were rarely looked after; in the inter-war years women often had all their teeth taken out by a dentist at the age of 21 in favour of a false set. On average, children from the poorest, overcrowded homes were 10 pounds lighter and five inches smaller than those who lived in the better working-class houses; children from

Soup kitchen in the crypt of St Peter's church, Walworth, south London, 1900–09. Every day, members of the church provided 1,000 penny meals and free soup and cake for children.

wealthier homes were bigger. In 1912 the annual report of the Chief Medical Officer of the Board of Education showed that 18.6 per cent of the children examined in Dorset, 12.7 per cent of those in Gloucestershire and 12 per cent of Somerset children were suffering from the effects of inadequate diet. The situation was even worse in towns, rising to 31.4 per cent of children in West Hartlepool.

In 1902 responsibility for providing elementary, secondary and technical education was given to 330 local education authorities under a central Board of Education. The old board schools now became council schools and a new emphasis was placed on secondary education. In 1918 the school-leaving age was raised to 14, but only a very small proportion of pupils went on to higher education. On the eve of the First World War just 22,234 students attended English universities and fewer than a thousand of these came from grant-aided secondary schools. Education rarely provided opportunities to escape from the ravages of poverty.

IN BRIEF

- The East End of London was notoriously poor, but York had almost as many poor families.
- The first generation or two of Jewish immigrants lived in the poorest districts.
- The Liberal government elected in 1906 introduced old age pensions and a national insurance scheme.
- Free school meals and medical inspections improved the health of children.

Stability and mobility

Most people still lived their lives at a local level. Although the railways provided quick and cheap transport throughout the land, the great majority of English and Welsh men and women stayed within the neighbourhoods that had been familiar to their ancestors. The local newspapers that were so popular at the time are full of accounts of regular weekly events and seasonal festivities: the whist drives and dances in village halls, the football and cricket matches, the annual fairs, Whitsuntide processions and Sunday school anniversaries. At their peak in 1906 British Sunday schools attracted over 6 million pupils, or more than 80 per cent of children between the ages of 5 and 14. The church or the chapel was often the centre of social life; the pub was the only rival attraction.

The motor car was as yet the prized possession of the rich. For most people, the only occasion when they left their home district was on a trip by rail to the seaside. By the eve of the First World War Blackpool was getting 4 million visitors a year. The late Victorian and Edwardian era was the golden period of seaside resorts, but central London was not yet an attraction to families in the provinces. Few ventured beyond the nearest towns to shop or to seek entertainment. Football teams were composed of young men who lived in the same streets as the club's supporters and patterns of mobility were little different from what they had always been. People were prepared to move home frequently, but most of them preferred to travel short distances within the neighbourhood that they had known since childhood. With few exceptions, the large towns and cities drew people from their traditional hinterland; only London attracted numerous immigrants from all parts of England and Wales. Even in the capital city, however, a strong attachment to a local district was evident. In the 1890s Charles Booth commented that in the poorest parts of the East End 'people do not usually go far, and often cling from generation to generation to one vicinity, almost as if the set of streets which lie there were an isolated country village'. Their relatives were all around them.

The persistence of families within the same neighbourhoods over the centuries helps to explain why local societies retained their own customs and their distinctive ways of

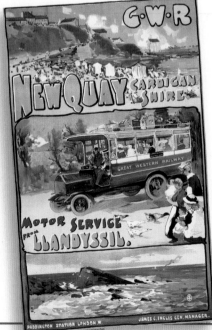

A Great Western Railway poster of 1908 advertising trips from Paddington station all the way to New Quay on the Cardiganshire coast.

speaking. The individual characters of English and Welsh towns in the late Victorian and Edwardian era were much more evident than now. Shops in the High Street bore distinctive local names, places were identified with the manufacture of particular products, and old attachments to one's place of birth and to the wider neighbourhood remained strong.

This continued association of families with particular districts or 'countries' is immediately apparent when we see lists of surnames in electoral rolls or directories, census returns or the indexes of civil registration. The railways had not changed the age-old preference of the majority of English and Welsh people to remain rooted in their native localities. Every county in England had its distinctive set of surnames, most of which had been formed locally back in the Middle Ages. Lancashire had its Cleggs, Fazackerleys, Ramsbottoms, and Sowerbuttses, Yorkshire its Bairstows, Barracloughs, Murgatroyds and Sutcliffes, Derbyshire its Heathcotes, Glossops, Ollerenshaws and Wildgooses, and

Staffordshire its Bloores, Fernihoughs, Salts and Tooths. In southern England the patterns were equally distinct. Kent was the home of the Chittendens, Hambrooks, Homewoods and Kingsnorths, the Akehursts were found in Sussex, the Riggses in Dorset, the Aclands in Devon, and the Annears in Cornwall. Even the Welsh names often had marked concentrations. The Bevans came from south Wales, the Eynons from Pembrokeshire, the Foulkeses from Denbighshire, and the Gittinses from Montgomeryshire. These patterns have been weakened in recent years but they are still evident in all parts of the land.

A street in Bagshot, Surrey, 1904, showing the drapery, millinery and footwear shops of W. S. Stanley, with the staff and a group of boys. Shops such as these had local origins and helped to give places their special identity.

STABILITY AND MOBILITY

IN BRIEF

- Most people still lived their lives at a local level, though cheap fares on the railways encouraged migration in search of a better life.
- Most towns and cities attracted immigrants from their immediate neighbourhood, but London drew people from all over the country.
- English and Welsh towns in the late Victorian and Edwardian era had strong individual characters.
- Every county in England had its distinctive set of surnames, most of which had been formed locally in the Middle Ages.

The First World War

The First World War is generally, and rightly, considered to be one of the great dividing points in the history of the nation. Before 1914, war was something that happened far away. Men went to war, some came back injured, and some never returned, but the mass of the population was not directly involved. The First World War was a new sort of experience. For the first time, men were conscripted to fight for their country and almost every family had someone who volunteered or who was 'called up' to fight. Over 8 million men and women served in the British forces between 1914 and 1918. The casualty figures were unprecedented and appalling. Nearly 1 million men and women from all over the British Empire were killed and very many more were injured. The memorials that stand in towns and villages throughout the land give an immediate sense of the loss of young lives. In Somerset, where the population was less than 450,000, more than 11,000 men were killed. The death rate varied between communities because some battalions were chosen to lead attacks, but perhaps about 13–14 per cent of those who served never came back.

Now that most of the lives of those who fought in the First World War have ended and surviving records have been made available for all of us to research, interest in the human stories of the ordinary men and women who went to fight has surged to unprecedented levels. The horror of it all is hardly believable. Even if our direct ancestors took no part in the war, nearly all of us have great-uncles or other close relatives who did. I have seen photographs of an uncle whom I never knew taken in the Middle East in the same places where his son was photographed in the Second World War. Neither of them had been abroad before they were called to fight, and afterwards both spent the rest of their lives

- Nearly one million men and women from all over the British Empire were killed in the First World War.
- For the first time, Englishmen and Welshmen were conscripted to fight in a foreign war. Previously, armies had consisted of volunteers.
- The War is one of the greatest dividing points in our history. Things were never quite the same afterwards.
- Interest in the human stories of those who fought has never been more intense, now that so many records have become available for study.

in their native parishes. In this, they were typical of countless others. The First World War was a significant divide in many ways, but it did not break the immemorial custom whereby the majority of the population remained rooted in their particular localities.

The worlds of our immediate ancestors were intensely local ones. In trying to understand their lives our task is to become immersed not only in family history but in the local history of the communities in which they lived. The images that are collected in our family albums or stuffed away in drawers are our starting points, but they make little sense on their own. Nor is there much satisfaction in simply finding names and dates. Our ancestors become real people only when we discover their homes, their places of work, leisure and worship and the peculiar nature of the towns, villages or hamlets where they lived and that of the wider neighbourhood that they knew so well.

LEFT
Marching towards the trenches, 28 June 1916. British soldiers from a battalion of the Worcestershire Regiment (29th Division) raise their helmets as they set off for France. Men were conscripted into the armed forces from 1916.

A simple war memorial on the village green at Biddestone, near Chippenham, Wiltshire. Most towns and villages have memorials erected in public places to those who died in both world wars. The list of names from the First World War is usually longer.

Gravestones

If your immediate ancestors lived in the same district as you do, a search for gravestones in a parish churchyard or a public cemetery is an obvious, and often rewarding, starting point. Gravestones usually record the age at death, and so even if this is a year or two out we are provided with an approximate date of birth. They may also explain family relationships and record the movements of individuals. In the south-west corner of the churchyard of St James, High Melton (Yorkshire) an inscription reads:

This Stone is plac'd here by John Harrop of Sheffield, in remembrance of his Parents who died at Doncaster, and are buried here, viz. George Harrop who was born at Barnborough April 1st 1762, and died July 22nd, 1814, Also Sarah Harrop his wife, who died December 6th, 1850 in her 80 year. Also two of their Children who were born at Melton and died in their infancy.

The earliest gravestones are those of the richer inhabitants of a parish who were interred inside the church. They date from the sixteenth century onwards. In earlier times the rich were commemorated by effigies, brasses and incised slabs. Monuments carved from alabaster or marble became fashionable from the reign of Elizabeth onwards. By the nineteenth century local worthies were being commemorated by wall plaques. The ordinary families of the parish were buried in the churchyard in unmarked graves, which were cleared whenever more room was required and the bones removed to charnel houses at the edge of the churchyard. From the seventeenth century onwards, when ordinary people were becoming more literate, farmers and craftsmen started to erect inscribed gravestones in churchyards in the same style as the tombstones inside the church. The earliest ones are found close to the church on the south, for the north was once thought to be the devil's side, where suicides, excommunicates and the unbaptized were buried.

Even in the nineteenth century, however, many families could not afford the expense of a gravestone. We might discover the record of a burial in a parish register but fail to find the place where our ancestor is buried because it is unmarked. I have failed to find any gravestones for my Hey ancestors earlier than that of my grandfather. The neglected condition of some churchyards hinders a search even when a stone survives. Inscriptions may be obscured by ivy or lichen, others may have been eroded where the local stone is soft,

Recording a gravestone in the churchyard of All Saints, Foots Cray, Kent. Some inscriptions are so badly weathered that they are now unreadable, yet others are as fresh as when they were cut. Family history societies have often surveyed all the churchyards in their area.

and in some churchyards the stones have been cleared away. Family history societies have often made a record of monumental inscriptions – MIs for short – and have deposited copies in local libraries and record offices or at the Society of Genealogists. The National Library of Wales has a large collection of transcribed Welsh inscriptions.

The designs of gravestones are often characteristic of a region and are confined to a particular period. Gravestones in the East Midlands, for instance, were often made from Swithland slate which could be carved with flowing letters and adorned with the mason's name at the bottom. Sentimental and whimsical verses became fashionable in the eighteenth and nineteenth centuries. For example, the sudden death of William Mather at Edensor (Derbyshire) in 1818 at the age of 29 was commemorated by:

When he that day with th' Waggon went,
He little thought his Glass was spent;
But had he kept his Plough in hand,
He might have longer till'd the land.

Gravestones sometimes provide genealogical information for two or three generations, but such information should be regarded as critically as any other record. Some gravestones that record a death in the seventeenth or eighteenth centuries were erected much later than the event. When a son was buried in the same grave as his parents, the stone that was placed in his memory might record their ages and dates of death. If all the lettering is of the same style it is likely that the gravestone was erected not long after the date of the last

recorded event. Gravestones may provide information about a relationship that was previously unknown. In some parishes they often note where exactly the deceased resided, down to the name of a farm or a mill. Make a full copy of the inscription and record the position of the tombstone for future reference. They are not always easy to find on a second visit.

It was a common practice in rural parishes to group family graves together. In the eighteenth and nineteenth centuries, for example, my mother's family, the Battys, are buried alongside each other in the neighbouring churchyards at Coxwold and Husthwaite in North Yorkshire. Even some of the Battys who died beyond the parish boundaries were brought back to the family's 'home' parish for burial. This practice amongst the moderately well-off inhabitants explains why a burial might be recorded in a different parish from that where a person died. In some places, certain surnames seem to dominate the churchyard. At Heptonstall, high on the Pennines to the west of Halifax, the Greenwoods are everywhere. The surname was derived from a local farm and was also used as a first name for children whose mother was a Greenwood. We can even find the gravestone of Greenwood Greenwood.

Browsing through a churchyard, we can also get a good sense of where local families originated, for many took their names from villages, hamlets or farmsteads. It is common to find that most of these were derived from places within a radius of about 20 miles, but that some came from further afield. The parish of Edensor, which serves the Chatsworth estate, has Peak District names such as Alsop, Darwind, Drabble, Eyre, Heathcott, Ollerenshaw and Shimwell, but its eighteenth- and nineteenth-century gravestones also record names such as Bland, Doungsworth, Greenhalgh, Hawkesworth, Holderness, Littlewood, Marsden, Oxspring and Penistone, which originated further north in Yorkshire. By contrast, the names on gravestones at Brighstone, Isle of Wight, are very different. An outsider cannot explain their etymology but is struck by such distinctive names as Buckett, Champ, Chipp, Creeth, Downer, Dozier, Gosden, Hippance, Munt, Pittis, Redstone, Scovell, Shotter, Swatheridge, Tolfree and Urry, all of which probably originated on the island or in neighbouring counties on the mainland.

A gravestone in the overgrown cemetery at Nunhead, south-east London. Jenny Hill was a music hall star, whose marriage to John W. Woodley failed after the birth of two daughters.

Public cemeteries

The erection of gravestones as memorials to the dead stopped the old practice of clearing graves to allow new burials. As this happened at a time when the national population was rising rapidly, churchyards soon became full and private and public cemeteries had to be opened. The burgeoning industrial towns, such as Liverpool, Manchester, Norwich and Sheffield, took the lead in the 1820s and 1830s and London soon had major public cemeteries at Kensal Green (1827), Norwood (1837), Highgate (1839), Brompton (1840), Abney Park (1840), and Tower Hamlets (1841). During the 1850s local authorities throughout England and Wales opened non-denominational cemeteries run by Burial Boards. The records of these municipal cemeteries have sometimes been deposited at local record offices, but many are still kept at the site office, where they may be consulted. They usually record the name, address, age, and occupation of the deceased, the dates of death and burial, and the position of the grave. As this information is filed in chronological order and is not indexed alphabetically, a search is quickened if you already have an idea of the approximate date of death.

The large numbers of Victorian memorial cards that survive amongst family mementoes from the mid-Victorian period onwards, edged in black and designed in a variety of styles, note the place of burial. The grave number in the burial register enables you to locate the grave on a cemetery plan. Where a private grave was purchased for family burials, the plot number will be recorded in any deed that survives amongst family papers.

Finding where an ancestor was buried in the public cemeteries and churchyards of large cities, especially London, can be a difficult and time-consuming task. The first step is to look at a large-scale Ordnance Survey map to locate possible burial grounds. Of course, a civil registration death certificate does not say where the deceased was buried. My wife's ancestor, Moses Downer, died on 7 July 1950 at 400 Ringwood Road, Poole. He was not buried in the churchyard of his home parish, St Andrew's, Kinson, nor could we find his grave during lengthy searches of three large public cemeteries at Branksome, Parkstone and Poole. On the suggestion of the officer at the last cemetery that we visited, we eventually tried the churchyard of the small church of St Clement's. We did not find the grave, but a churchwarden eventually confirmed from the register that Moses was buried there, probably in one of the graves where the inscription is now illegible. The church has no record of the position of the grave.

Cremation became legal in 1884, but in the following year only three people were cremated in the whole of Britain. The Cremation Act which came into force in 1903 allowed public burial authorities to provide and maintain crematoria out of the rates, but the fashion spread slowly. Even by 1947 only 10 per cent of the dead were cremated. Nowadays, however, the proportion has risen to two out of every three.

Photographs

Relatively few of us have portraits of our ancestors, but during the 1840s and 1850s the new art of photography started to provide cheap, but accurate images of ordinary people. Posed studio photographs reproduced on mounts the size of visiting cards (and so known as cartes de visite) were immensely popular from the 1850s and became more ornate in the 1870s and 1880s. In the late 1880s and for much of the 1890s larger, dark-coloured cards were fashionable, then a simpler style was adopted towards the end of the century. The serious looks on the faces of our ancestors and their tense poses were the result of long exposures with their heads in a clamp. Wedding photographs were often taken in the studio rather than at church. The need to travel to a studio means that baptism photographs are relatively rare, nor do we usually find photographs of groups of mourners at funerals. Informal 'snaps' became popular after 1900, when Kodak's Box Brownie sold for five shillings.

Many people inherit an album or a collection of photographs stuffed in a drawer, some of them creased or torn. These can now be improved by commercial photographers or by the skilled use of a scanner and computer software. It is now also easy to make copies of photographs that belong to relatives. But most of these old photographs have no names or dates attached to them. The

Often the physical properties of a photograph can be as helpful as the subject's dress and hairstyle to help you date a family picture – for example, ambrotypes like these generally date from the third quarter of the nineteenth century.

JANE MARLES

April 20/1903

Wishing you many Happy returns of the day from your affectionate Mother

Jane Marles

images stare at us teasingly, offering clues but no positive proof of identity. I can recognize some of the people in my grandmother's album and make informed guesses about others, but I have no idea who the rest are and am resigned to the conclusion that I will probably never know.

☛ R. Pols, *Family Photographs, 1860–1945* (Public Record Office, 2002) gives useful advice on how to interpret collections by looking at the whole body of evidence.

☛ The way in which pictures are arranged in an album might tell a story through the grouping together of couples and their children.

☛ Family likenesses are sometimes striking, but we need to take care that our hunches do not lead us astray, for albums often contain photographs of close friends as well as relatives.

☛ We need to pool information with other members of the family, for even if they do not know a name older relatives might identify someone on a picture as 'your grandfather's younger brother'.

We might be able to date our photographs approximately by hairstyle and dress, though we have to remember that the 'Sunday best' of old countryfolk might be 20 years out of date and that some studios provided unusual costumes for the occasion. A trip to a seaside resort often included a visit to a studio in order to send photographs to friends and relatives. Some of these studios did not last very long and their names and addresses might be located in trade directories, which will thus give a rough date for a photograph. Changing fashions in poses also offer clues.

The huge collections of picture-postcards with views of streets and rural scenes, which became popular towards the end of the nineteenth century and were used on a very large scale from 1900 to 1920, enable us to place our ancestors in the communities in which they lived. Most public libraries or museums have large collections of local photographs of special events such as coronation celebrations, Whitsuntide processions, fairs and markets, or of football teams, brass bands, church choirs and outings. Towns and villages throughout the country now have their own books of local photographs. The National Archives has an extensive collection from the mid-1850s to 1912 in the COPY 1 series, which consists of innumerable small collections; an information leaflet is available.

Photographs from an Edwardian family album.
The montage shows (clockwise from top left): Mr and Mrs W. H. Bulley with their two sons, William and Reginald, c. 1914; unnamed family friends in a photographer's studio in Exeter, c. 1914; Jane Marles (Mrs Bulley's mother), c.1903, together with the note she enclosed in the album; the album itself, bound in brown leather embossed with a horse-chestnut pattern, and with an ornate brass clasp; Reginald Bulley in RAF uniform, c. 1932.

Newspapers

The composing room of Lloyd's Weekly News, *Fleet Street, 1911. Printing remained a hand craft until the computer age.*

Local newspapers are of limited value for the family historian before the Victorian period, but from the middle of the nineteenth century they provide a wealth of information, ranging from announcements of births, marriages and deaths, obituaries, coroners' inquests and lists of those who attended weddings and funerals to advertisements of businesses and sales, notifications of bankruptcies, and reports of court cases, sporting events, flower shows and whist drives. Sales depended on naming as many local people as possible, so there is a good chance of finding ancestors (and possibly photographs) in their pages. Unfortunately, most newspapers are

available only on microfilm and very few are indexed. J. Gibson, B. Langston and B. W. Smith, *Local Newspapers, 1750–1920* (FFHS, 2nd edition, 2002) is a guide to their whereabouts.

The national collection is housed at the Newspaper Library (part of the British Library), close to Colindale underground station in north London. This library is open from Monday to Saturday from 10 a.m. to 5 p.m., except on public holidays. Proof of identity is required to get a reader's ticket and it is best to book a microfilm reader in advance of a visit. An online catalogue is available on the website at <www.bl.uk/collections/newspaper>. Other large collections of newspapers are held at the Bodleian Library, Oxford, and the National Library of Wales, Aberystwyth. Local newspapers can be consulted on microfilm in local studies departments of public reference libraries and sometimes in local record offices. They are particularly valuable for the first three-quarters of the twentieth century, when local newspapers flourished.

A report of my great-grandfather's death illustrates the sort of personal detail that can be found in local newspapers.

On Tuesday, 27 December 1887 the *Sheffield Daily Telegraph* reported:

Sudden Death at Thurlstone. Mr George Hey, farmer, of Thurlstone, died suddenly on Saturday morning. Not hearing him about the premises one of the family went to see where he was, and he was discovered lying under one of the cows in the cowshed. He was raised and taken to the house, and medical aid was sent for, but he expired shortly after. The deceased, who is 70 years of age, has been subject to bronchitis for several years. An inquest was held yesterday, when a verdict of 'Death from natural causes' was returned.

'Local worthies' were given long and fulsome obituaries. Anyone lucky enough to find one for an ancestor will find the personal details and career information that most of us will never discover.

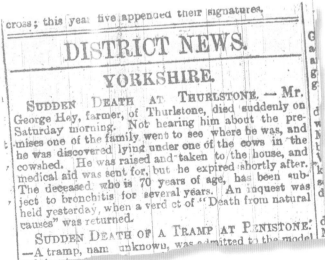

Land surveys

Although they do not provide genealogical information, national records concerning land ownership provide useful information about how some of our ancestors lived.

The National Farm Survey, 1941–43

During the Second World War the Government surveyed all farms of five acres or more, noting the farmer's name, whether he was owner or tenant, the amount of rent that was paid, the crops and livestock, and the number of farm workers, if any. The 300,000 or so farms that were visited were graded A, B or C, according to the competence of the farmers. The records are kept in the National Archives in MAF 32, with accompanying maps in MAF 73. An information leaflet is available.

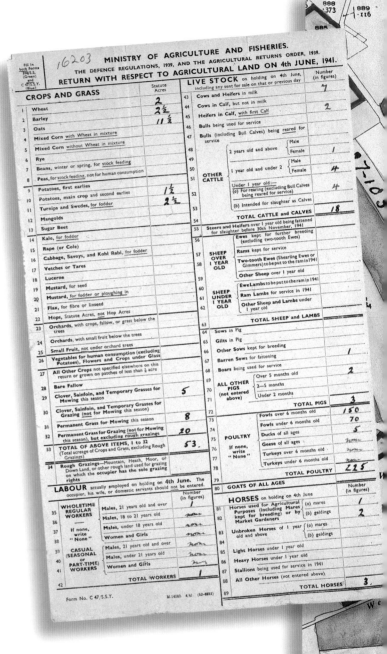

Records relating to Towngate Farm, Thurlstone, Yorkshire. The map from the Inland Revenue valuation records of 1910–11 identifies the farmhouse in Towngate, the village street, and colours in the land that was farmed, numbered 327–79. The individual record from the National Farm Survey in 1941 gives details of the crops and livestock. The farmer was Oliver Hey, the son of my grandfather's elder brother. This was where my great-grandfather, George Hey, died in 1887 (see p. 45).

Inland Revenue valuations and surveys

The Finance Act of 1910 required the Board of Inland Revenue to value all the land and property in England and Wales, so that a new tax could be assessed. The surveys and valuations were completed by 1915 and the records are now a major historical source in the National Archives, in IR 58, IR 121 and IR 124–35. An information leaflet on the rather complicated procedure for finding a particular property is available. You will need the assistance of an archivist on at least your first visit. See also B. Short, *The Geography of England and Wales in 1910: An Evaluation of Lloyd George's 'Domesday of Landownership'* (Cambridge, 1989). The fieldbooks in IR 58 name the property owner and any tenant (but not necessarily the actual occupier) and details of any tenancy. They note the floor area, the

condition and use of the property, the number of rooms and the valuation, but they do not survive for some parts of the country.

It is worth enquiring at county record offices to see whether they have any records from this valuation process. See also G. Beech and R. Mitchell, *Maps for Family and Local History* (The National Archives, 2004).

The Return of Owners of Land, 1873

Further back in time, a survey to ascertain the number of owners of land of one acre or more in the whole of the United Kingdom (except London) gives minimal information that might indicate the size of an ancestor's farm. The returns for each county in England and Wales, which were published by HMSO in 1874 as the *Return of Owners of Land, 1873* are available in good reference libraries or on microfiche or CD-ROM. They list owners' surnames in alphabetical order, note the acreage and rental value of the land, but not its precise location. Nearly 270,000 people or organizations are recorded.

The Valuation Office field book for Bateman's, Rudyard Kipling's house in Burwash, Sussex, 1910. The information in the return was re-worked and published as J. Bateman, The Great Landowners of Great Britain and Ireland (1883).

First World War records

Researching the story of an ancestor who served in the armed forces during the First World War has become an extraordinarily popular activity since the gradual release of soldiers' personal files, which started on Armistice Day 1996, and the release of approximately 216,000 officers' personal files, which began in February 1998. The microfilms of the records in WO 363 are by far the most heavily used in the National Archives at Kew. Over 8 million men and women served in the British armed forces during the war, so a significant proportion of the British population were directly involved. By the end of the war 7,712,772 men and women had enlisted in the Army, 407,360 in the Royal Navy and 293,522 in the Royal Flying Corps or the Royal Air Force.

☛ There is no longer such a thing as a standard First World War record of service. A search may produce little or nothing; on the other hand it might prove very rewarding.

☛ The essential guide to these and other records that have survived is W. Spencer, *Army Service Records of the First World War* (Public Record Office, third edition, 2001).

The Army

The 'burnt' records
Unfortunately, two-thirds of the Army other ranks service records that were kept at the War Office repository in Arnside Street, London, were destroyed by bombs on 8 September 1940, and many of the remaining third were badly damaged by fire and water.

The surviving records are now kept at the National Archives, where they have been microfilmed in a major project financed by the Heritage Lottery Fund and undertaken by the LDS Church. The service records of 2.8 million soldiers, most of whom saw operational service overseas, are thus available for study, at either the National Archives or the various LDS (Mormon) Family History Centres.

Documents from Wilfred Owen's service record. The famous war poet was a Lieutenant in the Manchester Regiment.

☛ The surviving 'burnt' records, which are kept in WO 363, were put into alphabetical sequence after the Second World War. These records are for soldiers and non-commissioned officers who completed their service at any time between 1914 and 1920, including those who survived the war, soldiers who died of wounds or disease or who were discharged on medical grounds, men who were killed in action, and those who were executed by firing squads. All of the files are unique and individual records vary in length from a single sheet to over 60 pages.

☛ The first step is to consult the WO 363 catalogue for the letter of the alphabet you require in order to find the relevant surname and forename(s) and a file

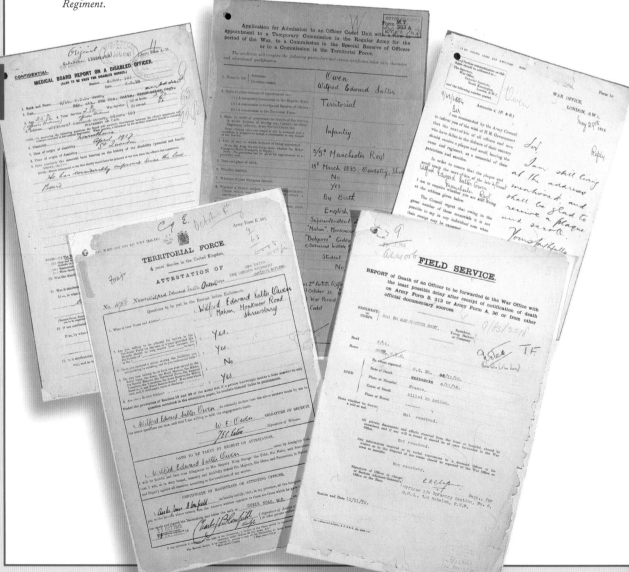

number. One third of all surviving service records is to be found in this series.

☞ The various types of attestation sheets that were filled in at the time of enlistment may note a soldier's age and physical appearance, his place of birth, occupation, and any former service.

☞ A conduct sheet and a medical history sheet are often filed with the attestation documents, and upon discharge another set of forms was completed.

The 'unburnt records'

☞ In WO 364 at the National Archives are the records which the War Office recovered from other government departments at the end of the Second World War. Most of these came from the Ministry of Pensions and are detailed medical histories of men who were discharged from the Army on account of sickness contracted or wounds suffered between 1914 and 1920. Curiously, they also include some records of soldiers who were discharged as far back as 1875. They are arranged in four sequences of A–Z.

☞ Another 22,801 files of those who were discharged from the services during the First World War because of sickness or wounds are kept in PIN 26.

☞ The records of those who served in the Women's Auxiliary Army Corps are held in WO 398.

☞ The main source for the 180,130 servicemen of all ranks who were taken prisoner (over half of them in the last eight months of the war) is WO 161/95–100, but only 5 per cent were recorded.

The war medals of Norman McQueen. From left to right the medals are the DSO (with double gallantry award), the 1914–15 Star, the British War Medal, the Allied Victory medal (with mention in dispatches), the Second World War defence medal (awarded for service in the Home Guard), the Coronation medal (for taking part in the procession in 1953) and the French Légion d'Honneur.

Officers

You are more likely to find information about the 250,000 Army officers than about the NCOs and ordinary soldiers, but not all of them have personal records: the main file was destroyed in the Second World War and only a subsidiary file survives.

☞ The *Army List* was the official listing of all those officers who held a commission in the British Army, just as it is today. It can be seen at the National Archives.

☞ The contents of officers' files vary greatly. They can be searched on the online catalogue of the National Archives. Otherwise, the first series to see at the National Archives is WO 338, the microfilmed name index for the records preserved in WO 339. The information is presented in six columns: surname; initial(s); regiment/corps; long number; rank; remarks. The 'long number' is crucial, for it identifies the relevant file in WO 339. Here are the records of 139,906 officers who saw service during the First World War.

☞ Another important series, in WO 374, contains the records of the officers of the Territorial Army, a number of officers who came out of retirement, and miscellaneous others. They are arranged in alphabetical order, which includes all initials and rank. They too can be searched on the catalogue.

Medals

Six different campaign medals were awarded for service during the First World War.

☞ The Medal Index Cards (MIC) in the record series WO 372 are available in 10,000 sheets of microfiche, each of which contains 360 separate cards. These cards provide a name index in alphabetical order, which points to the medal rolls in WO 329.

☞ E. C. Joslin, A. R. Litherland and B. T. Simpkin, *British Battles and Medals* (Spink, 1988) is the major guide to war medals.

At sea and in the air

☞ The essential guides are B. Pappalardo, *Tracing Your Naval Ancestors* (The National Archives, 2003) and W. Spencer, *Air Force Records for Family Historians* (Public Record Office, 2000).

☞ Registers of naval deaths during the First World War are to be found in ADM 104 and ADM 242 at the National Archives. These include date and place of birth.

☞ The service records of officers in the Royal Flying Corps are kept in AIR 76 at the National Archives and in those of the Royal Naval Air Service at ADM 273. Other ranks might be found amongst Army records in WO 363 or 364 or amongst naval records in ADM 188 or in AIR 79.

Other sources

☞ Local newspapers often published stories about local units, reports of promotions and awards for gallantry, and photographs of local men in

The service record of John Travers Cornwell (pictured left). He was only sixteen when he was mortally wounded at the Battle of Jutland on 3 May 1916.

home address in order to vote in their home constituency.

🖝 The Family Records Centre has indexes to the death certificates of those who died in the First World War. These are also available on microfiche at the National Archives.

🖝 The names of those who were killed are recorded on the 50,000 to 60,000 local war memorials that have been indexed in a joint project of the Imperial War Museum and English Heritage.

🖝 One of the most important collections of genealogical data that has gone online is the Debt of Honour Register on the website of the Commonwealth War Graves Commission, at <www.cwgc.org>. This is a database of the 1.7 million members of the Commonwealth forces who died in the First or Second World Wars, which records name, rank, regiment, date of death, place of burial or, for those with no known grave, of commemoration. It is very easy to search.

🖝 Army service records from the Second World War have not yet been deposited at the National Archives for public consultation. Next of kin can write to Army Personnel Centre, Historic Disclosures, Mailpoint 400, Kentigern House, 65 Brown Street, Glasgow G2 8EX.

uniform. They are kept at county or borough libraries and at the British Library's Newspaper Library at Colindale, in north London. If you have no idea of the service details of your ancestor, you should see whether the appropriate local record office has lists of absent voters in the 1918 election. Servicemen were allowed to register their name, rank, number, unit, and

2 Through the Nineteenth Century (1800–1900)

Genealogy was her favourite insanity.

Anthony Trollope, *Barchester Towers* (1857)

EXPLORING YOUR PAST

Introduction	56
Urban and rural	58
Farming	62
Industry	66
Families	72
Stability and mobility	76
Emigrants and immigrants	79
Houses	83
Progress	88

FINDING YOUR ANCESTORS

Civil registration	92
Census returns	106
Trade and commercial directories	116
Military records	120
Education records	131
Enclosure and tithe awards	133
The New Poor Law 1834–1930	138
Working men	142
Prison records	144
Protestant Nonconformity	146
Roman Catholicism	150
Jewish records	152

Introduction

A friend of mine who died in 2002 at the good old age of 101 told me that he could remember that in his younger days he listened to his grandfather, who recalled the stories of two old soldiers who had fought against Napoleon. This amazing link with the distant past shows how ancient memories could be preserved and passed on down the generations. Yet when we start to trace our family trees, few of us have any knowledge of our direct forebears before the reign of Queen Victoria. Indeed, it is common to find that nowadays memories go back no further than three generations. The information provided by census returns, civil registration records and parish registers is often a revelation to us. Because we know so little about the two or three generations before our grandparents, we tend also to think that they had similar lifestyles. In fact, the nineteenth century was a period of remarkable and continuous change. This was the time when Britain became the 'Workshop of the World' and the British Empire covered more than one-fifth of the land surface of the globe. The pace of change was unprecedented.

Throughout the nineteenth century the population of England and Wales rose at an astonishing rate. The 1801 census recorded 8.9 million people, a figure that is usually adjusted to 9.2 million, to take account of

Britannia and Industry, a poster of 1887 commemorating Queen Victoria's Golden Jubilee.

under-recording. Fifty years later, it had just about doubled to 17.9 million, and by 1901 it had almost doubled again to 32.5 million. The second decade of the nineteenth century experienced the fastest rate of growth ever and the rapid rise continued in each decade up to the First World War. In 1801 England and Wales were still largely rural countries, with only one in three people living in towns, but during the next 50 years the proportion of urban dwellers rose to 54 per cent, if a town was defined as a place with more than 2,000 inhabitants. For the first time in history countryfolk were in a minority. At the end of the nineteenth century three-quarters of the population lived in urban districts and Britain as a whole had become the most urbanized country in the world.

Peckham Rye, 1882. By the 1860s the suburbs of south London had spread over Camberwell, Peckham, Dulwich, Clapham and Streatham. They could be reached by horse-drawn omnibus.

IN BRIEF

- The population of England and Wales in 1901 was 32.5 million, nearly four times higher than it had been 100 years earlier.

- Three in every four people now lived in towns.

- Britain was the 'Workshop of the World' and its empire covered more than one-fifth of the land surface of the globe.

Urban and rural

The number of people living in towns continued to grow enormously in the second half of the nineteenth century. As always, London led the way. The capital city had long been a giant compared with the provincial towns. In 1801 it already had over 900,000 inhabitants, whereas Manchester, the second largest place, had a relatively modest 84,000. Victorian London sprawled in all directions, swallowing neighbouring settlements, until by the end of the nineteenth century over 6.5 million people considered themselves Londoners. In the provinces, the old hierarchy of towns was overturned as the new industrial centres outpaced the ancient cities; of the leading

medieval centres only Bristol and Newcastle-upon-Tyne remained in the ranks of the top dozen. By 1901 Liverpool had 684,958 inhabitants, Manchester 543,872, Birmingham 522,204, Leeds 428,968, Sheffield 380,793, Bristol 328,545, and Bradford, Kingston-upon-Hull, Nottingham, Salford, Newcastle-upon-Tyne and Leicester each had over 200,000. The great ports and the centres of the manufacturing and mining districts in the Midlands and the north of England now dominated the national economy. Meanwhile, Wales had changed fundamentally. In previous centuries the Welsh had been spread fairly evenly across their country, but during the reign of Victoria the coal mines, iron works and docklands of the south-east attracted immigrants on a huge scale. The population of Wales rose from about 587,000 in 1801 to 2,012,900 in 1901, and whereas at the beginning of the nineteenth century Glamorgan and Gwent accounted for 20 per cent of the Welsh population, by the end of Victoria's reign this proportion had risen to 57.5 per cent.

This spectacular growth of the towns and their surrounding industrial districts was the result not only of the natural increase of the population but of migration from the countryside. Most migrants came from the traditional catchment areas up to 30 miles away (except, as always, for London), but poor farm labourers from the southern

English counties reversed the trend of centuries by moving north in the hope of higher wages and better houses. The first four national censuses reveal that the sharp rise of the rural population since the last quarter of the eighteenth century continued until the 1840s, but because of migration to the towns and industrial districts it did not keep up with the population increase in the country as a whole. Having reached a peak of about 8.25 million in the middle decades of the nineteenth century, the number of people who lived in the countryside shrank slowly during the rest of Victoria's reign. By the later nineteenth century many rural settlements had fewer inhabitants than they had in the early Middle Ages. The drain of population was particularly evident in estate villages where squires turned away the rural poor who might have become a burden on the parish. As the young left in search of better opportunities the composition of rural societies became noticeably older than those of the vibrant towns. In the nation as a whole, agricultural labourers

Church Street, Liverpool, 1894. Liverpool had become the largest English city after London and a great world trading centre. It achieved city status in 1880.

(the 'Ag. labs' of census returns and parish registers), who had formed 23.5 per cent of the total occupied labour force in 1851, accounted for only 9.5 per cent 50 years later.

Much of the countryside was drained of its young people as men went in search of industrial work, where wages were higher, and as girls sought domestic employment in the middle-class suburbs. In the 1850s, and again in the 1870s, a large proportion of the agricultural labourers of Dorset, Somerset and Wiltshire, whose wages were the lowest in England, left with their families for a new life in the industrial districts of south Wales, the Midlands and the north of England, or they emigrated to the United States of America or the colonies. Amos Garland, one of my great-grandfathers, was a Somerset farm labourer who caught the train to Yorkshire, found manual work at some new coke ovens and then brought his family to a newly-built terraced house

Gleaning after harvest, 1896. The custom of collecting stray ears of corn and straw from a field after harvest was an ancient one that made a welcome contribution to the incomes of labouring families.

nearby. One of his brothers emigrated to America, another to South Africa. In the first half of the nineteenth century Somerset had shared in the general rise of population, growing from 274,000 in 1801 to 444,000 in 1851, but during the second half the natural increase did not match the number of people who left, so that by 1901 the county's population had dropped to 433,000. In the north of England rural wages were pulled up by those in the nearby industrial districts. Even so, many places in the northern countryside shrank in size during the later nineteenth century, especially during the 1880s, as the agricultural depression began to bite.

Some of the industrial villages also lost population in the late Victorian period as seams of lead were exhausted or old hand-crafts withered in face of mechanization. The south Midlands counties – Bedfordshire, Buckinghamshire, Northamptonshire – suffered when the men could not find regular work as labourers during the agricultural depression and the women and girls could no longer sell their hand-made lace or their straw hats and bonnets. The number of straw plaiters in

Bedfordshire dropped from 20,701 in 1871 to 485 in 1901. Families moved away or faced a life of debilitating poverty. At the same time, however, large-scale coal mining and quarrying businesses in distant parts of England and Wales were creating a new type of industrial village, where most of the men shared the same occupation and lived in monotonous rows of terraced houses close to their place of work. Many of these new villages were as large as some of the old market towns, but they lacked the social and commercial facilities.

The great industrial cities remained rooted in their localities and served their neighbourhoods in time-honoured fashion. During Victoria's reign all the leading towns rebuilt their market halls and corn exchanges, developed their retail markets, built department stores, widened their streets and became shopping and entertainment centres. But, as yet, the suburbs had not stretched far from the city centres. The Ordnance Survey maps of the late nineteenth century show that, before the age of the motor car, even the largest towns did not extend far into the countryside. Meanwhile, small market towns, that were rather dull except on market days, either grew at a modest pace or practically stood still. Immediately beyond the edges of the towns, great or small, an older, less hurried, way of life was preserved.

'The Hill at Norwich on Market Day', 1871, by F.B. Barwell. Livestock and provision markets were still held in traditional spaces in our great Victorian cities.

Farming

Oil painting entitled 'Suspense', by Archibald Thorburn (1860–1935), showing the old method of hunting grouse by dog and gun before shooting butts were introduced. The grouse-shooting season extended from 12 August to 10 December.

Although the proportion of the national workforce that was engaged in agriculture fell relentlessly during the second half of the nineteenth century, in many counties farming remained the major employer. Within each county, the old differences between, say, the corn-and-sheep husbandry of one 'country' and the dairy farming of another were still marked, both in the prosperous era of 'High Farming' in the first part of Victoria's reign and in the prolonged agricultural depression of the last quarter of the nineteenth century.

The long drawn out process of parliamentary enclosure of open fields and commons accelerated during the Napoleonic wars and was largely complete by the middle of the nineteenth century. During this time, the remaining parishes on the heavier soils and those on the lighter soils of East Anglia, Lincolnshire and the East Riding of Yorkshire, together with the heathland districts of Surrey, Middlesex and Berkshire and the moors of northern and south-western England were enclosed by hawthorn hedges or drystone walls. The Welsh uplands were enclosed a little later, half of them after 1840, but the Welsh pastoral tradition was hardly affected. In midland England red-brick, Georgian farmhouses and barns were built in the former open fields immediately after enclosure, and straight lanes and rectangular, hedged fields produced a planned countryside that looked very different from the older, irregular patterns of fields, lanes, woods and dispersed settlements in the rest of the country. On the edges of towns, some of the old commons were soon covered with housing, while the wildest parts of the countryside were converted into grouse-shooting moors. The passion for shooting game increased with improved gun technology and reached its peak in the years immediately before the First World War.

Parliamentary enclosure may have hastened the decline of the smallholder and helped to create the threefold division of landowner, tenant farmer and labourer in the cereal-growing regions, but it was not the major cause of these developments. Studies of the estate records of great landowners show that the general trend towards larger farms was evident before 1750 and that this trend continued in corn-growing regions whether or not a parish was enclosed. Other studies have demonstrated the remarkable survival of small family farms in certain parts of the country. In Lincolnshire, for instance, large farms were created on the wolds but small farmers survived in the fens and marshlands. In Wiltshire, large farms were formed on the chalkland, but small ones remained the usual type of holding in the cheese-making districts. The great increase in the national population meant that more and more families, especially those that were descended from younger sons and daughters and had no farm to inherit, had to seek employment as waged labourers. The 1851 census suggests that the ratio of labourers to all farmers was 3:1, and that of labourers to those farmers who were employers was 5:1. Meanwhile, the custom for servants living-in declined in southern England, though in districts such as the Yorkshire Wolds it continued well into the twentieth century.

Farm labourers were far from being unskilled workers, for they had to perform a variety of jobs according to the season and the type of farming that was practised in the neighbourhood. On large farms the workforce was graded strictly, on small farms most or all of the work was done by members of the family. Those men who worked solely for one landowner lived in 'tied cottages' that went with the job, but the

'Dinner Time', 1895. A posed photograph by F.M. Sutcliffe, taken in Foulbriggs Field, Lealholm Hall Farm, north Yorkshire. The plough was a local type, based on that invented at North Cave in the East Riding.

day labourers rented or even owned a cottage and garden or perhaps an allotment whose produce helped them through the hard times when they were 'laid off'. The winter months and long spells of bad weather brought great hardship, when families drew on the resources of their friendly society or were dependent on parish relief. The suppers provided by farmers once the harvest was safely gathered in were seen by the labourers as part of their earnings, while gleaning the corn that was left on the ground was considered a traditional right. Flora Thompson reckoned that in north Oxfordshire in the 1880s a family could get two bushels or more of corn through careful gleaning. Poaching was widely regarded as a risky but legitimate way of getting enough to eat and in some districts labourers tenaciously clung on to rights of grazing and collecting fuel. All the members of a family were expected to earn what they could, though the contributions of women and children were under-stated in the census returns. In the eastern regions, especially Lincolnshire and East Anglia, women and children, under the direction of a gang master, moved from farm to farm to meet the demand for

RIGHT
'The Great Egg Question, Sketches at a Poultry Farm', from The Illustrated London News, *2 April, 1887. Letters to a daily paper complaining about the price of eggs in London had started a lively discussion.*

seasonal labour. At harvest time, Irishmen spread into most parts of England and families left the East End of London for the hop fields of Kent.

The depression after the Napoleonic wars hit both agriculture and manufacturing, but during the first half of Victoria's reign an unprecedented period of prosperity formed a golden era for farmers that became known as the time of High Farming. Between 1830 and 1880 agricultural output rose by 60 per cent as farmers invested in new buildings, machinery, underdrainage, and the use of phosphates to supplement traditional manures. The countryside had never looked better. Labouring families did not share this prosperity, however, for the huge rise in population meant that demand for work exceeded supply and so wages were kept low. The prosperous era came to an end in the mid 1870s, when imported corn, particularly from the American prairies, forced wheat prices down by a half and those of barley and oats by about a third. At the same time, Australian imports caused wool prices to fall sharply. A series of wet summers between 1878 and 1882 made matters worse. Many farmers were eventually forced into bankruptcy, but the effects of the depression were not equally severe across the country. The corn-growing districts fared badly, but farmers who concentrated upon livestock, dairy products and fresh vegetables continued to do well. The rapid growth of towns and the creation of a national railway network encouraged farmers to specialize in milk and dairy produce or in market gardening. Those whose soils enabled them to change from cereals managed to survive if they were prepared to adapt.

1. Field with poultry coops.
2. Specimens of good breeds.
3. Incubators, for artificial hatching.
4. Artificial foster-mother, for newborn chicken.
5. Sleeping-house for older chicken.
6. Fattening chicken with the "cramming machine."
7. Higgler and boy collecting poultry.
8. Coops in barn, with chicken fattening.
9. Plucking chicken (killed by the man).
10. Chicken being pressed for packing.
11. Packing-cases for chicken.

THE GREAT EGG QUESTION: SKETCHES AT A POULTRY FARM.

Industry

For most of the nineteenth century Britain was the most advanced industrial nation in the world. 'King Cotton' led the way in making the whole world its market. By 1803 cotton had overtaken wool as Britain's leading export and by the 1880s Britain's share of the world's cotton goods exports had reached 82 per cent. The cotton industry was also the first where all the processes were performed in factories. From 1769 water-powered cotton mills had been erected by Sir Richard Arkwright and other self-made men in remote valleys. They had to attract a workforce by providing better-quality housing than was normally available for working men and their families, and as they were largely dependent on the labour of children, they made much use of pauper apprentices. Before the Factory Act of 1833 several thousand children grew up in apprentice houses. The surviving one at Quarry Bank Mill, Styal, where Samuel Greg developed one of the first great cotton empires, housed 100 children close to the works and near to the cottages, chapel and school.

When steam replaced water as the source of power, the cotton industry moved from Derbyshire to Lancashire, which rapidly became the most urbanised county in Britain. The towns of east Lancashire became dominated by their cotton mills, though weaving did not become factory-based until the widespread adoption of the power-loom in the 1830s and 1840s. The population of Blackburn rose from

Green's Economiser, 1900. The Wakefield firm of E. Green & Son, Ltd claimed substantial savings from their steam boilers. Their advertisement provides a graphic picture of the brick-built cotton mills of Lancashire.

IN BRIEF

- ☞ For most of the nineteenth century Britain was the most advanced industrial nation in the world.

- ☞ The Lancashire cotton industry led the way and was Britain's biggest exporter. Regions that had once been backward now had a leading role in the national economy.

- ☞ The Industrial Revolution was founded on coal. Britain had well over one million coal miners by the First World War.

- ☞ The service sector was another large employer and domestic service was by far the most common occupation for unmarried working-class women.

Meanwhile, the West Riding of Yorkshire was developing in much the same way. In two generations from the 1770s the woollen industry was changed out of recognition by water-powered mills, though the preparation and spinning processes were mechanized long before weaving. Before the late eighteenth century cloth had been made in the villages, hamlets and farmsteads that were scattered on the hillsides high above the river valleys. When workers' houses were built around the mills in the valley bottoms, the ancient pattern of settlement was transformed. In 1822 Edward Baines remarked that in Holmfirth:

> *The houses are scattered in the deep valley, and on the aclivities of the hills, without any regard to arrangement, or the formation of streets ... The traveller, at his first view of this extraordinary village, is struck with astonishment at the singularity of its situation and appearance ... This is a place of great trade, and the principal part of the inhabitants are employed in the manufacture of woollen cloth.*

11,980 in 1801 to 63,126 in 1861, that of Burnley from 3,918 to 28,700 and that of Bury from 9,152 to 30,397; their neighbours grew in similar fashion. For the first three-quarters of the nineteenth century the majority of cotton mill workers were first-generation incomers, many of whom had left the countryside to live in a brick terraced house close to their place of work. The whole nature of work was changed as employees became subject to factory discipline, with its regular hours and routine tasks performed under supervision. Men were put in charge of the spinning mules, while women did the carding and the children were employed at piecing. Women and children outnumbered men, and though the Factory Acts of 1833–74 restricted child labour, families and neighbours continued to operate as working units within a mill. Throughout the nineteenth century large numbers of women and girls were employed in the Lancashire cotton mills. In times of full employment they were better off than females in any other occupation in the kingdom.

For a time, the hill villages continued to grow as rows of weavers' cottages were built to cope with the increased output of yarn in the mills. The number of West Riding woollen mills rose from 129 in 1833 to 880 in 1850, by which time steam engines rather than water wheels were the major source of power. The old methods of making woollen cloth nevertheless remained more productive than the mills until the second quarter of the nineteenth century, and afterwards small mills and workshops long remained more typical than the larger units. Handloom weaving in the cottages continued well into Victoria's reign and other rural workers were able to find employment as coal miners or quarrymen and at the usual range of village crafts. Edward Baines reported that as late as 1859 as many woollen workers were employed outside the factories as within. In the Halifax–Bradford district, which specialized in worsted cloth, the transition to factory production in the early nineteenth century was much more rapid. Population growth was not restricted to the towns; for example, the parish of Birstall at the centre of the textile district had no urban centre but the combined population of its numerous settlements rose from 14,657 in 1801 to 67,424 a hundred years later.

The Industrial Revolution was founded upon coal. The number of British coal miners rose from about 50,000 in 1800 to well over 1 million by the eve of the First World War. When Victoria came to the throne, only a few mines were worked by more than about 50 men, but in the second half of the nineteenth century deep mines were sunk to the most productive seams and

the railways opened up a national market, so that by 1900 a typical pit employed well over 300 men and boys. The different coalfields lost many of their peculiarities as the miners became the country's most numerous and distinctive group of workers. As the industry grew, miners moved from pit to pit and often to other coalfields in search of better wages. They were the most mobile group of workers in the country until they settled in their new communities towards the end of the century. The early

Two miners with an empty and a loaded truck of coal on an endless rope-haulage system, 1894.

census records show that young miners were recruited from all parts of the country, but the later ones demonstrate that the majority of mining families had restricted their movements to the coalfield with which they were familiar. In the first half of the nineteenth century the usual accommodation for a coal miner and his family was a single-storey cottage, but during the second half of the century a two-up, two-down house in a long terrace became normal, as pit villages were built to high densities in unimaginative layouts. In south Wales, a new type of community was forged in the valleys. The Rhondda Valley had less than 1,000 people in 1801, but more than 114,000 a hundred years later. The pit villages offered a sharp contrast to the older villages around them, though of course some miners lived in ordinary villages or in isolated rows near the pithead.

The new quarrying settlements were similar in appearance to the pit villages. The most famous quarries were those in north Wales, where the largest slate quarries in the world were found at Penrhyn, Llanberis and Blaenau Ffestiniog once the railways had opened up a national market for Welsh blue slates. Wherever suitable clays could be found, brickworks catered for the increased demand for buildings, but many of the works were small and open only during the summer months. By contrast, Cornwall and the Yorkshire Dales experienced a mass exodus of workers and their families, often to foreign countries, as the mining of lead, copper and tin declined dramatically.

The Great Exhibition of 1851 triumphantly demonstrated that Britain had become the leading manufacturing country in the world. Incredible quantities of finished goods, machines and tools were exported from the metalworking districts to distant parts of the globe. The metal trades ranged from highly-skilled crafts such as the making of surgical instruments to repetitive and simple jobs such as nailmaking. Hand tools were not only the basis of the old agricultural economy, they shaped the modern industrial world. The production of tools for a global market increased considerably from the second half of the eighteenth century and reached its peak in the Victorian period, when Sheffield was the world's major centre

A celebration of industrial progress in Queen Victoria's Golden Jubilee year.

69

INDUSTRY

of tool production with an amazing range of files, saws, planes, hammers, spades, and other products. During the nineteenth century steam replaced water as the source of power in the metalworking industries. Typical of the new units in Sheffield was Butcher's Works, which in its heyday from the 1830s to the 1860s made steel files, razors, chisels, planes, high-quality table cutlery, pocket knives and Bowie knives for Americans. Three-storey brick workshops were arranged around a yard, from the centre of which soared a huge chimney. During the second half of Victoria's reign the traditional hand-craft basis of tool production gave way to mechanization. By the 1870s Sheffield had well over 250 tool firms, most of them small-scale, but several employing 200–400 men. By that time, the major cutlery factories – Rodgers', Wostenholm's, and Mappin's – also employed hundreds of men, but the industry remained characterized by numerous small workshops rented by independent craftsmen. Close parallels could be observed in the metalworking district known as the Black Country.

The primary production of iron and steel by puddling, rolling, smelting and casting, using coke fuel rather than charcoal,

required huge capital investment in large works that sometimes employed thousands of men. Whole new towns, notably Middlesbrough and Barrow-in-Furness, were created as migrant workers from far afield were housed close to the works. Middlesbrough was a hamlet of 25 people in 1801, but a thriving town of 91,302 inhabitants 100 years later. Elsewhere, industrial towns had new working-class districts grafted on to them. From about 1840 the east end of Sheffield was transformed by the huge steel works of Cammell, Brown, Firth, Hatfield, Jessop, Vickers and others and new terraces were built on the valley sides to house the workers. This 'heavy industry' district, which drew part of its workforce from neighbouring counties and beyond, was very different from the districts in and around the old part of the town where the traditional 'light trades' were performed by men whose surnames were often distinctly local. Other industrial towns, such as St Helens and Widnes, sprung up around

Regent Street, London, looking north, with Dickins & Jones on the right and the Hanover Chapel on the left, 1835, by G. S. Shepherd.

the new chemical works (the alkali trade, dyestuffs, bleach, soap and glass). The poor immigrants who came to live in this polluted landscape near the Mersey were of different stock from the traditional textile workers in the eastern half of Lancashire. About the same time, the railways transformed the old towns of Doncaster and Swindon and created the new town of Crewe.

The industrial towns of Victorian England were known for their particular products. Manchester was 'Cottonopolis', Bradford was 'Worstedopolis', and Stoke-on-Trent was an amalgamation of the six settlements of the Potteries. These specializations produced towns that were very different in appearance and character from each other. In the Victorian era people still lived in intensely local worlds. They rarely visited other major towns or even the capital city. Working life in the East End of London was very different not only from the West End but from the pit villages or mill towns in the rest of England, where most men had the same occupations as their neighbours. The work places of East Enders provided space for a small number of permanent craftsmen, while a large pool of unskilled labourers earned an irregular living at home, assembling furniture, stitching silk cloth, and making consumer goods such as carbonated drinks, vinegar, cigars and cigarettes, and artificial flowers.

Manufacturing is the dominant image of the Victorian era, but even then the service sector was substantial. The basic consumer industries – those concerned with the processing of food, drink and tobacco – employed over 1 million workers by 1901. In the growing industrial towns fortunes could

be made from brewing, the making of confectionery and the founding of department stores. The number of men in the building trades grew from half a million in 1851 to 1.3 million half a century later, though their methods and organization hardly changed. Towards the end of the nineteenth century three out of every four building firms employed fewer than ten workers and half of them had less than five. The transport sector also grew considerably with the coming of the railways and the need to move people to and from their place of work in the expanding towns. In 1901 those 'employed in the conveyance of men, goods and messages' numbered 1,267,825, including 18,825 women.

Domestic service was by far the most common occupation for unmarried working-class women. By 1901 they numbered 1,330,783. Many married women worked at home, taking in washing as 'manglers' or as out-workers for local firms, and others walked to neighbouring suburbs to do the housework for middle-class families. The census returns do not reveal the full story of female employment. In both the towns and the countryside working-class women took whatever employment opportunities presented themselves to add something to the family's income.

RIGHT
Maid ironing, 1899. About one in three women in Victorian England worked as a domestic servant when young.

Families

An advertisement of 1894 for one of the many home improvements of the time.

The huge population rise in the nineteenth century came about because of a combination of earlier marriages, and therefore more children, and declining death rates. During the late eighteenth century and for much of the nineteenth, couples had married at younger ages than in the preceding centuries, but during the 1870s the picture began to change throughout the whole of western Europe. In 1881 the median age at marriage for spinsters in England and Wales was 23.2, by 1891 it had risen to 23.7, and by 1901 it had reached 24.0. This upward trend might seem marginal at the level of individual decisions, but across the nation it represented a significant shift. At the same time, the proportion of English women who never married rose to 14 per cent by 1901. Yet for most of this period real incomes were rising.

People were deliberately choosing to have fewer children or not to marry at all in order to enjoy a more comfortable way of life.

The local societies of nineteenth-century England and Wales were youthful compared with today, with relatively few old people and numerous youngsters. Families had little space for privacy in their cramped houses. In the first half of the century the average family had six children, one of whom would die in infancy and another in childhood. Of course, averages disguise a considerable range of experience, but it is clear that from the 1870s both the crude birth rate and the fertility rate began to fall. By 1901 they were about 25 per cent lower than their peaks. Later ages at marriage and increasing numbers of people who never married explain half this fall; the rest must have been the result of birth control. The size of a family varied according to the father's occupation, with miners and farm labourers having more children than textile workers, and also from place to place whatever the occupation. Birth certificates show that babies were usually born at home, with unofficial midwives in attendance. The proportion of brides who were pregnant when they married fell from about 40 per cent in the early nineteenth century to under 20 per cent in the early twentieth century. At the same time, the number of illegitimate births fell from 6 per cent of all live births in the mid-nineteenth century to 4 per cent in 1900, though illegitimacy rates remained higher in the countryside, where social attitudes were less disapproving.

Death rates were particularly high in the first year of a child's life, even among the upper classes, though they were worse for illegitimate children and those whose parents were the least educated and the heaviest drinkers. Crowded homes, dirt and poor sanitation increased the risks. The common gastro-intestinal disorders, which lead to diarrhoea and dysentery, came from contaminated water and from food and drink infected by flies. Horse dung in the streets attracted flies, cesspools and open drains bred disease in the countryside. Living in the countryside was healthier than living in the towns, in terms of both greater expectation of life and lower death rates. Infant mortality remained high throughout Victoria's reign, but between 1870 and 1900 death rates for children under 15 declined by about a third because of a higher standard of living and better nutrition, public health reforms, and effective medicines for some infectious diseases.

FAMILIES

A group of poor people pose for a photograph entitled 'Out cast London' in 1884.

Children were most prone to illness in winter and spring, leading to secondary pneumonia, though autumn deaths were often caused by diarrhoeal infections caught in the summer months. School log books frequently mention not only coughs, colds and sore throats, but bronchitis, influenza, whooping cough, mumps, chicken pox, skin disease, and outbreaks of the three most dreaded diseases – measles, scarlet fever and diphtheria – which struck at any time of the year. Measles had been a feared killer of children since the late eighteenth century. It was endemic in London and other large towns and industrial districts and often spread suddenly into the surrounding countryside. Scarlet fever caused 10,000

Mary ward, Guy's Hospital, London, 1897.

deaths per annum in the middle of the nineteenth century, especially among children of all social classes under the age of six. It spread through the whole of England and Wales between 1868 and 1870, but by 1900 effective medicines reduced the number of deaths to about a fifth of what they had been. Diphtheria was a new disease of Victorian times. The first epidemic came in 1858–65 and it was feared until a serum treatment was introduced successfully in 1894. Whooping cough was another disease that killed infants and children from all classes of society; two out of every three of those who succumbed were under the age of two. During the second half of the nineteenth century local authorities achieved

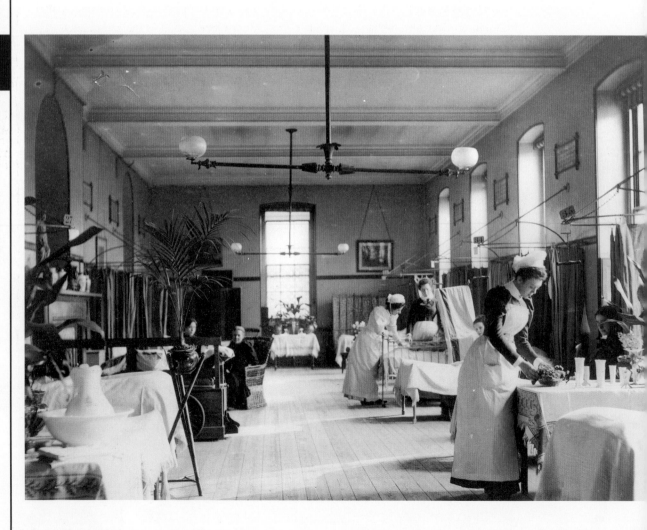

some notable successes in the war against infectious disease. Smallpox had killed thousands of children in the eighteenth and early nineteenth centuries and had maimed many others, but compulsory vaccination proved largely effective. Even so, local epidemics continued and major outbreaks across the country occurred in 1870–3 and 1902–5.

Those who survived childhood could not expect to live to a ripe old age. By the end of the nineteenth century upper-class people were living on average for nearly 60 years, twice the life expectancy of the poorest section of society, who were no better off in this respect than their Tudor forebears. In 1861 it was calculated that 38 per cent of women and 45 per cent of men died between the ages of 25 and 65, figures that compare with 15 or 16 per cent at the present time. Although some people lived as long as the oldest people of today, they formed a small proportion of the population. The leading causes of adult deaths were heart disease and tuberculosis (TB), or consumption as it was usually known. Even in the first decade of the twentieth century 75,000 British people from all classes of society suffered a lingering death from TB every year. In the first half of the nineteenth century, water-borne diseases, such as cholera and dysentery, had killed thousands, but public health reforms had removed these threats, while a general improvement in personal cleanliness had stopped the outbreaks of typhus, which had been spread by body lice. The great advances in medical knowledge and the higher standard of living in the later nineteenth century reduced the mortality rates, but most working-class families could not afford a visit from a doctor and so relied upon folk remedies and patent medicines

IN BRIEF

- By the late nineteenth century couples were marrying later and the proportion of English women who never married rose to 14 per cent.
- Society in late-Victorian times was much more youthful than it is today. Far fewer people lived to a good old age.
- Infant mortality rates began to fall in the late nineteenth century but were still very high by modern standards.
- In 1901 the average household size was 4.6 people, more or less the same as it had been for centuries.

that were often ineffective. Children in the smoke-filled towns where the sun shone weakly were deformed by rickets or stunted by their inadequate diet. The working classes were noticeably smaller than the wealthier sections of society. Britain was the richest country in the world, but thousands of volunteers for the Boer War were rejected on medical grounds.

Old people lived in their own house as long as they were able to look after themselves, but near to their children, if they could, sometimes with an unmarried child, an elder grandchild or a lodger to accompany them. The census returns of the nineteenth century show that most households consisted just of husband, wife and unmarried children. In 1901 the average household size was 4.6 people, more or less the same as it had been for centuries, but of course this figure conceals a wide range of experience at different stages of the life cycle. The average disguises the number of extended families at one end of the scale and the houses with just one or two people at the other.

FAMILIES

Stability and mobility

In Victorian England and Wales most families had close relations living nearby, in the next village or hamlet or in neighbouring streets in the towns. Families were spread out across the district they recognized as their 'country', a term for a neighbourhood that was still in common use. In every part of the kingdom core groups of families continued to inhabit the 'country' of their ancestors for generation after generation. The constant movement of people across parish boundaries hides this underlying pattern of residential stability, but the persistence of farming and craft families within a restricted area, and their dynastic connections, were remarkable features of the Victorian countryside, just as they had been in the past. In the towns, too, families tended to move only a few streets at a time; the London boroughs were no

different from the rural 'countries' in this respect. The 1851 census revealed that 80 per cent of the people who had been born in England and Wales were living in the county where their birth was registered.

Even when the railways provided quick and cheap transport to other parts of the country, most people stayed within the same districts as their forebears. The great majority of English and Welsh people never visited London and never met a foreigner. A study of 1,388 family histories compiled by amateur historians has shown that though people often moved, most of them were prepared to travel only short distances

'Outside the Church', c.1860, by an anonymous artist in 'Hymns and Prayers', published by the SPCK, shows a family leaving a service in a country church.

The entrance to Rugby station, 1880s, with a queue of horse-drawn taxis waiting for incoming passengers.

within the neighbourhood with which they were familiar. Until about 1880 mean average migration distances were around 22 miles, though they then rose steadily to around 35 miles in the early years of the twentieth century. Despite the improvements in communications and growing affluence, migratory patterns had changed little over time. All over Britain the trends were essentially similar. Most movement was local, though London and new towns such as Middlesbrough attracted people from far and wide. The only difference from the past was that by mid-Victorian times the large industrial boroughs were drawing workers from ever-widening circles, but even there the majority of immigrants came mainly from the surrounding districts. Those who stayed in the countryside kept to the neighbourhoods or 'countries' of their

ancestors. They spoke differently from outsiders and observed their own customs.

The inhabitants of the scattered settlements of the Blean district in nineteenth-century Kent were often on the move. In each ten-year period about half the population left their parishes, a few of them venturing as far as North America, Australia and New Zealand. The censuses of 1851–81 show that between 60 and 70 per cent of the population aged 15 years and over came from beyond the parish boundary, yet the majority of those who moved in and out stayed within comfortable walking distance. Of several hundred emigrants from Dunkirk and Hernhill, who were living in parishes within a ten-mile arc in 1851, nearly 90 per cent had moved less than five miles away. This pattern of localized movement was typical of every other rural district.

A horse-drawn omnibus at Waterloo, 1900, serving a route into the West End.

In the nineteenth century short-distance movements were made much easier in the towns, first by omnibus services and then by trams. Horse-drawn omnibuses carrying 12–15 passengers were introduced into London in 1829. By the middle of the century companies were providing regular services into central London from the northern and western suburbs. Provincial towns were soon provided with their own omnibus services. In 1870 London led the way with horse-drawn trams, which ran on rails and carried more passengers than the omnibuses. Then, in the late nineteenth and early twentieth centuries local transport became a municipal responsibility and horse-drawn services were replaced by electric trams. Meanwhile, in 1865, London had acquired the first underground railway in the world when the Metropolitan railway began to run between Paddington and Farringdon Street and then on to Moorgate. In the 1890s deep tunnelling methods greatly extended the system and enabled men and women to travel quickly from the suburbs to their places of work. The rapid expansion of cheap transport in all towns during Victoria's reign meant that working-class and lower middle-class suburbs could be built away from workplaces for the first time and that city centres could be turned into shopping and entertainment centres.

The 'railway mania' of the late 1830s and 1840s offered quick and cheap travel to distant places and connected the provincial towns and cities to each other and to London. By 1852 nearly all the main lines of the modern railway system were complete. Families could move to districts where wages were higher and employment was more regular, and if they could afford it they could have a day or even a week or two at the seaside, where new resorts like Blackpool or Skegness were growing rapidly. The Lancashire cotton factories led the way in shutting down for a week or a fortnight in summer. The Saturday half-holiday (from 1850) and the annual bank holiday (from 1871) soon became other occasions for family excursions to the seaside or the countryside.

IN BRIEF

- Most Victorian families had close relations living nearby, in the surrounding streets or in the district they thought of as their 'country'.

- People often moved beyond the parish in which they were born, but on the whole they did not move far, unless they were attracted to London or they decided to emigrate.

- Even when the railways provided quick and cheap transport, most people continued to live in the same districts as their ancestors.

- But short-distance mobility was made easier in the later nineteenth century by omnibus services, trams, railways and the London Underground system.

Emigrants and immigrants

The astonishing rise of the population of England and Wales during the course of the nineteenth century would have reached even greater heights had not hundreds of thousands of families, from every level of society and every form of occupation, emigrated across the Atlantic to the United States and Canada or over much longer distances to Australia, New Zealand, South Africa and other lands in the southern hemisphere. The exact number of people who left these shores is not known, for the records are inadequate, but as the population of the United States rose from about 4 million in 1790 to 23 million in 1850, at a time when the majority of immigrants came from Britain and Ireland, the figure was obviously enormous. In the early part of the nineteenth century the typical emigrants were members of a young family who went in search of cheap land on which to build a permanent home. Some had their journeys paid for by official and charitable schemes, but most had to find their own fares. They travelled 'steerage', crammed together below decks with hundreds of others. Two out of every three emigrants left these shores from Liverpool. Crossing the Atlantic became quicker and cheaper from the 1840s, when

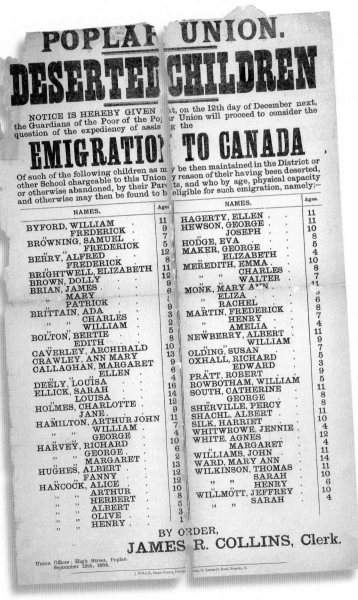

A notice from the Poplar Poor Law Union announcing the assisted passage to Canada of 76 deserted children between the ages of 2 and 16 in 1884.

poor people whose passage was paid by the Government or charity. During the first 30 years of Victoria's reign about 1 million people migrated from the United Kingdom to Australia and New Zealand, compared with some 3.5 million migrants to the United States and 750,000 to Canada. The number of emigrants from England and Wales rose from 160,000 in the 1870s to over 600,000 in the next decade, the peak time for emigration. About two-thirds of those who left were from the towns and industrial districts; only one in six were farm labourers who were leaving the depressed countryside.

As emigrants sailed from Liverpool, large numbers of Irish immigrants came the other

steamships, linked at both ends of the journey by railways, began to replace the old sailing vessels, but it was not until the 1860s that virtually all passengers to the United States and Canada went this way. From then onwards, the typical migrants were young, single adults, with men outnumbering the women by two to one, people who sought not land but industrial employment in the mills and mines. Nearly 40 per cent of English and Welsh people who emigrated between 1861 and 1913 did not settle permanently, for they always intended to return once they had made enough money.

After the American War of Independence Britain had to find a new place to send its convicts. In 1788 a penal colony was founded in Australia and in time 162,000 people were transported there. They were always outnumbered by the 'free settlers' who were prepared to pay their own fares and endure the three months' journey in the hope of a better life and by thousands of

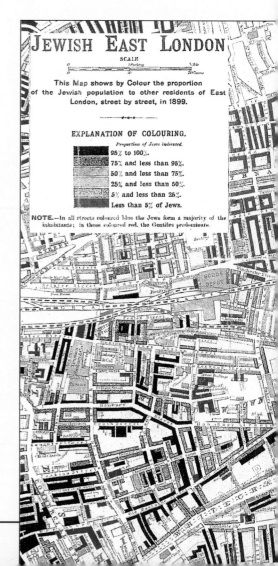

JEWISH EAST LONDON

SCALE

This Map shows by Colour the proportion of the Jewish population to other residents of East London, street by street, in 1899.

EXPLANATION OF COLOURING.

Proportion of Jews indicated.

95% to 100%.
75% and less than 95%.
50% and less than 75%.
25% and less than 50%.
5% and less than 25%.
Less than 5% of Jews.

NOTE.—In all streets coloured blue the Jews form a majority of the inhabitants; in those coloured red, the Gentiles predominate.

way. The 1841 census for England and Wales listed 289,404 people who had been born in Ireland and who had crossed the sea well before the potato famine started five years later. By 1861 the number had risen to 601,634, even though the children of earlier immigrants were not included. The Irish continued to arrive in considerable numbers during the later decades of the nineteenth century, particularly in the late 1870s and 1880s. Between 1851 and 1901 the population of Ireland fell by a half. Most emigrants headed for the New World across the Atlantic, but perhaps as many as 1 million settled in England, Wales and Scotland. Their chief destinations were London, Liverpool, the chemical towns near the

Mersey and the cotton towns of east Lancashire. As early as 1851 Irish-born people formed 22 per cent of Liverpool's population and 13 per cent of Manchester's. The 1881 census revealed that 82 per cent of Irish-born immigrants were day-labourers. They clustered together in the slum districts, often in smaller groups based on their counties of origin. Everywhere they went they faced a hostile reception, for not only were they poor and unskilled, they were looked down on as foreigners (even though they were in fact internal United Kingdom migrants) and Roman Catholics. Most Irish families remained poor and lived in squalid conditions throughout the reign of Victoria and often beyond.

Map of the East End in 1899 from The Jews in London *by C. Russell and H. S. Lewis. The darker colours show where these recent immigrants were concentrated. The letters refer to Jewish burial grounds.*

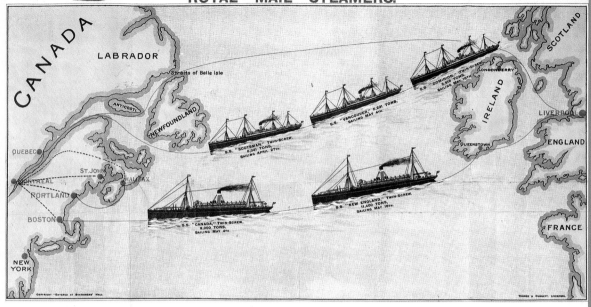

DOMINION LINE
ROYAL MAIL STEAMERS.

REGULAR WEEKLY SAILINGS
BETWEEN
LIVERPOOL AND **BOSTON**, VIA **QUEENSTOWN.**
LIVERPOOL, QUEBEC AND **MONTREAL**, VIA **LONDONDERRY.**
FOR FURTHER PARTICULARS **APPLY HERE.**

An advertisement of the Dominion Line of the regular weekly sailings from Liverpool to the United States and Canada, 1899.

The second largest group of immigrants were the Jews who had escaped from the pogroms of Tsar Alexander III's Russian Empire. The 1901 census enumerated 61,789 people from Russia and 21,055 from Russian Poland who had settled mainly in the East End of London or in particular districts of Manchester and Leeds. Like all immigrants, they sought help and reassurance by living together in well-defined areas. Many were forced to earn a poor living in the 'sweated workshops' that were run by the more enterprising of their fellow immigrants, making clothes, boots and cabinets or hawking cheap goods around the streets. By 1901 the East End of London, particularly

the borough of Stepney, housed 53,537 Russian and Polish Jews. Four years later, the Aliens Act brought this movement to an end. Few of these immigrants chose to become British by naturalization, perhaps because of the costs involved, but perhaps also because they did not fear ejection. The other groups of foreigners – Germans, French, Italians, Chinese and small numbers of other nationalities – were far less noticeable, except when they congregated in certain districts. The 1901 census noted that 99 per cent of the residents of England and Wales had been born within the British Empire.

Houses

During the long reign of Queen Victoria the middle classes stopped living over their offices and shops and moved to new suburbs a mile or two away from the smoke, the dirt and the noise. They journeyed into town each working day on the horse-drawn omnibuses or the railways, or perhaps on foot. The working classes remained close to their places of work until electric trams provided cheap transport at the end of the century. Towns were socially segregated as never before. Sheffield, for example, became divided between the working-class settlements around the new steelworks in the east end and the leafy suburbs that stretched into attractive countryside in the west, where all the steel masters and other businessmen lived.

Most middle-class families rented their suburban villas. Landlords often exercised strict control of the new estates by inserting clauses in the leases which prevented the building of industrial premises and even

Plans and elevations of the 'semi-detached villas' on the Bedford Park estate, Turnham Green, London, 1878.

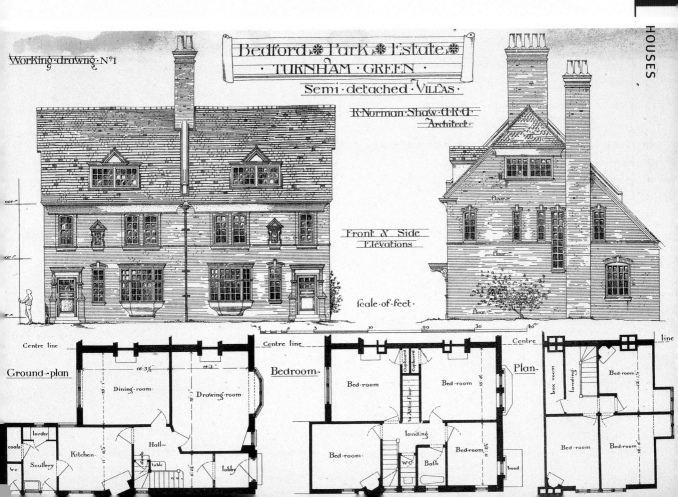

Working·drawng·Nº1

Bedford ❋ Park ❋ Estate
· TURNHAM · GREEN ·
Semi·detached·VILLAS·

R·Norman·Shaw·A·R·A·
Architect

Front & Side Elevations

scale·of·feet.

Ground·plan   Centre line

Dining-room   Drawing-room

larder
coals
Kitchen   Hall~
Scullery   lobby
w.c

Bedroom   Centre line   Plan.   Centre line

Bed·room   Bed·room   box room   landing   Bed·room
to Attic floor
Bed·room   landing   Bed·room   Bed·room
w.c   Bath

Charlotte Road, Edgbaston, a leafy suburb of Birmingham, c.1900.

shops. Food, goods and other services were delivered to the door. Thus, Edgbaston became a green suburb for Birmingham businessmen, with fine walks lined by trees and three elegant churches erected in dignified squares, the middle classes of Leeds were housed at Roundhay and those of Huddersfield at Edgerton.

The vernacular tradition of building survived well into the nineteenth century, until the railways reduced the transport costs of Welsh blue slates and machine-made bricks. At first, labourers' cottages remained very small and low and often consisted of just one room. The houses of the mill workers were built in terraced rows or arranged around folds and yards, often as back-to-backs, which had become the typical form of working-class accommodation in the industrial towns of northern England from the late eighteenth century. Their walls were shared by three other houses and the accommodation consisted of one room on the ground floor and one or two rooms above. It has been calculated that half the houses that were standing in Leeds on the eve of the First World War had been built before 1841 and that two-thirds of these were back-to-backs. In the middle decades of the nineteenth

century most local authorities passed laws forbidding further buildings in this style.

In 1849 the *Bradford Observer* published an outsider's report on the town:

Bradford may be described as an accumulation of main streets, steep lanes and huge mills – intersected here and there by those odious patches of black, muddy waste ground, rooted up by pigs, and strewed with oyster shells, cabbage stalks, and such garbage, which I have noticed as commonly existing in manufacturing towns …

Cellars are very numerous in Bradford, and not one operative family in a hundred possesses more than two rooms – 'a house and a chamber'. In respect of dwelling accommodation the worst feature of the stuff and woollen towns is that they seem to be making little or no progress. In the case of ranges of houses, even of a comparatively superior class, the privies are built in clusters, in a small space, left open behind, instead of each being placed in a quiet, decent situation, close to the house to which it belongs.

Nevertheless, the corporation had recently paved and drained over 30 streets and some of the worst Irish colonies had been 'materially improved'. Trade was exceedingly brisk and the relatively few paupers were mainly 'Irish and English agricultural labourers who have not as yet learned to be useful in their new sphere'. In the second half of the century the town centre of Bradford was transformed by civic pride into one of the finest in England.

Titus Salt's Saltaire works and part of his model community: an engraving by W.H. Prior for The Illustrated Times, *8 October 1859.*

In 1853, five years after he had been made mayor of Bradford, Titus Salt opened his enormous alpaca and mohair mill in the countryside and laid out the model village of Saltaire. Eventually 820 houses were erected in a grid pattern of 29 streets. Built of good-quality stone, each house had a parlour, kitchen, two or three bedrooms and a back yard, though no garden. Salt provided Congregational and Methodist churches, an institute and a school, an attractive park, but no pubs. Saltaire attracted enormous interest but few other enlightened businessmen followed his example until the closing years of the century. The model villages of paternalist employers housed only a small fraction of working-class families.

By the second half of Victoria's reign, the typical house of the better-off 'artisans' had a wider street frontage, a bow window, and sometimes a little railed-in garden. The

IN BRIEF

- In Victoria's reign the middle classes left the town centre for new suburbs. The working classes stayed close to their places of work until electric trams provided cheap transport at the end of the nineteenth century.

- Back-to-back terraced houses were usual in the towns of the industrial North in the first half of the nineteenth century. Some towns were notorious for housing their working-class families in cellars.

- Model communities such as Saltaire set high standards, but they housed only a small fraction of the population.

- In the countryside, the cottages in estate villages were often far superior to those in the 'open' villages that had no resident squire.

few had a bathroom. A tin bath in front of the fire had to suffice. Much more common were the two-up, two-down houses with back yards and narrow alleys that were the standard design for those with moderate but regular wages. Most of them had neither cellars nor attics. Often jerry-built, they were erected in narrow streets and were dull and dreary in appearance. Worst of all were the slums with only two or three rooms that had been built in the years before the Public Health Acts and local by-laws insisted on higher standards. They were dark, dirty, damp and overcrowded, arranged around yards with communal ashpits and earth closets.

Living conditions in the working-class districts of Victorian towns improved during the later nineteenth century as local authorities began to provide proper sanitation and to oversee the building of houses, while smaller families and rising wages meant more space and a little money

sitting room or parlour fronted the street, the kitchen or living room was at the back, leading to a small scullery with a water tap and a sink and a 'copper' for washing. A water closet stood in a small, flagged yard at the rear. Floors were covered with linoleum and pegged rugs that had been made by the family in the winter months. Each of these better-class workers' houses had three bedrooms, two of which had fireplaces, but

to spend on domestic comforts. Overcrowding gradually eased, though all towns still had serious problems at the end of the century. In London, a typical solution was to divide buildings into two or three houses, with separate families on each floor. By the end of Victoria's reign all towns had a supply of piped water, though the Monday washing in the kitchen or scullery still relied on the 'set pot' or copper, heated by a coal fire. Another improvement in the last few years of the nineteenth century was the provision of gas, regulated by slot meters. Families in the towns, though not yet in the countryside, were able to throw away their paraffin lamps and to use gas cookers instead of pans on the open fire in the kitchen.

RIGHT
A woman and boy drawing water from a village well, 1895.

A typical Victorian terrace with polychromatic brickwork, in suburban London.

Those who lived in the industrial villages surrounding the towns were housed in much the same way as urban dwellers, though sanitation facilities remained poor. In the farming villages and hamlets families still had to rely on pumps and wells for their water and the pervading smell of cesspits competed with that of farm manure. Though many a squire had built an estate village with superior accommodation for the workers, and life in the countryside was undoubtedly healthier than in the towns, the cottages of the rural poor were a disgrace. The worst ones were found in south-western England, where farm workers' wages were the lowest in the land.

As the national population rose rapidly in the last quarter of the eighteenth century and the first quarter of the nineteenth so did expenditure on the poor. Parish rates not only supported more people but paid for a greater range of goods and services than before. Many districts throughout the country now had a sub-group of families who were always poor and who passed on the culture of being poor to their children. By the early 1800s it was not uncommon to find communities where over half the population was directly dependent on poor relief. The burden was spread unevenly between the 'open' villages, which had no squires and which admitted immigrants, and the 'close' villages where a squire or a small group of farmers could bar entry to anyone whom they feared would become dependent on the parish. Many 'close' villages were surrounded by 'open' ones from which farm labourers walked to work. The clamour to lessen the poor rates and to make all who were capable pay their share led to the passing of the Poor Law Amendment Act in 1834, which transferred responsibility for the poor from parish vestries to the elected Boards of Guardians of the new Poor Law Unions and ushered in the harsher system that was immortalized in the novels of Charles Dickens.

Progress

The numerous reminiscences and local histories that were published towards the end of Victoria's reign leave no doubt that life had become much better than it had been in the tough times of the first half of the nineteenth century. Higher wages and lower food prices, improved housing and sanitation, gas lights and cookers, better transport, restrictions on the hours of work, provision of schools and compulsory attendance, medical advances, the more efficient enforcement of law and order, the benign influence of churches and chapels, clubs and societies, and organized sport all contributed to a higher quality of life.

The writers recalled the savage conduct, drunkenness and coarse language of their childhood days, the brutal sports of bull- and bear-baiting, dog- and cock-fighting, the casual cruelty and the running battles between villages. Joseph Lawson, who was born in Pudsey, at the heart of the West Riding textile district in 1821, remembered an insular world where

there were only two places to go to in spending spare time away from one's own house – the church or chapel, and the alehouse; the former were seldom open, while the latter was seldom closed.

Yet they all felt superior to the inhabitants of neighbouring villages:

It was a common remark … that Yeadon was the last place that God made, and that He made it out of the refuse.

Weddings and the birth of children were celebrated by heavy drinking, while funerals were often even noisier. The most important event of the year was the local feast, when families gathered together and former residents returned home. The unruly crowds and the rough nature of many of the attractions led to calls for their suppression, but many feasts faded as railway excursions to the seaside became popular. In the first half of the nineteenth century the hours of work were long and holidays were few. Sundays and the afternoons of Good Friday and Christmas Day were the only official

IN BRIEF

- By the end of Victoria's reign, improvements including higher wages, lower food prices, and better housing and sanitation, had produced a higher quality of life.
- Most working-class houses had gas light, running water and drainage, carpets, rugs and comfortable furniture, and perhaps even a piano.
- Britain led the way with organized sport, especially football, rugby and cricket, at both professional and amateur levels.
- Britain had become the richest country in the world, but the lives of our ancestors seem humdrum to us.

An advertisement of 1887 showing the sports equipment manufactured by Richard Allen.

times off, though semi-independent craftsmen could organize their working weeks so that 'Saint Monday' became a day of beer drinking and relaxation. Legislation began to shorten working hours, then the churches and chapels turned Easter and Whitsuntide into public festivals and from the 1850s Christmas began to be celebrated in a modern way.

Sporting events were changed radically as the century advanced. Football games between rival villages, like that still celebrated at Ashbourne on Shrove Tuesdays, ranged over miles of fields and rough ground, with few or any rules. Even when nowhere near the ball, men kicked each other ferociously. The Saturday half-holiday that was granted in 1850 was instrumental in a change of attitude. By the 1860s and 1870s association football, rugby and cricket became organized sports with agreed rules and competitions at both professional and amateur level. Local rivalries could now be expressed in more civilized ways by participants and spectators alike.

Music was another improving influence that played a large part in many people's lives. Joseph Lawson thought that 'perhaps there is nothing in which Pudsey has made so much progress during the last sixty years as it has in music.' The performances of the Pudsey Old Red Band were 'child's play' compared with later standards. Brass bands, orchestras, choirs and handbell ringers attracted enthusiastic audiences for their concerts. Members walked long distances to and from practices after working all day and large crowds took part in outdoor local sing-songs organized by the churches and chapels. Book clubs, lending libraries and mechanics' institutes encouraged

self-improvement and countered the old ignorance and beliefs in ghosts, fairies and witches, but it was not until elementary education became compulsory that real improvements were made. In 1850 only about half the grooms were able to sign the marriage register; by 1900 almost all could do so.

The published reminiscences of life in the early decades of the nineteenth century depict homes that were devoid of comfort. In the weavers' cottages little room was available for the simple furniture and turn-up beds amidst the looms and spinning wheels, and the stink of the urine that was used in the warping process was abominable. The vile communal privies in the folds or yards added to the smell and general discomfort. Even in the 1840s many houses and cottages had no proper drainage and were lit by dim rushlights or whale-oil lamps or just by the light of the fire. By the

Sea-bathing at Sandown, Isle of Wight, 1887, when horse-drawn bathing machines were still in use.

An undated advertisement promoting the joint benefits of Wright's gas cooker and Coombs' aerated pastry flour.

AN ADMITTED ANTIDOTE FOR INDIGESTION.

COOMBS' AERATED PASTRY FLOUR Coombs Flour

To Secure Delicious & Well Cooked Pastry USE COOMBS' "EUREKA" FLOUR. & WRIGHT'S "EUREKA" GAS COOKER.

end of the nineteenth century, however, much improvement was evident. Most working-class houses not only had gas light, running water and drainage, a great many had a carpet or rugs, horsehair-padded chairs, a mahogany sideboard, soft furnishings, and perhaps even a piano.

Before Victoria came to the throne, masters and men spoke the same dialect and the master's clothes were little better than the workman's. Men and women took snuff or smoked long clay pipes and men often shaved only on Sunday. Many people were undersized through malnutrition, their faces disfigured by missing teeth or the ravages of smallpox. Families lived on oatcakes and porridge, supplemented whenever possible with potatoes, a little bacon and skimmed milk, and with whatever vegetables they could get. In the early nineteenth century each neighbourhood still relied on a communal oven for baking, but after the Napoleonic wars foundries turned from the

manufacture of cannon to the production of cast-iron ranges with fireside ovens at prices that were cheap enough for the working classes to buy. By the 1850s most families had an oven range, just as the repeal of the Corn Laws lowered the price of cereals. The following decades have been seen as a golden era of home baking.

Even the workhouses became more humanitarian towards the end of the century. From 1885 old couples in workhouses were officially allowed to stay together. Soon afterwards newspapers and books, tobacco and snuff were provided and individual clothing allowed instead of uniforms. But although the standard of living was certainly higher for most people at the close of the Victorian era than it had been in the early nineteenth century, and Britain had become the richest country in the world, to us the lives of our ancestors seem humdrum and full of everyday problems.

Civil registration

The finest set of records available to family historians in England and Wales are the certificates of births, marriages and deaths that were registered by the state. The system began on 1 July 1837, ten days after Queen Victoria came to the throne.

The Family Records Centre

☞ The indexes of all these registered events were once held at St Catherine's House, Kingsway, London, but they are now kept at the Family Records Centre, 1 Myddelton Street, London EC1R 1UW.

☞ The centre is open on Mondays, Wednesdays and Fridays, from 9 a.m. to 5 p.m., Tuesdays from 10 a.m. to 7 p.m., Thursdays from 9 a.m. to 7 p.m., and Saturdays from 9.30 a.m. to 5 p.m. The centre is closed on bank holidays.

☞ Entry to the building is free and neither a reader's ticket nor a prior appointment is needed.

☞ FRC information leaflets can be picked up near the enquiry desks or downloaded from the website <www.familyrecords.gov.uk/frc>.

At the Family Records Centre the indexes are stacked on shelves that are arranged in separate sections for births, marriages and deaths, running right up to the present day. The earliest ones are handwritten and so are bulky and awkward to fit on the tables, where sufficient space is difficult to find at the busiest times. Many readers lift the indexes on and off the shelves with that frenzied, concentrated look which we normally associate with exercising at a fitness centre. Others chat in pairs, look puzzled and sigh deeply, or exclaim in triumph when they find that elusive ancestor. It is sometimes possible to find what you want straightaway, but just as often it takes more than one visit to find an entry, and sometimes the information simply isn't there when it ought to be. The civil registration records are amongst the most informative documents that a family historian is likely to find, but the indexes can be maddeningly frustrating. If you can't find what you want, it isn't always your fault, though it is usually because you are starting with the wrong information.

☞ Up to 1893, the indexes are handwritten and arranged in years, divided into quarters, ending in March, June, September and December.

☞ The surnames in each quarter are listed alphabetically and several volumes are needed for each quarter, e.g. A to C, D to G, and so on.

- ☞ In the second column the forenames for each surname are also arranged alphabetically.

- ☞ From 1984, the indexes are arranged in annual volumes. From 1894, indexes are typewritten.

The indexes are generally easy to use, but complications arise if names are spelt differently from what we expected. The surname Coomber, for example, might be spelt Comber or Coumber, or someone known in the family as Harry might have been registered as Henry, or perhaps William Henry, so a wider search of the indexes will be necessary. Usually, we don't have a precise date to look for, but perhaps have a rough idea of when an ancestor was born from an age recorded on a gravestone or a death certificate, so several indexes may have to be consulted. Marriages might be found by working backwards from the birth of a child, or deaths discovered by moving forwards from a census return.

After listing the surname and forename, the indexes of births name the superintendent registrar's district where the event was registered. The names of these districts, which were much larger than parishes, will often be unfamiliar to us. They were based on the poor law unions which had been created in 1834. An index to the registration districts is provided on the website: <www.genuki.org.uk/big/eng/civreg/GROIndexes.html> and in B. Langston, *A Handbook to the Civil Registration Districts of England and Wales* (privately published, 2001). The Institute of Heraldic and Genealogical Studies, Canterbury, has published three maps, covering the periods 1837–51, 1852–1946, and from 1947, which show the position of these districts, though

Using the birth indexes at the Family Records Centre.

not their precise boundaries. In 1852 the original 619 districts were increased to 623 and some minor boundary changes were made.

Each district was divided into sub-districts which were the responsibility of local registrars. Every three months the local registrars sent copies of the certificates that they had issued to the Registrar-General. At the same time, ministers of churches sent copies of marriage certificates. Up to 1899 a marriage ceremony in a Protestant Nonconformist or Roman Catholic church had to be held in the presence of a civil registrar. From 1837 marriages could be performed in a civil registry office. Couples used this option in London, and perhaps other large towns, especially when the bride was pregnant, but in many parts of the country the fashion for civil marriages did not start until the second half of the twentieth century.

✍ All the details that are recorded in the index, i.e. surname, forename, registration district, volume and page number, together with the year and quarter on the spine of the index, should be noted for use in filling in an application form for a certificate.

✍ Up to this point, the information that has been discovered has been free. We may be satisfied to know that the birth of a brother or sister of an ancestor was registered in December 1858 and so decide to pursue the matter no further. With a direct ancestor, however, we need to purchase a certificate.

✍ Application forms are available near the counter at the Family Records Centre, where they should be filled in and a fee paid. In 2003 a copy of a certificate cost £7.00. It may be collected after four working days, but most people will await the postal delivery of the large

Ordering certificates at the Family Records Centre.

envelope that they have addressed at the counter.

📄 Postal applications are not dealt with at the Family Records Centre. These should be addressed to the General Register Office, PO Box 2, Southport, Merseyside PR8 2JD. The current fees for postal applications are £11.50 or £8.50 if the full index reference is supplied or £7.00 for online orders at <www.statistics.gov.uk/registration>. A search of the indexes can also be requested, with the understanding that over half the fee is forfeited if the search is unsuccessful.

📄 The copy of the certificate that is provided upon payment of a fee is usually a scan of the microfilm of the original registered copy of the certificate. A handwritten copy is supplied if the quality of the original is poor. As with all copying, this runs the risk of transcription error. James Downer died in 1894 at Stuckton in the parish of Fordingbridge, not at Shicklow as it says on my copy of his death certificate. The place of death of my maternal ancestor, Thomas Batty, who died in 1882, was copied as 'Morker, Mastington', but I knew from other information that his farm at Morker was near Markington. Morker, incidentally, was normally written as Morcar. If the original certificate is difficult to read, a photocopy may be issued, leaving the problem of transcription to us.

We cannot always be certain that we have chosen the correct entry. Many of us have had the annoying experience of paying for a certificate which is not the right one. There is no easy way of deciding which John Clark or Mary Johnson is the ancestor that is being sought, but the registration district might provide a clue and other evidence, perhaps from a gravestone or a census return, might be suggestive. Identifying an ancestor becomes easier once the fashion of having a second forename became widespread, unless, of course, he or she was usually known by his second name and we are unaware of the first one. A reference checking system is available on the reverse side of the application form, which provides a partial refund if we have chosen the wrong person. For example, we might specify that the father of the ancestor whose birth certificate we are seeking should be named George. However, the search will fail if his full name was William George. The reference checking system is not always an appropriate option.

Birth certificates

A birth certificate is of great value to a family historian in providing the names of the parents and thus enabling us to go back a further generation. Before 1875, the mother of an illegitimate child could state the name of the father if she wished and this would be recorded on the certificate. From 1875, the father had to appear at the registry himself if he wanted to acknowledge parentage. If the name of the father of an illegitimate child was not recorded, we may have come to an end in tracing that particular male line. A serious problem in some districts is that of the under-recording of births in the early years. It seems that many people were under the mistaken

Birth certificates provide the following information:

the name and maiden name (and any
previous married name) of the mother

the date and place of birth
In the case of twins or more
the time of birth is noted.

the occupation of the father

the name of the child

the gender

the name of the father

the signature or mark, name and
address of the informant
(usually a parent)

CERTIFIED COPY OF AN ENTRY OF BIRTH

GIVEN AT THE GENERAL REGISTER OFFICE, LONDON

Application Number.......... 6979B

REGISTRATION DISTRICT   Bethnal Green

1882   BIRTH in the Sub-district of Church Bethnal Green in the County of Middlesex

Columns:—	1	2	3	4	5	6	7	8	9	10*
No.	When and where born	Name, if any	Sex	Name and surname of father	Name, surname and maiden surname of mother	Occupation of father	Signature, description and residence of informant	When registered	Signature of registrar	Name entered after registration
287	Thirteenth March 1882 24 Nelson Street	Jenny	Girl	Henry Bull	Jane Susannah Bull formerly Golding	Pork butcher	J.S. Bull Mother 24 Nelson Street Bethnal Green	Twentieth April 1882	Joseph Hooper Registrar	

CERTIFIED to be a true copy of an entry in the certified copy of a Register of Births in the District above mentioned.
Given at the GENERAL REGISTER OFFICE, LONDON, under the Seal of the said Office, the 19th day of February 1982

*See note overleaf

BXA 730147

This certificate is issued in pursuance of the Births and Deaths Registration Act 1953. Section 34 provides that any certified copy of an entry purporting to be sealed or stamped with the seal of the General Register Office shall be received as evidence of the birth or death to which it relates without any further or other proof of the entry, and no certified copy purporting to have been given in the said Office shall be of any force or effect unless it is sealed or stamped as aforesaid.

CAUTION:—Any person who (1) falsifies any of the particulars on this certificate, or (2) uses a falsified certificate as true, knowing it to be false, is liable to prosecution.

Form A502M D4 82642(8 110M 1/81 Mcr (2015)

impression that a baptism which was recorded in a church register was sufficient. The Births and Deaths Act (1874) tightened up procedures for civil registration from 1 January 1875.

An example from my wife's family tree illustrates this problem. When Thurza Evans married George Wakefield at St Marylebone parish church on 6 August 1871 she was said to be 'of full age, spinster', but her actual age was not recorded. Her father was named as George Evans, carpenter. The 1881 census (held on 3 April) noted that she was 38 and had been born in Chelsea, the 1891 census (held on 5 April) recorded her age as 47 and her birthplace as Westminster. These discrepancies are minor and do not present too much of a problem. Her death certificate, issued on 5 October 1895, after she had been burnt in a horrific fire, gave her name as Thurza Collins Wakefield and her age as 52. The three recorded ages suggest that she was born between 1842 and 1844. A search of all the birth indexes from 1837 to 1851, including the surnames Evan and Evens and Collins and various spellings of Thurza, failed to find her. The only possible candidate was Thirza Caroline Evans, whose birth was registered in June 1843 at Hartlepool, far from London. Could she have moved to London when young? Could Caroline be a mistake for Collins, or vice-versa? A check had to be made. It turned out, however, that the father of this Thurza was Henry John Evans, a miner, not George Evans the carpenter. It seems as if the birth of our Thurza Evans was one of those that was not registered under the new civil system. A search of the numerous London parish registers is now my only option. So far, I have searched the ones for Chelsea but have not come across her.

Marriage certificates

Several problems arise in interpreting what was actually written under the certificate headings.

- The recorded ages are sometimes incorrect, especially when the wife was older than the husband.

- Often the partners are simply said to be 'of full age'. This should mean 21, but the legal age of marriage was 16 and before 1929 might have been as low as 14 for boys and 12 for girls, though this was very rare. When one of my great-grandmothers married in 1857 she was said to be 'of full age', though she was only 19. Her husband was her first cousin, which was not unusual, for this had been legal since the sixteenth century.

- Although the recorded addresses at the time of marriage can be useful in following a family's movements, particularly after the streets were numbered, we need to be aware that they could be those of temporary residences which allowed a couple to marry at their chosen parish church. A minimum of four weeks' residence for one of the partners was necessary and if both gave the same address or lived close to each other they saved the cost of an extra set of banns.

- If one of the partners was illegitimate, his or her father's name might have been invented. When Moses Downer, an illegitimate boy who was brought up in the Fordingbridge workhouse, married in 1888, he gave his father's name as Charles, the same name as that of his wife's father. No father's name was recorded on his birth certificate.

In searching the marriage indexes it is sensible to check the entries for both partners if their names are known and it saves time to look for the rarer name first. From March 1912 the index entry for one spouse also records the surname of the other. The maiden name of a widow can be deduced from her father's name. A common practice is to work backwards through the indexes from the date of a child's birth or from the information in a census return, though of course the birth that we are starting from may be that of the last child in a large family. Finally, we need to note the names of witnesses, for they were often relatives and so they can confirm that we have indeed purchased the correct certificate and sometimes help us in pursuing a line further.

The marriage certificate of Henry Bull and Jane Susannah Virgin, 25 April 1881.

Marriage certificates give the following information:

where and when the marriage took place

the names and ages of the spouses
though in the early years this is often written simply as 'of full age'

the names and occupation of the spouses' fathers

the spouses' occupations and 'conditions'
(bachelor, widower, spinster, widow)

the spouses' place of residence

CERTIFIED COPY OF AN ENTRY OF MARRIAGE   GIVEN AT THE GENERAL REGISTER OFFICE

Application Number   W 005933

the signatures or marks of the spouses and two witnesses

whether the marriage took place after banns or by licence

PRACTICAL DIFFICULTIES:
THE CASE OF HENRY AND JANE SUSANNAH BULL

The trouble that I have had in finding the birth and marriage certificates of my wife's great-grandfather, Henry Bull, illustrates how seemingly-straightforward enquiries can go down blind alleys before we discover the truth. In the 1881 census returns Henry Bull was aged 21 and unmarried, working as a butcher, and living in Bethnal Green with Thomas and Eliza Crump, aged 70 and 54, respectively; Henry was described as Thomas's son-in-law, which was rather puzzling until I discovered that he was Thomas's step-son. An obvious first step was to search the indexes of births for 1859–60, where I found two possible candidates. The first was eliminated when I sent for the birth certificate of Henry Bull, registered in Hoxton New Town, Shoreditch in September 1859 and was told that the entry in the index was a mistake for Henrietta, daughter of Robert Bull! The only other entry for a Henry Bull in the East End of London during the right period was for the boy who was born on 22 December 1859 in Hoxton New Town, the son of Henry and Adeline Henrietta Bull, formerly Coomber. I assumed (reasonably) that this was our Henry, but subsequent discoveries did not fit. I would have remained baffled had it not been for Andy Wotton, who turned out to be descended from Henry's elder brother, informing me that although the index reference for Henry's birth was missing, upon enquiry he had found that the certificate existed at the General Register Office in Southport and that it showed that Henry was born on 23 August 1859, the son of George William and Eliza Bull. Eliza later

Henry Bull and his daughters, Annie Alice (left) and Jenny.

took Thomas Crump as her second husband. Numerous other facts have since confirmed these relationships.

Henry was a bachelor when the 1881 census was taken, but he married soon afterwards. The birth certificate of his daughter, Jenny, dated 13 March 1882, named her mother as Jane Susannah Bull, formerly Golding. I searched the CD-ROM of the 1881 census for Jane Susannah Golding and found that only one woman with that name was living in the East End of London at that time. Her home was in the next street to where Henry Bull was born and she was three years younger than him, so there seemed little doubt that she was the right one. When I searched the indexes for their marriage, however, the only reference to a Henry Bull that I could find was not matched under Golding. In the end I had no option but to send for this certificate, which showed that Henry had married Jane Susannah Virgin, a widow who was six years older than he was and whose father was Henry Thomas Golding.

It was some consolation to find Henry's death certificate without any trouble. The difficulties that I had with his birth and marriage certificates are, fortunately, untypical, but they do show that after many years of experience you can still get it wrong.

Death certificates

Again, the recorded information on these certificates is not always straightforward.

🖙 The place of death was not necessarily the same as the normal residence of the deceased or where he or she was buried.

🖙 The 'cause of death' is unreliable or too vague in the early certificates. When my great-grandfather, John Hey, a fancy weaver, died in 1855 the cause was recorded as 'decay of nature'. The

Death certificates give the following information:

the date and place of death

the name of the deceased

the age of the deceased

(However, the indexes only show the age from the March quarter of 1866 until June 1969, from when the date of birth is given.)

the deceased's occupation

and his or her usual residence if different from their place of death.

the cause of death

the signature or mark, name and address of the informant, who was 'present at death' or 'in attendance'

Certificates also include the name of the deceased's father if the deceased was a child or an unmarried woman. The name of the deceased's husband is given if the deceased was a married woman.

CERTIFIED COPY OF AN ENTRY OF DEATH

GIVEN AT THE GENERAL REGISTER OFFICE

Application Number W00S933

	REGISTRATION DISTRICT	Edmonton			
1935	DEATH in the Sub-district of Edmonton		in the County of Middlesex		

Columns:–

No.	When and where died	Name and surname	Sex	Age	Occupation	Cause of death	Signature, description and residence of informant	When registered	Signature of registrar
1	2	3	4	5	6	7	8	9	
362	First April 1935 North Middlesex County Hospital U.D.	Henry Bull	Male	76 years	of 77 Langham Road Tottenham U.D. Retired Butcher (Master)	1a Bronchopneumonia 2. Cerebral haemorrhage No P.M. Certified by M. R. Thomas M.E.	J. Clark Daughter 24 Langham Road Tottenham	Second April 1935	W.H. Miller Registrar

CERTIFIED to be a true copy of an entry in the certified copy of a Register of Deaths in the District above mentioned.

Given at the GENERAL REGISTER OFFICE, under the Seal of the said Office, the ....22nd............day of ......November...... 2000

DXZ 783411

See note overleaf

CAUTION: THERE ARE OFFENCES RELATING TO FALSIFYING OR ALTERING A CERTIFICATE AND USING OR POSSESSING A FALSE CERTIFICATE ©CROWN COPYRIGHT
WARNING: A CERTIFICATE IS NOT EVIDENCE OF IDENTITY.

DXZ Series Dd 0659 32M 9/00 SPSL(207217)

quality of the information improved from 1875, when a medical certificate had to be supplied by a doctor.

☞ The informant might not have known the deceased's real age and it was common to add a year, thinking that someone was 84 after he had passed his 83rd birthday.

☞ A man's occupation could well have changed over time, so it might not tally with that recorded in a marriage certificate or a census return. When one of my grandmothers married in 1900 she gave her father's name and occupation even though he had died eight years previously.

Nevertheless, death certificates provide important pieces of information.

☞ The recorded age points to a date of birth.

☞ The date of death directs a search for a will or administration.

☞ The address might suggest where to look in a census return or where to find a gravestone.

☞ The informant was often a close relative, perhaps a wife from a second marriage whose name was not previously known, or perhaps the name of a daughter-in-law. It was usually a woman who was 'present at death'.

The Family Records Centre also houses special registers and indexes in a section labelled 'miscellaneous returns'. The most important include the records of British citizens overseas whose births, marriages and deaths were registered at HM British

The death certificate of Henry Bull, 1 April 1935.

Consulates from 1 July 1849; registers kept by clergymen abroad; the births and deaths of people at sea since 1851; the deaths of those serving in the armed forces during the two world wars; and various registers (some dating from 1761) of the births, marriages and deaths of people serving in the armed forces. Many of these indexes are also available on microfiche at the National Archives and the Society of Genealogists.

Other repositories

The indexes at the Family Records Centre cover the whole of England and Wales, so a visit to London is usually worthwhile. There are other possible approaches, however.

☞ Microfiche or microfilm copies of all or part of the indexes are held by the National Archives and many local record offices or libraries, the Society of Genealogists and numerous family history societies, and the various Family History Centres of the LDS Church (which allows free access to anyone).

☞ Another approach is through a local registry office if we are confident that a birth, marriage or death occurred within that district and we have fairly precise details of name, place and date. Sooner or later, however, most family historians decide that they must visit the Family Records Centre, where a blanket search of all the indexes of civil registration produces an enormous amount of genealogical information.

No system of registration has ever been perfect. A thorough search of the indexes sometimes fails to produce a name that ought to be there. Often, this is because the information that has prompted a search is incorrect, but a failure to find an entry might be the result of error by the clerks who compiled the indexes. We might need to look for every possible variant spelling, for names where the letter H has been dropped, where B has been substituted for P, M for N, etc. and for variant first vowels. Most errors and omissions in the civil registration indexes are in the older, hand-written indexes. As the records are not computerized, mistakes can only be rectified after FRC staff have been notified. On the whole, however, the problems that might arise are minor compared with the rewards. The indexes and certificates of civil registration are the family historian's major source.

Changing access to records

A project named FreeBMD aims to provide free internet access to the civil registration indexes. A large group of volunteers are using scanned or photocopied pages of the indexes to create an enormous database which currently contains 70 million entries. Searches are possible by surname only, by district, by county, by part-year, or whole year, or group of years, even by volume and page number. The researcher will still need to buy the certificates to get the full details. The FreeBMD website is at <www.freebmd.org.uk>. A mirror site is available at <http://freebmd. rootsweb.com>. A commercial site at

<www.1837online.com> is reviewed by Peter Christian in *Ancestors* 15 (Aug/Sep 2003).

The Government's White Paper *Civil Registration, Vital Change* (2002) proposes the eventual deposit in local record offices of records that are more than 100 years old and the end of the requirement to buy a certified copy of a birth, marriage or death certificate in order to see the information contained in it. The intention is to restrict the access to information on entries less than 100 years old in order to protect the privacy of individuals and to prevent fraud. This will mean that for these entries addresses, occupations and causes of death will not be disclosed except to members of the family or other authorized persons.

Change of name

Men and women may call themselves by whatever name they choose, unless there is intention to defraud. Various methods of changing a name legally have been available. Some preferred a statutory declaration before a JP or Commissioner for Oaths, others an advertisement in the newspapers. Only a minority changed their name by deed poll before a solicitor, for this involved an extra payment. Before 1903 deed polls were enrolled in the Close Rolls, which are held at the National Archives under C 54. Since 1903 the enrolment of deeds has taken place after an application to the High Court of Justice. These deeds are kept in books which are deposited at the National Archives under J 18 when they are three years old.

Adoption

Records of guardianship or fostering rarely survive. The formal adoption process began in 1927. The Family Records Centre has annual indexes of the Adopted Children's Registers at Southport which give the name of the adopted child and the year of adoption, but not the child's name before adoption. Adopted people over the age of 18 can apply for their original birth certificate. Brief information on adoption records is available online at <www.familyrecords.gov.uk/>.

About 300,000 children were taken care of in Dr Barnardo's homes. Detailed records from 1867 onwards, including admission registers and photographs, can be searched by postal application to Liverpool University. They are confidential for 100 years, except for children who are now adults (or with their written consent) or their next of kin.

Divorce

Before 1858 only the very wealthy were able to get a divorce; others had to turn instead to separation or bigamy. From 11 January 1858 the new Court for Divorce and Matrimonial causes heard all divorce and matrimonial cases. See A. Bevan, 'Divorce 1858 Onwards', *Ancestors* 10 (Oct/Nov 2002) for an account of the gradual extension of the right to divorce. By 1900 over 10,000 separation orders were being issued each year, but it was not until the 1920s that divorce became available for all classes. County courts were given the

An unidentified Dr Barnardo's boy, 1875.

responsibility of hearing suits in the late 1960s and 'No fault' divorces were introduced in 1971.

Decrees and files are kept in two places.

- Records of the result of successful divorce suits are still kept by the Principal Registry of the Family Division and cannot be searched by the public. Instead, officials will carry out a paid search of the index, and certified copies of the decrees can be bought.

- Records of the filed papers in divorce suits from 1858 onwards (but with a 30-year rule), are kept at the National Archives under J 77 and are indexed in J 78. Microfilm copies of the indexes are also available at the Family Records Centre. Most of the records from 1938 have been destroyed.

Surname distributions

The early civil registration indexes can be used to plot the distribution of surnames across England and Wales at the time when railways were opening up the country. See D. Hey, *Family Names and Family History* (Hambledon & London, 2000) for examples of this technique, using the indexes of deaths for a five-year period commencing 1 January 1842. Very many names were still concentrated in the districts where they had originated in the Middle Ages.

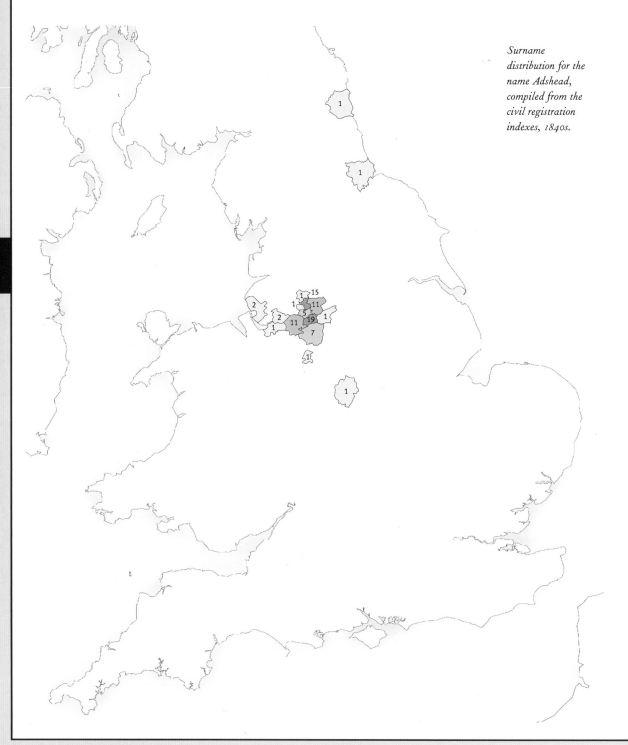

Surname distribution for the name Adshead, compiled from the civil registration indexes, 1840s.

The 82 entries for the surname Adshead show that it is a north Cheshire and south Lancashire name that is derived from a small settlement called Adshead Green.

Death is revealed to be an eastern England name. Pronounced Deeth, it seems to have been an occupational name for a maker of tinder that originated in Suffolk and Essex in the fourteenth century. These counties were still the stronghold of the name at the beginning of Victoria's reign.

Surname distribution for the name Death, compiled from the civil registration indexes, 1840s.

Census returns

The census enumerators' books that are available every ten years from 1841 to 1901 are the second major source of genealogical information for the Victorian period. A census for the whole of England and Wales has been taken every decade since 1801, except during the war-time year of 1941, but the records of the first four censuses are of little use to the family historian. All the official schedules were destroyed once the official statistical tables had been compiled, but a few unofficial lists have survived in some local record offices. The 1841 census was the first to be the responsibility of the newly-established General Register Office, and from that time onwards the census enumerators' books are a storehouse of genealogical information.

The purpose of each census was to inform the government about the demographic, occupational and social condition of the whole of England and Wales. It is only in recent decades that huge numbers of family historians have begun to use the census enumerators' books for genealogical purposes. Those that are available for study provide snapshots of all the households of England and Wales at ten-yearly intervals during the long reign of Queen Victoria and prompt many further searches of the civil registration indexes and other records. When we complete our census form the first

year of each decade we are assured that the personal details will be kept secret for 100 years. This means that, at present, census records have been released only up to 1901.

The nineteenth-century census registration districts were the same as the poor law unions and the civil registration districts. Each one was divided into enumerators' districts. The enumerator provided every householder with a form, or 'schedule', which had to be filled in on the Sunday that had been chosen as census night. The form was collected the following day and if necessary the enumerator helped the head of household to complete it. The information was then copied into the census enumerators' books and, once these books had been checked against the schedules by the registrar and by the superintendent registrar, they were sent to the census office in London.

The census enumerators' books for 1841 to 1901 are now freely available for study. The 1841 to 1901 returns at the Family Records Centre are on microfilm. The 1901 returns at the FRC and the National Archives at Kew are on microfiche. Census returns for all years can be ordered for viewing at Mormon Family History Centres. Copies of all Welsh returns and those for Cheshire, Shropshire and Herefordshire are kept at the National Library of Wales, Aberystwyth.

THE MAN WHO REFUSES TO FILL UP THE SCHEDULE,
AND DEFIES THE ENUMERATOR.

- Check whether indexes of surnames (blue label) or streets (white label) for the place you are interested in are available on the shelves.

- Find the place-name indexes (pink label) on the shelves for the year you require. Each place has a reference number for the registration district, highlighted in colour.

- Turn to this number in the reference book (yellow label) on the same shelves, which lists registration districts, sub-districts and parishes. Note the piece number(s).

- In the rows of cabinets, which are arranged by census years, find the microfilm with the same number. Place the box with your seat number in its place.

- Find your seat and insert the microfilm. Print-outs of pages from the microfilm may be purchased, if required.

- The microfiche copies of the 1901 returns are arranged in the same way as the previous years, but they are on microfiche rather than microfilm.

'The man who refuses to fill up the schedule, and defies the enumerator', cartoon from The Illustrated London News, *1891.*

Microfilm or microfiche copies of the census enumerators' books for a particular county or district are also normally available at county record offices and city reference libraries. The 1901 returns for the whole of England and Wales can be seen on the internet site <www.1901census.nationalarchives.gov.uk>.

Using the microfilms at the Family Records Centre

- Near the enquiry desk choose a black box with a seat number.

Increasingly, local family history societies have made indexes of names for one or more returns for their districts, which they have published as booklets, or on microfiche or CDs. The 1851 census has been particularly well covered and some counties are very well served. The Nottinghamshire Family History Society, for instance, has indexed the surnames for the whole county from 1841 to 1891. Images of the 1891 census returns are being published commercially on CD-ROM and DVD, accessible on both PCs and Macs, county by county, and this service is being extended to earlier censuses. Soon, we shall have full coverage of all the census enumerators' books that are more than 100 years old.

Using the 1881 census CD-ROMs

A transcription and index of the 1881 census returns for the whole of England, Wales and Scotland, which was compiled in a joint project between the National Archives, the LDS Church and family history societies throughout the land, is available on a set of CD-ROMs from the LDS Distribution Centre, 399 Garretts Green Lane, Birmingham B33 0UH or on the website <www.familysearch.org>. Microfiche copies of the index can be purchased from the Federation of Family History Societies. The transcripts are not error-free, so the information should be checked against the original returns. All the information recorded in the census of 1881 is included, so it is easy to find collateral lines or to see the returns for a whole community.

To use the CD-ROMs, proceed as follows:

☞ The program will ask you to insert one of the eight CDs of the National Index. These are arranged alphabetically.

☞ Type in a name. It helps if you know the approximate date and the county of birth, or the county of residence in 1881. If the search fails to find a match, try alternative first names, e.g. Jennie, Jinnie or Jane for Jenny, or try a middle name. Some of your information may

be incorrect, so if you don't succeed try the barest details.

☞ All the entries which match the name, together with alternative spellings of the surname, will appear on the screen. If there are far too many, you must narrow your search, e.g. to a particular year of birth.

☞ Click a likely entry, which gives name, year and county of birth, and county of residence. The program will ask you to replace the index CD with the appropriate British Census CD.

☞ Click the name you have chosen. The entry which appears is for the whole household. To get full details of each member of the household, e.g. occupation, or relationship to the head, click the icon under 'Search' in the menu bar (the sixth from the left).

☞ Click the fifth icon from the left (a picture of binoculars) to search another name, or click 'Neighbours' in order to see who else lived in the same street or village. In London and other large cities two or three households often shared the same address, on different floors.

The 1901 Census Online

Images of the census enumerators' books for 1901, full transcripts, and an index of individual names are available on the website <www.1901census. nationalarchives.gov.uk>. This online service may be accessed on a computer at home or at the Family Records Centre, the National Archives at Kew, most record

Person Search

Locate your English or Welsh ancestors, or someone famous, and obtain the digitised census images and transcription online. There is a wealth of information available, including a person's address, age, occupation, relationships and more. This search is probably the fastest way to trace an individual in the 1901 Census.

Last Name Search: Enter "Last Name" (other fields optional).
First Name Search: Enter "First Name", "Gender", "Age" and "Where Born" (other fields optional).

Once you have filled in the search form scroll down the page and click on the "Search" Button.

| Clear | Clear form for new search |

Census Home Page
Contact Us
Help
FAQs
Site Tour

Search
Person Search
Advanced Person Search
Address Search
Place Search
Institution Search
Vessel Search
Direct Search

Account Sessions
What are they?
Open/Resume
Suspend/Logout
My Account
Print Ordering

Useful Links
National Archives'
email updates

Enter Your Search Criteria — Help

Last Name		e.g. Youngs	?
First Name		e.g. John	?
Gender	▾		?
Age on 31st March 1901	☐ years +/- ☐ years e.g. 40 years +/- 5 years		?
Where Born		e.g. Lynn	?
Place Keywords		e.g. Islington	?
Limit result list to 10 ▾ entries per page			?

| Search |

Person search criteria box from 1901 census online (www.1901census.nationalarchives.gov.uk).

offices and reference libraries, the Society of Genealogists, and other institutions, including some family history societies.

☞ Click 'Person Search' and type in a name you are searching. The search is narrowed if you know the approximate age, birthplace, and district of residence. Access to the index is free, but this provides only minimal information – name, age, where born, administrative county, civil parish, and occupation. There is no cross-reference to alternative spellings of a name. I failed to find Jenny Bull at first because her name was written as 'Jennie' – a spelling which was not used in any other record of her.

☞ Charges are made for viewing the digitized pages of the returns, which provide full transcripts.

☞ The transcripts contain errors, so it is advisable to check them against the images of the original returns, at a cost of £0.75p. As the online census is a live system, any corrections that are reported can be made quickly, so the quality of the service should improve.

Census enumerators' books

A census enumerator's book starts with a brief description of the district, which is named at the top of each subsequent page. We can quickly find an ancestor who lived in the countryside, but may have a long search for someone who lived in London or one of the large industrial cities, which were divided into numerous enumerators' districts. The streets were rarely numbered before the 1850s and in the smaller towns this fashion did not catch on until much later. For example, the small West Riding town of Penistone did not give its houses numbers until November 1881. Once the streets had been numbered, the house of an ancestor can be located on large-scale Ordnance Survey maps, though we have to remember that in populous towns two or three households often shared the same address by living on separate floors. In heavily built-up areas the enumerators found it difficult to decide what actually constituted a 'house', as distinct from a 'room'. Rural dwellings had less need for numbers, but we need to be alert to the possibility that the name of a farmhouse changed.

The Family Records Centre has several finding aids at or near the enquiry desks. *The Survey Gazetteer of the British Isles*

provides a comprehensive list of place names compiled from the 1901 returns, together with a *List of Parishes in England and Wales*, a *Hamlet Index*, and separate *Welsh Place Names Indexes*. The specialist finding aids for London include lists of the registration districts in which each civil and ecclesiastical parish lay, and lists of street names, including those which were altered or abolished in Victorian and Edwardian times, but as streets often served as boundaries between enumeration districts, we may have to note more than one set of numbers. We may know the street in which an ancestor lived from a birth, marriage or death certificate or from a directory, so locating a street in a particular enumeration district can save an enormous amount of time in searching through the census returns. Street indexes are also provided for other large towns with a population of over 40,000, for most census years.

An extract from the 1901 census entry showing the parents and family of the late HRH Queen Elizabeth the Queen Mother (highlighted).

				Number of Rooms occupied if less than five	Name and Surname of each Person	RELATION to Head of Family	Condition as to Marriage	Age last Birthday of Males	Age last Birthday of Females	PROFESSION OR OCCUPATION	Emp Wo Own
					Claude George Bowes Lyon Lord Glamis	Head	M	46		Peero Son — Landowner Meaus	E
					Cecilia Nina do do Lady Glamis	Wife	M		38		
					Mary Francis do do	Daur	S		14		
					Rose Constance do do	Daur	S		10		
					Michal Claude do do	Son	S	4 months			
					Elizabeth Angelia do do	Daur	S		8		
					Hedwig Wolters	Servant Tutor	S		24	Governess	Dom
					Helen Searby	Servant	S		34	Housekeeper	domestic
					Marguerite Rodier	do	S		30	Cook	do
					Annie Harley Knight	do	S		30	Ladys-maid	do
					Clara Knight	do	S		22	Nurse	do

The undermentioned Houses are situate within the boundaries of t

MR. CHARLES DICKENS'S LAST READING.

The enumerator's handwriting can be difficult to read, especially on the microfilm copies of the 1841 returns, which the family historian soon finds has its limitations.

☞ The relationship of each member of a household to the head was not given.

☞ Although actual ages were recorded for children under 15, all other ages were rounded down to the nearest 5, for the aim of the census was to produce statistical tables, not to help genealogical research. We need to be aware that, for example, someone recorded as 25 years old in the 1841 census could have been any age between 25 and 29.

☞ The last column did not note actual birthplaces but simply asked whether or not a person was born in the same county as he or she resided, or whether the birthplace was in Scotland, Ireland, or 'foreign parts'.

The Registrar-General's office learned from their experience and made significant improvements by the time of the next census. From 1851 onwards they recorded the relationship of each member to the head of household, everyone's true age, and his or her place of birth. They also decided that census night should be in late March or early April, for the 1841 census had been taken in June and agricultural workers who were sleeping rough had not been counted. Nightworkers who were absent from home on census night but who returned the following morning were henceforth included with the other members of their household. The days on which the Victorian

The census return for Charles Dickens (top entry) and family, 1841, Devonshire Terrace, Marylebone.

censuses were taken were: 6 June 1841, 30 March 1851, 7 April 1861, 2 April 1871, 3 April 1881, 5 April 1891 and 31 March 1901.

The reliability of the information in the census enumerators' books depends upon the statements given by householders and the accuracy of the copies made by the enumerator. It is common to find that a few particulars vary from one census to the next.

- ✒ Some people apparently did not age ten years each decade, some had different names and some had changed their minds about where they were born.

- ✒ In the earliest censuses the terms son-in-law and daughter-in-law were sometimes used to mean (in modern terms) step-son and step-daughter.

- ✒ We need to bear in mind also that children who had been both born and buried since the previous census would not be recorded.

One of the chief problems is deciding whether or not a recorded age is accurate. It is common to find a difference of a year or two between two returns, but occasionally the gap is larger. Perhaps some people may have thought that having passed their 61st birthday they were in their 62nd year, but others deliberately gave the wrong information. The family historian who is searching for the baptism of, for example, someone aged 46 in 1851 may need to widen his search of the baptism registers beyond the years 1804–5.

We need to be equally cautious with the recorded place of birth. If a family had moved a considerable distance, they might have said that they came from a nearby town whose name would be known to their new neighbours, rather than the actual village or hamlet, just as we do today, or they might have claimed that they came from the place where they spent their childhood rather than the place where they were born. The information tends to be more accurate for the younger children. One of my grandmothers always said that she came from Chard in Somerset, but it turned out that she had lived nearby at Chardstock as a girl and had actually been born several miles to the north at Thurlbear, not far from Taunton. In 1881, when the family were living in Yorkshire, the census return noted her place of birth as Taunton, but it provided the clues that her younger sister had been born at Chardstock in 1871 and that her little brother had been born in Yorkshire in 1875. It is often possible to trace the movements of a family in this way.

A census return might record a place of birth that was different from the one noted ten years earlier, usually because of forgetfulness or ignorance, but sometimes because the name of a township or hamlet was replaced by that of the parish. In 1881 my wife's ancestor, Charles Sandy, gave the hamlet of Gorley as his birthplace, but in 1891 he said that he had been born in Fordingbridge, which was the name of the parish in which Gorley lay. In 1901 the birthplace of my wife's grandmother, Jenny Bull, was recorded as Hackney, though she had been born at Bethnal Green. Perhaps her step-mother (who was born at Hackney) was the informant and did not know the exact place of birth; and perhaps that is why Jenny's father was said to have been born at Chelsea when in fact he too had been born in Bethnal Green? These problems may frustrate us, but they can usually be overcome.

The census enumerators' books provide information that lead us to other sources of information, particularly to the indexes of civil registration, which are housed in the same building at the Family Records Centre. For example, if a person appears in the 1871 census but not in the one for 1881 the search for a death certificate should start in the index for June 1871. A search for a marriage certificate might profitably begin with the year of the birth of the eldest child in an enumerator's return, working backwards, with the realization that older children might have died or left home before census night. The recorded age and birthplace normally guide us to a registered birth or allow us to go back beyond the period of civil registration to parish or Nonconformist registers. The 1851 census gave me the vital information that my great-great-grandfather, John Hey, was born in Shelley in the parish of Kirkburton, five miles to the north of where he was living. He died four years later and if I had not found this piece of evidence I would have been uncertain about tracing the family back to another John Hey, who died in the township of Shelley in 1633.

Charles Darwin, photographed in 1882, with the census entry (below) for his family, dating from 1881.

CENSUS RETURNS

83

The undermentioned Houses are situate within the Boundaries of the

[or Township] of	City or Municipal Borough of	Municipal Ward of	Parliamentary Borough of	Town or Village or	Urban Sanitary District of	Rural Sanitary District of	Ecclesiastical Parish or District of
Down				Down		Down	Down

ROAD, STREET, &c., and No. or NAME of HOUSE	HOUSES In-habit-ed	HOUSES Unin-habited (U), or Building (B)	NAME and Surname of each Person	RELATION to Head of Family	CON-DITION as to Marriage	AGE last Birthday of Males	AGE last Birthday of Females	Rank, Profession, or OCCUPATION	WHERE BORN	If (1) Deaf-and-Dumb (2) Blind (3) Imbecile or Idiot (4) Lunatic
West Hill	1		William Atkins	Head	Mar	41		Police Constable	Lydd, Kent	
			Harriet L. do	wife	Mar		39		Rye, Sussex	
			Lewis W. do	Son		12			Lydd, Kent	
Luxtham rd	2		Charles Robert Darwin	Head	Mar	72		M.A, LLD (Cambs) FRS JP	Shropshire Shrewsbury	
Downe House	1		Emma do	wife	Mar		72		Maer, Staffordshire	
Luxtham rd			Elizabeth do	daur	Unm		33		Down, Kent	
"			William E. do	Son	Mar	42		Banker, B.A. (Cantab)	N. Ferraes Middlesex	
"			Sara do	daur	Mar		41		United States	
"			George H. do	Son	Unm	44		M.A (Cant) F.R.S Barrister	Down, Kent	
"			Francis do	Son	Widr	32		M.A. M.B. (Cant)	do do do	
"			Bernard R.N. do	Grandson		4			do do	
"			Herman Frank	Visitor	Mar	23		Music Director & Violinist	Saxony Germany	
"			Rose B. do	Niece	Mar		34		Clewis Staffordshire	
"			Charles Wood Fox	Cousin	Unm	23		Barrister	Hampstead Middlesex	
"			James Johnson	Serv	Unm	23		Footman Domestic Serv	Marylebone do	
"			Frederic Gill	Serv	Unm	20		Groom "	Bromley Kent	
"			Margaret Evans	Serv	Unm		50	Cook "	Edgalatton Shropshire	
"			Augusta Dickson	Serv	Mar		44	Ladies Maid "	Hamburg Germany	
"			Elizabeth Bradford	Serv	Unm		24	Housemaid "	Bullbeck Cambridgeshire	
"			Harriet Iroine	Serv	Unm		22	Housemaid "	Offham Kent	
"			Mary Wilkins	Serv	Unm		22	Kitchenmaid "	Sundrigae Kent	
"			Pauline Bedel	Serv	Unm		29	Nurse Dom.	Switzerland	
"			Harriet Wills	visitor	Unm		24	Ladies Maid "	Westwood Hants	
"			Leonard Darwin	Son	Unm	31	34	Lieutenant Royal Engineer	Down Kent	
Total of Houses.. 4					Total of Males and Females..	13	13			

Note:—Draw the pen through such of the words of the headings as are inappropriate.

Eng- Sheet D.

PRACTICAL DIFFICULTIES:
THE CASE OF GEORGE AND FANNY McCUIN

McCuin is a very rare name in the census returns for England and Wales, though it is likely to be a spelling variant of a Scottish or Irish name, such as McEwan or McCune. The only McCuin in the 1881 census return for London was George McCuin (whose name is mistranscribed as McCuen on the CD-ROM). He was one of 34 lodgers at 28 and 29 Dorset Street, Spitalfields, where he was described as a 23-year-old bricklayer's labourer, born at Gonigate, Glasgow. The next name in the list was that of Maurice McGregor, aged 27, also born in Gonigate, so it seems that they had travelled down together. Perhaps they had not been long at the lodging-house and were soon to move on? In which case, I was lucky to find him.

George McCuin was an omnibus driver, living at 11 Gladstone Street, Islington, when he married in 1888. His father was another George McCuin, bricklayer. It seemed a straightforward task to search for them on the excellent website linked to the Scottish Record Office, but I quickly found that no McCuins were recorded in the 1881 Scottish census and a painstaking search of parish records led nowhere. Then, on visiting the Mitchell Library in Glasgow, I was informed that there was no such place as Gonigate; perhaps a strong accent had disguised the name of the central street, Gallowgate, which appeared to be the only candidate?

The next step was to find him on the London census of 1891 to see whether the recorded birthplace would be more helpful. He was living across the road at 10 Gladstone Street, still working as an omnibus driver, but his birthplace was now said to be 'London, Whitechapel'! A check on the indexes of births at the Family Records Centre did not find him there. George died two years before the 1901 census, so I had no further source of information about his birthplace.

One of the witnesses to his marriage in March 1888 was F. McCuin, so I decided to search the indexes of marriages from that date. This long-shot proved spectacularly successful, for in December 1888 Fanny McCuin, aged 22, married Albert Edward Cary. She was described as living at 11 Gladstone Street, Islington and as being the daughter of George McCuin, builder. She was clearly George's younger sister. I returned to the census returns in high hopes of finding her birthplace, only to discover that in 1891 she was said to have been born in Islington and in 1901 to have been born in Holloway. A search of the marriage indexes at the Family Records Centre, looking at all variant spellings, failed to find her there. None of the handful of Fanny or Frances McEwans whom I found in Scottish records was the right person. My only remaining hope is to find these McCuins in Irish records, but that is not going to be an easy task.

The recorded occupations usually tally with those in other sources such as civil registration certificates and trade directories, but they rarely mention dual occupations, such as that of the weaver-farmer, or casual employment of a seasonal nature, such as brickmaking or the various ways in which an 'agricultural labourer' earned his living. The seasonal or part-time work of women and children was rarely recorded, especially as the home was the usual place of work, though in fact the earnings of the women and many of the 'scholars' in the census returns were essential to the well-being of working-class families.

Mapping surnames in 1881

Family historians can make their own distribution maps through the use of the software package *The British 19th Century Surname Atlas*, available from <www.archersoftware.co.uk>. Type in a surname and you immediately get a map of its distribution at the time of the 1881 census, arranged either by counties or by Poor Law unions (the basis of census and civil registration districts). Such maps regularly display marked geographical concentrations, even though the picture is often distorted by large-scale migration to London.

Kevin Schürer, the Director of the UK Data Archive at the University of Essex, has shown that in 1881 40 per cent of the British population shared just 500 different surnames. The figure rises to about 4,000 surnames for 80 per cent of the population and 9,000 surnames for 90 per cent. Counting each spelling variant as a single surname, there is then a huge 'tail', with the remaining 10 per cent of the population sharing 30,000 surnames.

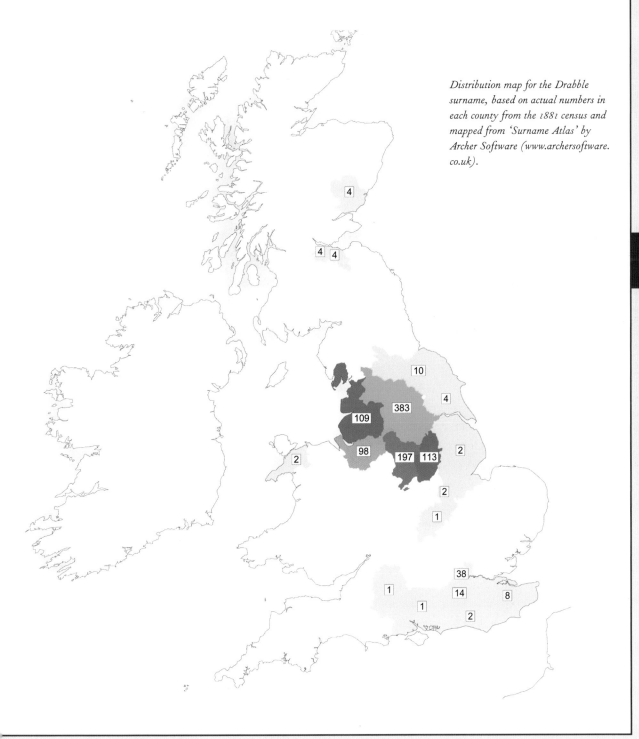

Distribution map for the Drabble surname, based on actual numbers in each county from the 1881 census and mapped from 'Surname Atlas' by Archer Software (www.archersoftware. co.uk).

Trade and commercial directories

The idea of publishing a trade and commercial directory for a particular place goes back to 1677, when Samuel Lee produced his list of the merchants of the City of London. Half a century later, Brown and Kent's *London Directory* was first issued in 1734 and revised each year until 1826. During the later eighteenth century the idea caught on, with William Bailey's *Northern Directory* (1781) and the five volumes of John Wilkes's *The Universal British Directory* (1790–99), and with directories of the leading provincial towns. These town directories soon began to include neighbouring villages and by the 1830s they were being published as county volumes. From about 1840 we can find entries for most of the villages in the land.

During the reign of Victoria substantial directories for all parts of the country were published at a rate of about two or three a decade. Some were the work of local publishers, but most formed part of a series, such as those of William White of Sheffield or James Pigot, whose firm was taken over in 1853 by Francis Kelly, the major publisher of directories in the south of England. Kelly's directories were the best known in the country until their production was interrupted by the Second World War, after which they were gradually replaced by telephone directories. Reference libraries and county and city record offices usually have a set of local directories. The Guildhall Library has a huge collection and the Family Records Centre has several hundred available on computer. The whereabouts of directories are listed in J. E. Norton, *Guide to the National and Provincial Directories of England and Wales, Excluding London, Published Before 1856* (1950) and G. Shaw and A. Tipper, *British Directories: A Bibliography and Guide to Directories Published in England and Wales (1850–1950) and Scotland (1773–1950)* (1988). London Metropolitan Archives has a large set of London directories available on microfilm, which are listed in an information leaflet. In recent years directories for many of the English counties have been published commercially on CD-ROM.

Another type of venture was the national gazetteer. Amongst the most famous is Samuel Lewis, *A Topographical Dictionary of England*, which was published in seven editions between 1831 and 1848–9, the last edition being in four volumes with an atlas of the poor law unions, which also formed

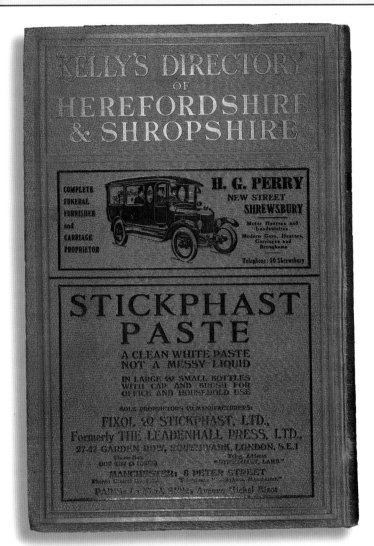

The back cover of Kelly's Directory for Herefordshire and Shropshire, *1926.*

lengthy account of the history, topography, economy and population of the county or district. Towns and their surrounding villages are then arranged alphabetically, perhaps by the ancient subdivisions of the county known as hundreds or wapentakes. Later directories have separate street sections for the towns and pull-out maps. Each group of settlements is introduced by a general survey that covers local history, land ownership and tenures, population, the economy, and local administrative units, including poor law unions, parishes, townships, and manors at a time when many changes were being made. Postal information and details of railway, coaching and carrying services are also provided. Then, the names, ranks or businesses, and addresses of the 'principal residents' are listed, followed by classified entries for the various tradesmen, arranged alphabetically.

The publishers employed full-time agents who consulted local clergymen, schoolmasters, overseers, etc. and went from house to house to gather information (which was not always given readily). Directories can be a great aid to family historians, for they record a large number of householders at specific points in time, but they did not

the basis of civil registration and census enumeration. Lewis also published three editions of *A Topographical Dictionary of Wales* between 1833 and 1849, in two volumes and an atlas. His brief accounts of each town and village included information on the contemporary civil and ecclesiastical arrangements. Fuller information is provided in the six volumes of J. M. Wilson, *The Imperial Gazetteer of England and Wales* (1870).

Trade and commercial directories soon adopted a common style. They start with a

try to cover the entire population like a census. They had no reason to include labourers, servants and other people of humble status, so it is common to find that a third or more of the local population was omitted. Indeed, at the head of the town entries in William White's *Directory of Leicestershire* (1863) is the statement: 'The following Alphabetical Directory contains the Addresses of all the Inhabitants, except Journeymen and Labourers'.

Directories are accessible and easy to search, so they are useful in narrowing a field of enquiry in civil registration or census records. For example, as directories were published at frequent intervals, we can soon find the approximate date that a head of household died and was replaced by the next generation, though we have to remember that the information collected for a directory was slightly out of date by the time it appeared in print. If a person appeared in the 1861 census but not the 1871 return, we can concentrate our search in the civil registration death indexes in the last few years if he is listed in a directory of 1868. Likewise, the addresses recorded in directories can be used to identify an enumeration district in a contemporary census return. A search of the entries for neighbouring settlements may be profitable in locating an ancestor who has moved or in identifying kin with the same surname. Some professions have their own publications, notably *Crockford's Clerical Directory*, first published in 1858, and the *Medical Directory* from 1845.

Successive directories show how some trades passed down the generations from

Page from Crockford's Clerical Directory, *1876, listing the senior clergy of the dioceses of York and London.*

father to son. D. R. Mills, *Rural Community History from Trade Directories* (Local Population Studies supplement, 2001) demonstrates how we can learn about the occupations of ancestors who were craftsmen and small businessmen, especially when the information is enhanced with old photographs, and how we can can get a good sense of the local communities in which our forebears lived and worked. Directories are particularly effective in evoking the local economy of the numerous market towns of Victorian England. They are invaluable in conveying a sense of the places where our ancestors spent most, or all, of their lives.

Although directories do not provide direct genealogical information, they record ancestors in particular places at certain points in time and note their occupations and addresses. They thus help us unravel a family's history. The rare surname Hukin, which appeared 57 times in the 1988 Sheffield telephone directory but only another 60 times in the rest of the United Kingdom, provides an example. The name was first recorded in Sheffield in 1744, when Joshua the son of Joshua Hukin was baptized at the parish church. In 1783 John the son of Joshua Hukin of Sheffield Park, basketmaker, was apprenticed to a local cutler. The nineteenth-century trade directories show how later members of the family earned their livings as razor makers, filecutters, silverplate manufacturers, beerhouse keepers or shopkeepers. There is a butcher, pig killer, tripe dealer, mason, and wood turner. The last one to work in the local cutlery industry was Billy Hukin, a razor maker who died in 1994. The Hukins were typical of the working-class families of this bustling, industrial borough.

Title page of the Post Office's London Directory, 1824.

UNDER THE PATRONAGE OF
HIS MAJESTY's POSTMASTER-GENERAL.

The Post-Office
London Directory
For 1824.

BEING A LIST OF UPWARDS OF
20,000

Merchants, Traders, &c. of London, and Parts Adjacent;

LIST of the LORD MAYOR, and COURT of ALDERMEN.
LIST of the BANKERS in LONDON.
LIST of 700 COUNTRY BANKERS, with the BANKERS they draw on in LONDON.
LIST of PUBLIC NOTARIES.
LIST of LONDON & COUNTRY

NEWSPAPERS, with the Places and Days of Publication.
LISTS of ARMY and NAVY AGENTS, DIRECTORS of the FIRE & INSURANCE OFFICES
LISTS of the LONDON, WEST INDIA & EAST INDIA DOCK COMPANIES, FOREIGN MINISTERS, &c. &c.

GENERAL INFORMATION relating to the
POST OFFICE,
INCLUDING the LAST RATES of POSTAGE.
Regulations of the Twopenny Post-Office, &c.
Also a List of the GENERAL and TWOPENNY POST
RECEIVING HOUSES.

By CRITCHETT & WOODS.

THE TWENTY-FOURTH EDITION.

London : Printed for the Proprietors by Chapman and Roe, 5, Sherbourn-lane;
And sold by J. Richardson, Royal Exchange; Cowie & Co. Poultry; Sherwood, Neely & Jones, and J. Walker, Paternoster-Row; Simpkin and Marshall, Stationers'-Court; Kingsbury, Parbury, & Allen, Leadenhall-Street; Black, Young and Young, 2, Tavistock-Street, Covent-Garden;
And by all the Booksellers and Stationers in the United Kingdom.
Price 3s. 6d. Sewed, 4s. Bound;
Or, with the COACH AND CARRIER'S GUIDE, 5s. Bound.

Military records

The records of military service are to be found in the National Archives at Kew and at regimental military museums. Local record offices rarely have much information. Records of military service are not available on the internet, but a number of sites point the researcher in the right direction.

Websites

☛ It is best to start at <www.catalogue. nationalarchives.gov.uk>, from which you can access information leaflets that the National Archives has produced about tracing careers in the British Army. A section devoted to the Army and Royal Navy is found in the 'Pathways to the Past' pages at <www.nationalarchives.gov.uk/ pathways/FamilyHistory/gallery3/>.

☛ A list of present-day regiments is available on <www.army.mod.uk/ unitsandorgs/>. This provides brief histories and lists of their main engagements.

☛ For regimental history, turn to <www.regiments.org/>, which explains the system in detail.

☛ For more leads, see <uk.dir.Yahoo. com/Arts/Humanities/History/ By_Subject/Military_History>.

☛ T. and S. Wise, *A Guide to Military Museums and Other Places of Military Interest* (8th edition, 1994) gives the addresses of museums with a brief description of their collections. A list of museums can be found on <www.army. mod.uk/ceremonialandheritage/ museums_main.html>.

No. CLXXIII.
2nd January, 1882.

PUBLISHED QUARTERLY.
Price 10s. 6d.

THE

NEW ARMY LIST,
MILITIA LIST,
YEOMANRY CAVALRY LIST,
AND
INDIAN CIVIL SERVICE LIST;

EXHIBITING THE

RANK, STANDING, AND A SUMMARY OF THE WAR SERVICES
OF EVERY REGIMENTAL OFFICER IN THE ARMY

SERVING ON FULL PAY,

INCLUDING

THE ROYAL MARINES

THE

INDIAN STAFF CORPS AND LOCAL INDIAN FORCES

DISTINGUISHING THOSE

WHO HAVE SERVED IN THE PENINSULA,
WHO WERE AT WATERLOO,
WHO HAVE RECEIVED MEDALS AND OTHER DISTINCTIONS,
AND
WHO HAVE BEEN WOUNDED, AND IN WHAT ACTIONS;
WITH THE PERIOD OF SERVICE BOTH ON FULL AND HALF PAY.

GIVING ALSO

THE DATES OF EVERY OFFICER'S COMMISSIONS

AND

DISTINGUISHING THOSE OBTAINED BY PURCHASE

WITH AN INDEX.

BY THE LATE

LIEUTENANT GENERAL H. G. HART.

EDITED BY HIS SON.

LONDON:
JOHN MURRAY, ALBEMARLE STREET.
1882.

Title page from
The New Army List, *1882.*

☞ Pages devoted to military records are
found at <www.genuki.org.uk/big/
MilitaryRecords.html>.

The Army

Regiments are the basic units of the
British Army. Finding records of Army
service is a difficult and time-consuming
task if the regiment of the soldier is not
known. The structure was greatly changed
in 1881, when many regiments were merged
and often linked to a county. From that time,
a typical regiment had two battalions, one
serving at home for a while and the other
stationed abroad. Local militia forces lost
their independence and became the third
battalion of the regiment. Each battalion
was divided between eight and twelve
companies. For full information, see
A. Bevan, *Tracing Your Ancestors in the
Public Record Office* (6th edition, 2002),
pp. 180–251 and S. Fowler and W. Spencer,
Army Records for Family Historians (Public
Record Office, 1998).

Officers

The most important source for tracing
the career of an officer is the *Army Lists*,
which have been produced since 1702
and published regularly since 1754. They
provide a broad outline of an officer's

STATEMENT of the Services of _Guy H. Colton Boynton_ of the _17_ Reg.t of _Lancers_ with a Record of such other Particulars as may be useful in case of his Death.

Where Born _Burton Agnes Yorks_ Date of Birth _16th May 1828_

Age on his first Entrance into the Army _26 3/12 Years._

Rank and Regiment, in which the Officer first entered the Army, and the successions of his Rank and Regiment on every subsequent Promotion, Removal, or Exchange, whether to Full or Half Pay.				FULL PAY. Whether obtained with or without Purchase; and, if by Exchange, whether with or without paying the Difference.	HALF PAY. Whether obtained by reduction, or by the Purchase of a Half Pay Commission; whether in consequence of his being from ill health incapable of Service, or under what other circumstances; and, if by Exchange, whether with or without receiving the difference.	List, and Dates of any Battles, Sieges, and Campaigns, in which the Officer was present; specifying the Regimental or Staff Situation he held on each occasion, and the name of the Officer in the chief command.
Ranks.	Regiments.		Dates.			
	Full Pay.	Half Pay.				
Cornet Lieut	17 Lancers do		30 Nov 54 by without purchase 12 Jan 55 by purchase			Present with the Regiment in the Crimea from 16. July 55. to the 25. October 55.

Retired by the sale of his Commission 29th August 1857

	Instances in which the Officer has distinguished himself by gallant, or skilful conduct, when, where, and on what occasion; and whether noticed in General Orders.	Wounds received in Action, specifying when, where, and on what occasion; what grant of Pay has been received; Rate of Pension; Date; and whether permanent or temporary.	Titles, Honorary Distinctions, and Medals, obtained; and if conferred for any specific Service, when, and on what occasions.	Service Abroad.		
				Period.		Station.
			Received Medal 1st Class for Service of Crimea in the Crimea	From.	To.	
				May 55	25 Oct 55	Balaklava

If the Officer be Married,* specify.					If the Officer has any legitimate Children, specify		
When.	Where.	To whom.	The Wife living at the Date of.	Minister who married the Parties, and of what Church.	Names.	Dates of Birth.	Where Baptized.

*Note. A Report to be made to the War Office within Six months of the Marriage.—See Regulations for Widows' Pensions.

Service on	Years.	
	Abroad.	At Home.
Full Pay		
Half Pay		
Total up to 31st December, 1829		
Full Pay		
Half Pay		

I do hereby certify, upon my honour, that, to the best of my knowledge and belief, this statement is in all respects correct and true.

G. H. Boynton Lt. Signature of the Officer.

We do hereby certify, that We are satisfied of the general correctness of this statement.

Signature of the Commanding Officer.
Paymaster.
Adjutant.

Cavalry officer's service record, 1871.

career. The lists are arranged by regiment and many have been indexed. They can be consulted in large reference libraries or at the National Archives, which has complete sets of the annual lists between 1754 and 1879 and of quarterly lists from 1879 to 1900 on open shelves. If an ancestor cannot be found in these lists he is unlikely to have served as an officer. The buying of commissions, up to the rank of colonel, was abolished in 1871.

Service records at the National Archives come in two forms: those kept by the War Office, which are in WO 25, and those produced by the regiments, which are in WO 76. Incomplete card indexes are available at the National Archives. These service records provide personal information about an officer at the various stages of his career – the grant of commission, promotion, resignation, placement upon the half-pay list, etc. The registers of officers who retired on half-pay between 1858 and 1894 are kept in WO 23/68–78. These note name, rank, regiment, date of commencement, rate, and a record of payments and they are often annotated with the date of death. Details of pensions for wounded officers during the period 1812–97 are found in WO 23/83–92. Several series of registers of those receiving widows' pensions are also kept in the National Archives.

Royal Artillery, discharge of Gunner John Hardy, 1876.

Those who were employed in government service had to show their loyalty to the Crown by producing evidence of baptism in the Church of England. These certificates can be found in two series: WO 32/8903–8920 (code 21A) covers the period from 1777 to 1868, and WO 42 has a set from 1755 to 1908, together with certificates of marriage, birth of children, death and burial. Indexes to both series are available at the National Archives. Reports by officers of their marriage are held in WO 25/3239–3245 for the period 1830–82.

Other ranks

As nearly all service records were originally kept by individual regiments or corps, for the period 1855–72 you need to know the approximate dates that an ancestor served in the Army and his regiment. Old photographs may help you to identify the regiment, for many soldiers who were about to serve overseas had their photograph taken to give to their next of kin. Such photographs rarely survive in the National Archives. See the article by D. J. Barnes on 'Identification and dating: military uniforms' in D. J. Steel and L. Taylor, eds., *Family History in Focus* (Guildford, 1984). Help on identifying cap badges is also available on the internet at <www.egframes.co.uk/indexbadge.htm>.

The basic service records were the regimental muster book and the regimental pay list. These record a soldier's Army career from the time that he enlisted, through his movements with the regiment throughout the world, to his discharge. The sheer quantity of muster books and pay lists, each of which covers only a short space of time, means that the task of searching

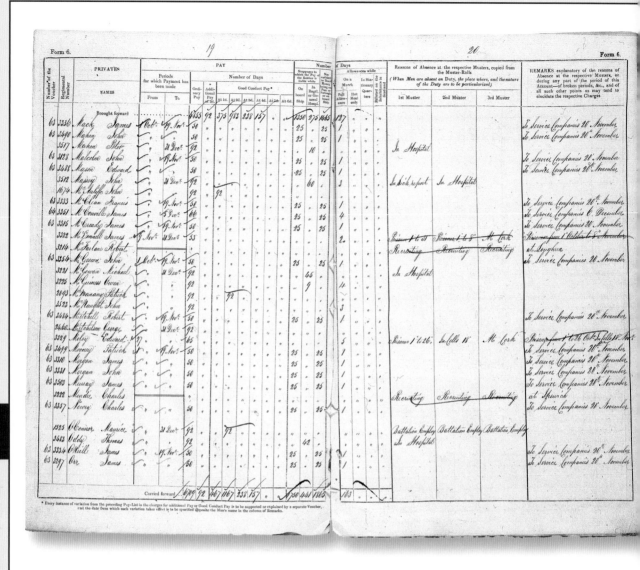

through them can be a very long one. It is worth looking at more accessible records first, especially the service records of soldiers who retired with a pension, even if you do not know whether or not your ancestor received a pension.

The most important soldiers' documents in the National Archives are attestation and discharge papers in WO 97, from 1760 to 1913. Up to 1882, these normally record only those who were discharged and received a pension. The records of soldiers who died whilst serving, or who did not

receive a discharge certificate, have not survived. Except for the early years, the documents give information about age, physical appearance, birthplace, and trade or occupation when the soldier enlisted. They also provide a record of service, including any decorations awarded, promotions or reductions in rank, crimes and punishments, and the reason for discharge to pension. Sometimes, the place of residence after discharge and the date of death are noted. The documents are arranged by date of discharge, but as the order in many boxes has been considerably altered over the years you may have to search through a whole box to find a particular individual.

The documents in WO 97 fall into four series:

☛ *1760–1854.* These are arranged alphabetically by name within regiments. Relatively few records survive for men who served before 1792. The series is available on microfilm at the National Archives and there is a computerized index which records name, regiment, birthplace, age at discharge and years of enlistment and discharge. This is searchable on the online catalogue.

☛ *1855–72.* These too are arranged alphabetically by name within a regiment.

☛ *1873–82.* These are arranged alphabetically by the name of the soldier within the categories: cavalry, artillery, engineers, foot guards, infantry and miscellaneous corps.

☛ *1883–1913.* These are arranged in order of surname and include soldiers discharged to pension and those discharged for other reasons, such as the termination of limited engagements or discharge by purchase. Details of the next of kin are given.

Other records which are kept in WO 121 are in very poor condition and access to them may be restricted. They include general registers of discharges from 1871 to 1884 in WO 121/223–238 and registers of men discharged without pension between 1884

Muster roll/pay list of 68ᵗʰ Foot, 1ˢᵗ Battalion, 1854–5.

and 1887 in WO 121/239–257. A large part is searchable on the online catalogue; see Jenny Bunn, 'Indexes to soldiers' discharge documents, 1760–1854', *Ancestors* 11 (Dec 2002/Jan 2003). The certificates of service of soldiers who were awarded deferred pensions, 1838–96, are in WO 131.

Description books are kept in two main series in WO 25 and WO 67. The regimental description and succession books of 1778–1878 are in WO 25/266–688, but not all regiments have books for the whole period, and only a small percentage of all soldiers were recorded. Some books are arranged alphabetically, others by date of enlistment. They provide a description of each soldier, his age, place of birth, and trade, and a record of his service. The depot description books for 1768–1908, which are held in WO 67, give the same information, which was obtained when recruits assembled at the regimental depot. They are usually much fuller than the series in WO 25. See A. Bevan, *Tracing Your Ancestors in the Public Record Office* (6th edition, Public Record Office, 2002), pp. 222–5 for the problems in using these records.

If the regiment in which a soldier served is known, then a long search through the muster rolls and pay lists could be undertaken. The main series of muster books and pay lists from 1769 to 1898 are kept in WO 10 to 16. They are arranged by regiment and are bound in annual volumes. A successful search reveals a soldier's date of enlistment, his movements during service, and his date of discharge or death. The muster rolls for Chelsea Pensioners from 1702 and admission books for 1778–96 and 1824–1917 are held in WO 23. The admission books are arranged chronologically and note the soldier's regiment, his name, age, service, rate of pension, and the date of his admission. An index of in-pensioners admitted between 1858 and 1933 is kept in WO 23/173. Some 5,000 personal files of soldiers (and sailors) who received a disability pension and who left the armed services before 1914 are held at the National Archives in PIN 71.

Nineteenth-century wars

1793–1815	French Revolutionary and Napoleonic Wars
1854–6	Crimean War
1857	Indian Mutiny
1860, 1862–4	Maori Wars
1878–9	Zulu War
1878–81	First South African War
1882–5	Egyptian and Sudan Campaign
1884–5	Sudanese War
1899–1902	Boer War

Campaigns and casualty returns

➳ The records of particular campaigns are listed in detail in M. Roper, *The Records of the War Office and Related Departments, 1660–1964* (Public Record Office, 1998). Most of these do not name individuals.

➳ Several series of monthly and quarterly casualty returns between 1809 and 1910 are kept in WO 25. These are arranged by regiment and many are indexed. They record a soldier's name, his rank, place of birth, and trade, the date, place and nature of the casualty, any debts and credits, and the name of his next of kin or legatee.

➳ Casualty rolls for many of the campaigns in which the Army fought during the second half of the nineteenth century are kept mostly in WO 25 or 32.

➳ Several casualty lists have been published, e.g. F. and A. Cook, *The Casualty Roll for the Crimea* (London, 1976), J. Young, *'They Fell like Stones'*:

The names of the following members of the

are entered on this Roll of Honour as a record of their patriotism in having fought for their Queen & Empire in the South African Campaign of 1899–1900.

Standard form of the Boer War Roll of Honour, 1899–1900.

Mens Names, Ages and Qualities.	When and where put on the Sick List.	Statement of the Case when put on the List.	Symptoms and Treatment while under Cure.	When discharged to Duty, Died, or sent to the Hospital.	REMARKS.
Admiral Nelson	25 July	Compound fracture of the right Arm by a musket ball passing thro' the little above the Elbow an Artery divided the Arm was immediately Amputated and the following give him Rx Opii gⁱⁱ ij f Pil statim s. Rep Pil Opii gⁱⁱ j Rep Pil Opii gⁱⁱ ij hora s. s.			
Jas Holden Seaᵐ Aged abt 27 Yrs	25 July	A Wound of the breast and Compound fracture of the right Arm close to the Shoulders, by a Musket ball passing thro' the Pectoral Muscle and afterwards thro' the Arm which shattered the bone very much and Divided the Humeral Artery. Amputation was immediately performed. the Tourniquet could not be applied, compression was of very little use on dividing the Artery. a large Hemorrage took place. which was immediately stopt by taking up the Arteries the stump was dress'd and the patient put to bed the following administed Rx Opii gⁱⁱ ij f Pil Statim s.		Diet. Tea Lemonade Sago Soups &c — A small Hemorrage from the surface of the Stump which stopt by applying flour &c
Jnᵒ Willson Seaᵐ Aged abt 29 Yrs	25 July	Received a Wound of the breast and Shoulder by a Musket ball passing thro' the breast and Scapula a large Hemorrage came on which was suppressed by Compression Rx Opii gⁱⁱ ij f Pil statim s. Rx Mixtura Salin ʒⁱ 6ᵗⁱᵉ		Diet. Tea. Lemonade. Sago Soup &c
Wⁱⁱᵐ ...	25 July	Received a Compound fracture of the left Arm by a musket			

casualties of the Zulu War, 1879 (1991), and South Africa Field Force Casualty List, 1899–1902 (London, 1972), a facsimile of WO 108/338 and S. Watt, In Memoriam: Roll of Honour, Imperial Forces, Anglo-Boer War 1899–1902 (University of Natal, 2000).

The medal rolls at the end of each campaign are kept in WO 100 and are available on microfilm at the National Archives. These are arranged by regiment, rank, and then alphabetical order of surname. Some medal rolls have been published. Details of all the medals awarded for campaigns between 1793 and 1984 can be found in E. Joslin, A. Litherland and B. Simpkin, British Battles and Medals (Spink, 1988), copies of which are available in the Research Enquiries Room and the library at the National Archives.

The records of those who served in the regular Army were mostly destroyed upon the soldier's death. In contrast, 98 per cent of the service records of the many thousands of men who enlisted in the Imperial Yeomanry during the Boer War survive in WO 129. They are sorted by battalion and then company. As companies had a loose county affiliation, knowing the county where an ancestor came from helps in the search for his number. Each of the first seven books of WO 129 name about 8,000 men, listed by surname (though not arranged alphabetically within each letter) and then by number; only the initial of the first name is recorded. See the alphabetical index of 39,8000 men in K. J. Asplin, The Roll of the Imperial Yeomanry ... (2 vols, Salisbury, 2000). The Boer War has a website at <www.anglo-boer.co.za>.

Extract from a surgeon's journal from HM Theseus, 1797, including a report of the amputation of Admiral Nelson's arm after a musket ball severed an artery just above his right elbow.

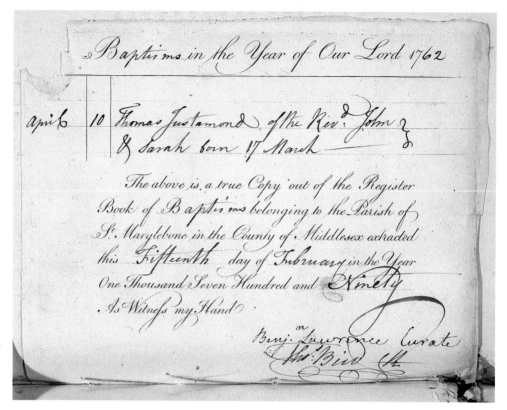

Baptisms in the Year of Our Lord 1762

April 10 Thomas Justamond of the Revd John & Sarah born 17 March

The above is a true Copy out of the Register Book of Baptisms belonging to the Parish of St. Marylebone in the County of Middlesex extracted this Fifteenth day of February in the Year One Thousand Seven Hundred and Ninety As Witness my Hand

Benjn Lawrence Curate

Evidence of baptism from lieutenant's passing certificate, 1790.

The Royal Navy

The essential guide to the extensive records is B. Pappalardo, *Tracing Your Naval Ancestors* (The National Archives, 2003), although A. Bevan, *Tracing Your Ancestors in the Public Record Office* (6th edition, Public Record Office, 2002), chapter 19 provides a good overview. The records in the Admiralty (ADM) section of the National Archives are searchable on the online catalogue. The main series are as follows:

Officers

☞ Officers were listed in *Steele's Navy List*, published at intervals between 1782 and 1817, and in the official *Navy List* from 1814. Copies are available at the National Archives, together with the unofficial *New Navy List* of 1841–56.

☞ Class ADM 196 at the National Archives has service registers from 1756 to 1920. From the second half of the nineteenth century these contain dates of birth, marriage and death, the names of next of kin, and information about pay and pensions.

☞ Passing certificates summarizing an officer's training and career, are held in various series under ADM. The most complete are those for lieutenants from 1691 to 1902 in ADM 6, 13 and 107; see Pappalardo for indexes and Bevan, pp. 259–61.

☞ Records of warrant officers include the Commission and Warrant Books, 1695–1849, in ADM 6, which has indexes for 1695–1745 and 1779–89, and the Succession Books, 1695–1849, in

ADM 6, 11, 29 and 104, which are indexed by ships' and officers' names.

Ratings

☛ Until 1853 ratings did not join the navy but signed up for a single voyage on a particular ship. A key source at the National Archives is ADM 29/1–96, covering the period 1802–94, which now has a personal name index incorporated in the online catalogue. This provides name, date and place of birth, age on joining the navy, rank or rating, dates served, and cross references. See B. Pappalardo, 'Indexing the Admiralty' in *Ancestors* 15 (Aug/Sep 2003).

☛ From 1853 ratings had to sign on for ten years initially. Continuous service records in ADM 139 (1853–72) note the date and place of birth and provide a physical description.

☛ ADM 188 has registers of seamen's services (1873–1923), which give date of birth, ship or shore establishment, and a record of service. Only the rating or his next of kin can apply to see records kept from 1924 at the Ministry of Defence.

☛ The census returns from 1861 list the personnel on board naval vessels. An index of the 1861 return is available at the Family Records Centre and at the Family History Centres of the LDS Church. The CD-ROM of the 1881 census can be searched by surname.

The Royal Marines

In 1755 soldiers who served on ships became a permanent force under the Admiralty based at Chatham, Plymouth and Portsmouth. From 1805 to 1869 another division was based at Woolwich. In 1802 these armed forces became known as the Royal Marines. Their records, which are kept mostly in ADM at the National Archives, are listed in Information Leaflet 74 and in G. Thomas, *Records of the Royal Marines* (Public Record Office, 1994). The survival rate for the records of each division varies considerably.

☛ The most important records for family historians are the registers of births, marriages and deaths. Those for the Chatham division in ADM 183 cover 1830–1913, those for Plymouth in ADM 184 cover 1862–1920, and those for Woolwich in ADM 81 are for 1822–69. The Portsmouth division has marriage registers for 1869–81 in ADM 185.

☛ Marine officers were named in the *Army Lists*. Their service records are in ADM 196.

☛ Attestation papers in ADM 157 give a marine's age, birthplace, trade and a physical description. They are arranged by division, then company, then date of either enlistment or discharge.

☛ Description books in ADM 158 provide further information, including promotions and casualties.

☛ ADM 159 has records of service from the middle of the nineteenth century. These record the date and place of birth, trade, religion, date and place of enlistment, physical description, conduct and promotions.

☛ Company pay lists are housed in ADM 96. Pension records are in ADM 165 and 166.

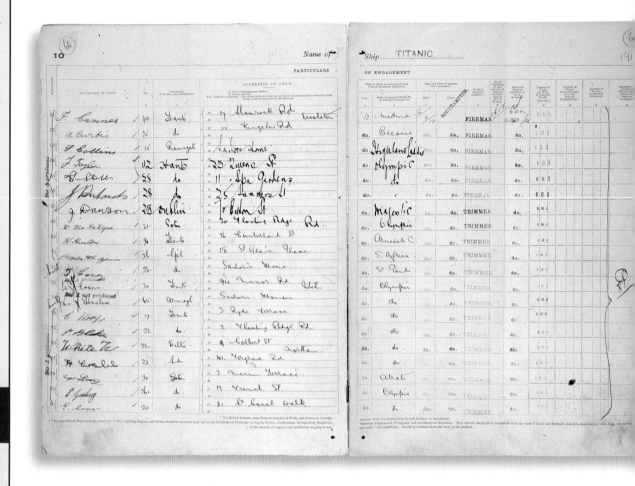

Crew list of the Titanic, 1912.

The Merchant Navy

The available records are discussed in K. Smith, C. T. Watts and M. J. Watts, *Records of Merchant Shipping and Seamen* (Public Record Office, 2001).

☞ Seamen's registers were compiled from crew lists after the passing of the Merchant Shipping Act (1835) until 1857. They are kept at the National Archives in BT 112, 113, 114, 119, 120. They provide the date of birth, position held, ship(s) served on, and sometimes a physical description.

☞ Nothing replaced this system until the Central Index Register was introduced in 1913. The main series of records before 1921 has not survived. The register from 1921 to 1972 is held at the National Archives in BT 348–350.

☞ Officers' records survive from 1845, especially the certificates of competency and service that are held in BT 143/1.

☞ Lloyd's captains' registers, compiled for insurance purposes from 1869 to 1948, are kept at the Guildhall Library, London.

☞ The Society of Genealogists has a collection on merchant seamen.

Education records

From 1880 attendance at primary school was compulsory. The records of local Board schools (from 1870) and Council schools (from 1903), and those run by the churches and chapels, are often held at local record offices, though individual schools may have kept their log books and the admission registers which name the child and give the date of admission, the father's name and address (and sometimes the mother's name), the child's date of birth, the name of any previous school, and sometimes the date when he or she left. Many of the schools that were built in the late Victorian or Edwardian period are still in use. The addresses of local private schools are named

Photograph of '23 scholars and 2 masters', Southport Modern School, Lancashire, June 1906.

in trade directories, but records are unlikely to have survived for those which are not still in existence. School photographs, reports, magazines, and sometimes examination and (from 1908) leaving certificates are often found amongst a family's own collection. Local libraries and record offices are copying as many of these photographs as possible.

The National Archives has relatively few education documents that name individuals. Instead, their records relate to the administration of education in England and Wales. An information leaflet is available on the website <www.nationalarchives. gov.uk>. Records of schools in ED 2 give the names and assessments of pupils in examination schedules from 1872 to 1894, listed alphabetically by county, then place. Other records in ED 2 include the reports and recommendations of inspectors on the returns made in 1870 by local authorities about population size, school accommodation, enlargements, closures, and elections of School Boards in towns and villages, but not in boroughs. See A. Morton, *Education and the State from 1833* (Public Record Office, 1997).

The two ancient universities have kept records of students since the Middle Ages and have published their names in J. Foster, *Alumni Oxoniensis* (8 vols, 1888–91), an alphabetical register of students at Oxford University between 1500 and 1886, and J. and J. A. Venn, *Alumni Cantabrigiensis* (8 vols, 1922–54), which covers the whole period from the late thirteenth century to 1900. The admission registers of Durham (founded 1832) and University College, London (founded 1836) have also been published. The universities that were founded in the late nineteenth and twentieth centuries often have an archives section in their libraries and many have published institutional histories. See *School, University and College Registers and Histories in the Library of the Society of Genealogists* (Society of Genealogists, 1996).

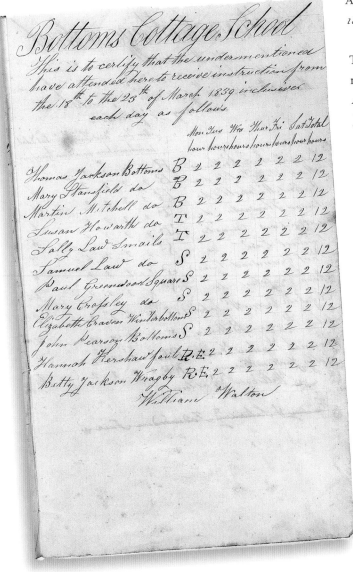

Bottoms Charity School, time book, showing the attendance records of children working in Ramsden Mill, Rochdale, Lancashire, 18–23 March 1839.

Enclosure and tithe awards

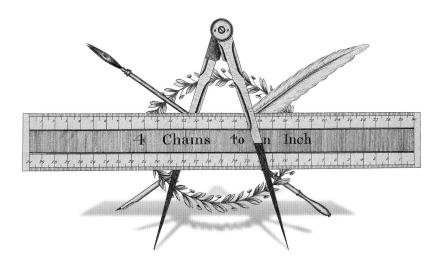

During the eighteenth and nineteenth centuries over 6 million acres of open fields, commons and wastes in England and Wales were enclosed by about 4,000 private Acts of Parliament, the great majority of them between 1750 and 1850. Much of the English and Welsh landscape was altered by the creation of rectangular fields divided by stone walls or hawthorn hedges, by straight roads and lanes, and by Georgian farmhouses set amongst the new enclosures or at the edge of moorland clearances.

☞ W. E. Tate, *Domesday of English Enclosure Acts* (ed. M. E. Turner, 1978) lists all the places that were enclosed by the parliamentary process.

☞ Some record offices and reference libraries possess catalogues of the whereabouts of awards for particular counties. For example, B. English, *Yorkshire Enclosure Awards* (1985), lists 33 different repositories which house records of enclosure for that county.

☞ An Act of Parliament was necessary only when agreement could not be reached amicably. Private agreements, including those of earlier times, are sometimes found amongst the records of the Court of Chancery at the National Archives or in deeds in miscellaneous collections at local record offices, but numerous manors and parishes that were enclosed privately have left no record of the process.

Local historians will be interested in the whole procedure and in the ways in which communities were affected, but family historians will be particularly concerned with the legal document known as the award, which was drawn up by the appointed commissioners after a thorough survey had been made and all claims had been settled. Their decisions were set out in a schedule of the new 'allotments'. Each 'allotment' was given a number so that it could be identified on the accompanying map. In the open field districts of the central parts of England, the schedule lists the owners and tenants of every piece of property in the parish. The awards for the many other places where only the commons and wastes were enclosed are less comprehensive in their coverage, unless the parishioners took the opportunity at the same time to convert their tithe payments to a fixed sum.

- The schedule enables us to find ancestors who were farmers, large and small, and tells us the size of their farms (though they might have held further land in an adjacent parish).

- The accompanying map shows where the farm was situated.

- An enclosure award map is often the earliest map available for a particular township or parish.

- Awards are a major source of information about open field parishes at the point of great change. They are still used as legal evidence, for they set out public roads, bridleways and footpaths, watercourses and drains, and other conveniences such as public wells, and

the maps showed (by a letter T on the inside boundary) which owners were responsible for the maintenance of field walls.

Tithe awards

Tithe was a tenth of a person's produce which had originally been paid to support the rector of the parish church. In many cases, however, tithes were granted to a monastery or a college, which then appointed a vicar to serve the parish. Upon the dissolution of these monasteries and colleges at the Reformation, the right to collect tithes was bought by, or was granted to, a lay landowner. If tithe payments were not converted to fixed money rents at the time of enclosure, the family historian whose ancestors were countryfolk at the beginning of Victoria's reign should look for a tithe award. You are unlikely to know this in advance, so the simplest thing to do is check on the off chance. Awards were made in the years following the Tithe Commutation Act of 1836; by 1852 the Tithe Commission had made awards for 11,395 parishes or townships. The coverage varies considerably from one part of the country to another. In some counties nearly all parishes have awards, but in Leicestershire the proportion is less than a third and in Northamptonshire it is less than a quarter.

Tithe award for the parish of Ashford, Middlesex, 1842.

Three copies of each award were made:

☞ one was deposited in the parish chest and should now be in a local record office

☞ a second went to the bishop and should be kept in the archives of the ancient diocese (in the case of Wales, at the National Library at Aberystwyth)

☞ a third went to the central government and is held in the National Archives at Kew.

The national reference work is R. J. P. Kain and H. C. Prince, *Tithe Surveys of England and Wales* (Cambridge, 1995), which refers to the tithe awards at the National Archives in IR 29 and the accompanying maps (with

No. 4.—London: Published (By Authority) by G. Routledge, 11, Ryder's Court, Leicester Square.

NERS.	OCCUPIERS.	Numbers referring to the Plan.	NAME AND DESCRIPTION OF LANDS AND PREMISES.	STATE OF CULTIVATION.	QUANTITIES IN STATUTE MEASURE.			Amount of Rent-Charge apportioned upon the several Lands, and Payable to the Vicar.			REMARKS.
					A.	R.	P.	£.	s.	d.	
ns	Richardson Henry & others	70	Three Cottages & Gardens		"	"	24				
			Carpenter's House Shop &c		"	"	12				
					"	"	36	"	"	"	
amin	Cornwall	53	The Field & 2 Cottages		2	"	"	"	6	"	R.38468
(late)	Sherborne George	126	Ashford Field	Arable	26	2	"	1	12	10	A.A.1.
rancis	Clifford Francis	131	Hanwell Field	Arable	12	3	9				
		132	do	do	3	1	25				
		133	Shrubbery	Wood &c	1	2	4				
		134	Mansion House Building Yard and Garden		1	2	22				
		141	Paddock on Common	Pasture	4	"	29				
		141a	Plantation in do	Plantation	"	1	12				
		142	The Park	Meadow	10	3	13				
		142a	Shrubbery in do	Wood	"	2	31				
		145	Small Paddock	Meadow	"	2	2				
		146	Garden Ground	Garden	1	1	34				
		154	House Yard & Garden		"	1	"				
		155	The Meadow	Meadow	2	1	25				
					39	"	6	5	6	5	A.A.1.
mas	Himself	21	Two Cottages & Gardens		"	"	25	"	1	6	R.17195.
mes Esqe	Himself	2	The Meadow	Meadow	2	1	5				
		3	The Gardens	Gardens	1	"	"				
		4	Mansion house Outbuildings Yards and Garden		1	2	17				
		5	The Orchard	Pasture	"	3	11				
		6	Front Meadow	Meadow	7	3	28				
		7	Next do	Arable	7	2	23				
					21	1	4	3	6	4	A.A.13.
e Esqe	Himself	40	Small Meadow	Pasture	"	2	"				
		40a	Plantation & Pond	Plantation	"	3	11				
		42	On the Common	Arable	5	"	22				
		42a	Plantation in do	Plantation	"	1	17				
		45	On the Common	Arable	8	"	8				
		51	Paddock	Meadow	9	"	10				
		61	Plantation in do	Plantation	"	1	12				
			carried forward		24	1	"				

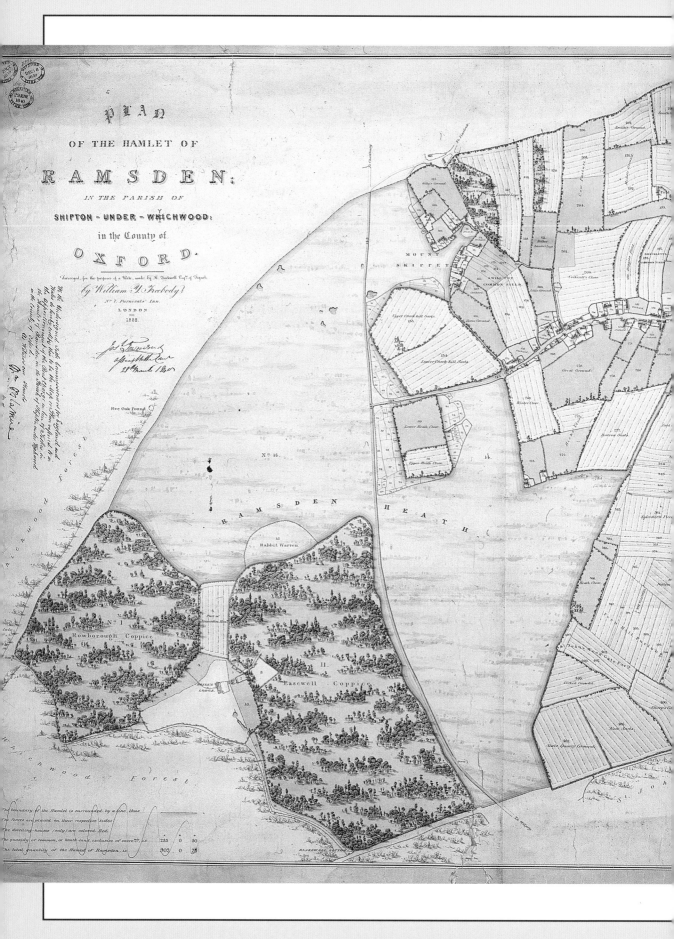

PLAN

OF THE HAMLET OF

RAMSDEN:

IN THE PARISH OF

SHIPTON – UNDER – WHICHWOOD:

in the County of

OXFORD.

Surveyed for the purposes of a Rate, made by H. Backwell Esq.ʳ of Siquet,

by William J. Freebody?

Nº 7. Furnival's Inn.

LONDON

1838.

Five Oak Pound

Nº 14.

R A M S D E N   H E A T H

Rabbit Warren

Nº 1

Rowborough Coppice

Part of
Ramsden Ho.

BRIZEW
LODGE.

Easewell Coppice

W h i c h w o o d   F o r e s t.

The boundary of the Hamlet is surrounded by a line, thus
The fences are placed on their respective sides
The dwelling-houses only) are colored Red.
The quantity of common, or heath-land, exclusive of encroachmts. is   255   0   30
The total quantity of the Hamlet of Ramsden, is   902   0   25

MOUN
SKIPPET

SWILL THE
COMMON FIELD

Upper Church hill Starts

Home Ground

Lower Church hill Starts

Great Ground

Binter Close

Lower Heath Close

Upper Heath Close

Barrow Starts

Heath Close

Nicked Ground.

Slats Quarry Ground.

Near Starts

BLAKEWELL BOTTOM

the same piece number) in IR 30. These are searchable on the online catalogue by parish name, but beware of odd parish names.

- ☛ Tithe awards list the owners and each of the occupiers of every piece of property in the parish. The properties are described as house, cottage, garden, orchard, field, etc. and their size is recorded.

- ☛ The awards are a valuable source of information about field names and some even say what crop was being grown at the time of the survey.

- ☛ The large-scale maps which accompany the awards were not drawn to a uniform scale, but they are often the earliest detailed maps that are available for a particular parish.

- ☛ The maps can be used with the 1841 and 1851 census returns to construct a detailed picture of a parish in the middle years of the nineteenth century and they can be compared with later six-inch Ordnance Survey maps and the valuation records of 1910–13.

- ☛ The family historian who becomes deeply interested in the history of the places where his or her ancestors lived will examine the enclosure and tithe awards in much greater detail than the researcher who at this stage is merely trying to find out where exactly the ancestors resided.

Tithe award map for Ramsden, Shipton under Wychwood, Oxfordshire, 1838.

The New Poor Law, 1834–1930

The old system by which parishes or townships were responsible for relieving their poor inhabitants came to an end with the 1834 Poor Law Amendment Act, which divided England and Wales into Poor Law unions run by elected Boards of Guardians, who were responsible to central government. The Act aimed to reduce expenditure on the poor by discouraging paupers from seeking assistance until they had tried all other means of maintenance. It insisted that the able-bodied poor were to receive relief only in a workhouse, where their standard of living would be marginally lower than that of a labourer. In practice, the Guardians rarely enforced the full rigour of the new law and most unions continued to subsidize paupers who lived at home, but there is no doubt that the new system was a harsh break with past practice.

The boundaries of the New Poor Law unions followed those of groups of ancient parishes but sometimes encroached into another county. For example, the Middlesex parishes of Finchley, Friern Barnet, Monken Hadley, and South Mimms formed part of Barnet Union, the rest of which was in Hertfordshire, and the Middlesex parishes of Hampton and Teddington were in Kingston Union, most of which was in Surrey. Some workhouses were situated outside the area that they served. For instance, the Holborn Union Workhouse was in City Road in the borough of Shoreditch. Stanford's *Map of the Poor Law Administration in the County of London* (1905) shows the location of metropolitan workhouses. In other parts of the country, early editions of large-scale Ordnance Survey maps, together with trade and commercial directories, help us to identify union workhouses. Many were later converted into hospitals, whose sites are still in use.

Background information

🖙 J. Gibson and F. A. Youngs, Jr, *Poor Law Union Records: 4. Gazetteer of England and Wales* (FFHS, 1993) and the three other booklets in the series on the range of records that are available.

Poster satirising the punishments inflicted on the 'incorrigible' poor under the New Poor Law Act of 1834.

The New Poor Law with a description of the new Workhouses

Look at the Picture — See

THE NEW POOR LAW, 1834–1930

INTERIOR OF AN ENGLISH WORKHOUSE UNDER THE NEW POOR LAW ACT.

☞ N. Longmate, *The Workhouse: A Social History* (Pimlico, 2003) provides useful background.

☞ The website <www.workhouses.org.uk>, which is an enormous project that is still in progress, provides detailed maps of the unions, a list of workhouses and a guide to records.

☞ The workhouse at Southwell (Nottinghamshire), which was the prototype of the Poor Law union workhouses, has been restored and opened to the public by the National Trust.

Records

The survival rate for records of the New Poor Law unions that are useful to the family historian is not good and little is available online. The place to search is the county record office, not the National Archives, which holds instead official correspondence between the workhouses and central government. By the mid-nineteenth century the main types of registers of inmates had become standardized.

☞ Admission and discharge books or registers. These are daily lists of everyone who was admitted, discharged or died. They are not usually indexed, nor are there normally any cross references from an admission entry to show when that person died.

☞ Creed registers. These give the religious creed or faith of each inmate. Inmates were recorded in alphabetical sections, starting with everyone with a surname beginning with 'A' and then listing them in order of date of admission. The date of discharge or death is normally added to the admission entry.

☞ Registers of births. From 1904 a birth certificate should not state that a birth took place in a workhouse; instead the street and number occupied by the workhouse was recorded as the place of birth. Examples of euphemistic names for London workhouses include Twyford Lodge for Willesden Workhouse Infirmary and the Lodge, Bancroft Road, for Mile End Workhouse.

☞ Registers of baptism are sometimes to be found amongst the records of the Board of Guardians.

☞ Registers of deaths were frequently kept, but not records of burials, for these normally took place in a local parish burial ground or public cemetery. Metropolitan unions often entered into contracts with local authorities for the burial of the poor in large private cemeteries beyond London.

☞ Records of patients who were admitted to a workhouse infirmary may be found either with the records of the Board of Guardians which was responsible for running it until 1930 or with the archives of the NHS hospital which it became in 1948.

🖝 Guardians' records usually include registers of people whom they sent to county lunatic asylums, private asylums, or to Metropolitan Asylums Board hospitals.

The records in the National Archives at Kew are not easy to search. They help to explain the circumstances under which paupers lived, but they rarely provide personal details of workhouse inmates. The voluminous records of the MH (Ministry of Health) series do, however, provide information about staff, e.g. masters and mistresses, doctors and midwives, or teachers. The MH volumes are listed in alphabetical order by county and within each county by union. Registers of staff, 1837–1921, are found in MH 9 and personal details, 1834–1900, in MH 12; later files were destroyed by fire in the 1940s. MH 12 is a huge series with 16,741 volumes, largely of official correspondence, arranged by union.

The census enumerators' books at the Family Records Centre (or widely available on microfilm) list the occupants of workhouses on census nights, though sometimes only by their initials. I found my wife's ancestor, Moses Downer, in the Fordingbridge Union Workhouse on census night 1871, aged 4, and again in 1881, aged 14. His birth certificate shows that he had been born there on 2 January 1867, the illegitimate son of Elizabeth Downer of Gorley in the parish of Fordingbridge. The original workhouse has gone and the later one on the same site has been converted into a hospital. No workhouse records survive.

NOTICE

TO THE UNEMPLOYED INDUSTRIOUS POOR.

The Guardians of the Blofield Union, being desirous of finding work for the industrious and unemployed poor, hereby inform such persons that there is at present a great demand for labour in several of the manufacturing counties of England, and especially for large families of children, provided the greater part of them are above 12 years of age; and *the more girls the better.*

The Wages given to families are as follows;—and an agreement will be entered into for that purpose for a term of 3 or 4 years.

A labouring man, about	12 Shillings per week.
A lad of 17 or 18	8 ditto.
A boy of 16	5 ditto.
A boy of 14	4 ditto.
A girl of 15 to 20 or upwards	5s. 6d.
Ditto of 14	5s.
Ditto of 12 or 13	4s.
Ditto of 11	1s. 3d.

and increasing after the first year.
and schooling.

There is also an opening for girls who are orphans, or otherwise unprovided for, between the ages of 12 and 18, who may be bound as Apprentices to a Master who has not a large family of his own, and be employed under an agreement, the same as if they were his own children.

Every attention is paid to the religious and moral education of the younger children.

Application is to be made to the Guardian, Churchwardens, and Overseers, of each Parish, who will communicate with the Board of Guardians.

None but persons of steady industrious habits will be accepted.

H. N. BURROUGHES,
CHAIRMAN OF THE BOARD OF GUARDIANS.

October 21st, 1835.

PRINTED BY WILLIAM DURRANT PAGE, GENTLEMAN'S WALK, NORWICH.

Notice of employment in 'the manufacturing counties' and the wages that might be earned there, issued by the Guardians of Blofield Union, Norfolk, 1835.

Working men

☛ Most records of employment are likely to be held in local record offices rather than in national collections. The police, for example, were organized at county level, not centrally.

☛ Many large businesses have deposited their archives at local record offices. These may include the names of the workforce, but in most cases there are no systematic lists and a search may be lengthy and unproductive.

☛ Few records relating to occupations are available online.

A few organizations have large collections of archives which contain valuable information for the family historian.

☛ The Post Office records at Freeling House, Mount Pleasant, Farringdon Road, London EC1A 1BB (entrance in Phoenix Place) start in the late seventeenth century. POST 58 records all staff appointments from 1831 to 1952.

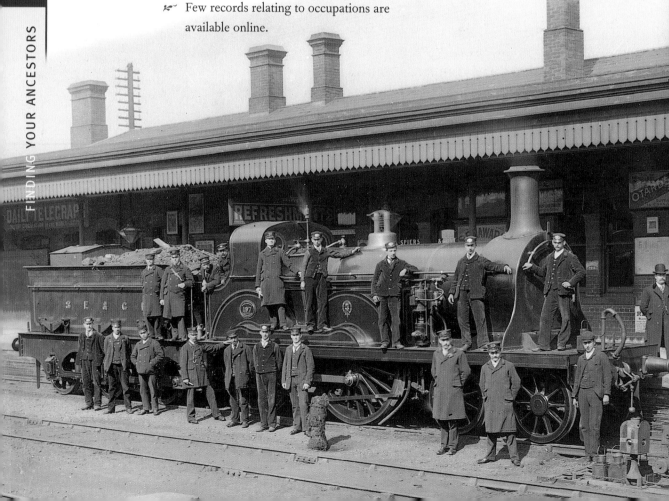

Staff pensions are the subject of detailed correspondence files, and a large collection of photographs is available.

☞ The archives of many railway companies have survived and many are kept in the National Archives (which has an information leaflet; see RAIL). A search may not be straightforward, for even if we know where an ancestor lived he could have worked for one of three or four different companies. D. T. Hawkings, *Railway Ancestors, A Guide to the Staff Records of the Railway Companies of England and Wales, 1822–1947* (Sutton, 1995) is the essential guide.

☞ London Metropolitan Archives houses the large collection of London Transport records.

☞ The trade union records that are kept at the Modern Records Centre, University of Warwick Library, or at local record offices include some registers of members which note men's ages, occupations, addresses and dependants, and any benefit payments. Many branch records have not survived. See H. Southall, D. Gilbert and C. Bryce, *Nineteenth Century Trade Union Records* (Historical Geography Research Series, 1994).

☞ Friendly societies were established as benefit clubs in times of sickness and

Police service record, detailing the examination of E. T. D. Williamson of Minster, Kent, upon his application to join the police force, 1894.

death in the late eighteenth and nineteenth centuries. Where membership records survive, they have sometimes been deposited at local record offices. The rules of friendly societies are kept under FS at the National Archives.

Railwaymen with a Stirling F Class locomotive at Tonbridge station, Kent, 1900.

Prison records

Since 1877 prisons have been administered by the Home Office. Prison registers from that time, together with many earlier registers, may be seen at the National Archives, though records up to 100 years old may be closed to the public. Registers giving details about convicts in prison or on prison ships that were moored in British waters, covering the period 1770–1951, are in PCOM 2. HO 26 and HO 27 contain criminal registers for London and Middlesex from 1791 onwards and for the rest of England and Wales from 1805. These list all those who were charged with indictable offences, the date and place of the trial, the verdict and (if convicted) the sentence. Where the sentence was transportation, the name of the prison ship is recorded. The registers are arranged by year and then alphabetically by county. HO 27 is indexed up to 1828.

Before the Home Office assumed responsibility, crime was dealt with at county level. The most serious criminal cases were referred to the assizes. The records are kept in the National Archives in class JUST 3, switching in 1558 to ASSI 1–54 (England) and 57–77 (Wales). They are written in Latin up to 1732 and the handwriting is notoriously difficult to read. A. Bevan, *Tracing Your Ancestors in the Public Record Office*, 6th edn (PRO, 2002) and a TNA leaflet indicate the survival rates for each county, many of which do not have anything before c. 1820. Lesser offences were the concern of quarter sessions, especially from the sixteenth century onwards. Records are kept at county record offices and some of the early order and indictment

THE

METROPOLITAN
POLICE GAZETTE,
AND
Criminal Recorder.

(Price Threepence.)

On SATURDAY, the 29th of June inst. will be Published, (to be continued Weekly,) No. 1, of the " Metropolitan Police Gazette, and Criminal Recorder."

This Publication which will be of the size of a Weekly Newspaper and of a form suitable for Binding, will contain (expressly written for the Gazette) Reports of the proceedings at all the Twelve Police Offices in the Metropolis during the Week.—Interesting Trials at Assizes, Sessions, Courts of Law, &c.—Records (most useful to every Police Officer) of all Serious Offences and Criminals, with descriptions of their persons and the amount of rewards offered for their apprehension.—Hue and Cry.—Police Anecdotes.—False and Cowardly attacks made on the New Police exposed, and their authors DISPATCH'd —Gang of Miscreants, Prigs, Fences, Flash Houses and Gaming Houses.—Swell Mob.—Ascot and Hampton.—Feats at Windsor and Ben Lewis's Gang—The Spa-fields affair considered a Radical Murder.—Caution to persons attending Theatres.—Criticisms, &c.—The whole forming an entertaining and useful Miscellany.

No Police Constable connected with the Force will hesitate to become a Subscriber to a Work so useful, so cheap, and so devoted to his interest and the interests of the Public generally ; and which at all times will fearlessly, zealously, and impartially vindicate the Commissioners and Officers from the hebdomadal and systematic attacks of a certain Sunday Paper, which has (like the Boy in the Fable) cried " Wolf " " Wolf" so long, that at last the cries are almost unheeded.   Some dirty work of a certain junta in the Kilburn case of ADAMS v. SOPER and others exposed.

To be Sold by all respectable Booksellers and Newsmen,   Advertisements respecting Property Lost, Stolen, &c. and of Servants Wanted and wanting Places will be inserted.

J. W. PEEL, Printer, 9, New Cnt, Lambeth.

Poster announcing the publication of the weekly Metropolitan Police Gazette, 1833, a good source of information on criminal ancestors.

LEFT
Prison photograph and details of Rosa Hieldson, aged 14, who was given a short sentence at Lambeth in 1873.

books have been published by local record societies. County gaols and houses of correction (also known as Bridewells) for criminals, beggars, etc. were erected in county towns. The surviving prison registers and calendars (lists) of prisoners who were tried at assizes or quarter sessions should be at county record offices if they were not transferred to the National Archives. From the late eighteenth century many of these registers were printed. They record a prisoner's name and alleged crime, and sometimes his age, marital status, trade and the date when he was committed to custody. A few, notably those for Bedfordshire, provide a physical description

and a 'mugshot'. The verdict or sentence may have been added after the trial. A full account is given in D. T. Hawkings, *Criminal Ancestors: A Guide to Historical Criminal Records in England and Wales* (Sutton, 1992).

🖙 Census enumerators' books include the names of those in prison on census night. The 1861 returns and some of those for 1851 just give initials, but normally the details are the same as for anyone else.

🖙 Local newspapers usually reported cases that were brought before the courts. They also reported the verdicts of coroners' inquests into sudden or suspicious deaths.

🖙 Many of the records of coroners' inquests have been lost or destroyed; surviving ones are open to the public after 75 years. J. Gibson and C. Rogers, *Coroners' Records in England and Wales* (FFHS, 1992) lists their whereabouts.

🖙 An online searchable edition of the Old Bailey Proceedings, 1674–1834, the printed accounts of all criminal trials held at London's central criminal court, is available on <www.oldbaileyonline.org>. See P. Christian, 'Proceedings of the Old Bailey', *Ancestors* 16 (Oct/Nov 2003).

Protestant Nonconformity

The original Nonconformists or Dissenters were those who refused to subscribe to the Act of Uniformity of 1662 and the other Acts that re-asserted the authority of the Church of England after the Restoration of Charles II. At first, the main sects were the

Florence Nightingale's birth entry from a register of Dr Williams' Library.

Presbyterians (some of whom eventually became Unitarians), the Independents (who were otherwise known as Congregationalists), the Baptists, and the Society of Friends (commonly known as Quakers). Over time, the doctrines and affiliations of some congregations changed. Collectively, they are known as the Old

Dissenting sects, those whose history goes back much further than that of Wesleyan Methodism.

The Old Dissenters formed only a small proportion of the national population. In 1676 Bishop Compton's enquiries suggested that the figure was about 4 per cent, though in some parishes the proportion was much higher. At that time, the Nonconformist sects commonly used the Church of England for their marriage and burial services, and sometimes for their baptisms (though not, of course, the Baptists or Quakers). Parish registers do not distinguish Dissenters from the members of the Church of England. When a Nonconformist denomination first kept a separate register, the entries were normally only a record of baptisms. The registers of Upper Chapel, Sheffield and of the parish church of St Peter and St Paul show that many Dissenters baptized their children at both church and chapel – sometimes on the same day – but that others were content with the chapel service. Between 16 May 1681 and 30 July 1702 the Dissenting minister baptized 277 Sheffielders whose names do not appear in the Anglican baptism register and a further 129 who were baptized at both the chapel and the parish church. The fashion for duplicating services declined dramatically in later years. Between 1721 and 1735 only 17 children were baptised at both chapel and church in Sheffield, whereas 290 children were baptised at the chapel only.

The law of the land applied pressure on Dissenters to conform to the Anglican services. Before the introduction of civil registration in 1837 anyone applying for a government post had to produce proof of baptism in the Established Church. After the passing of Lord Hardwicke's Marriage Act in 1753 Nonconformists were no longer able to celebrate weddings in a chapel where a couple simply made a declaration before witnesses; only the Quakers were exempt from the new measure. Many Roman Catholics defied the Act, but most Protestant Dissenters seem to have accepted it reluctantly. Their records of vital events are nonetheless worth pursuing. If the

baptism of a child of a Nonconformist family cannot be found in an Anglican parish register, it may be worth trying the voluntary General Register of Births for Dissenters from 1 January 1743 to the beginning of civil registration, which was formerly held at Dr Williams' Library, London. This facility was used by families from many parts of Britain, though especially, of course, by Londoners; nearly 50,000 births were recorded. The register is

RIGHT
Anonymous portrait of Elizabeth Fry, from William Penn House, Buckinghamshire.

147

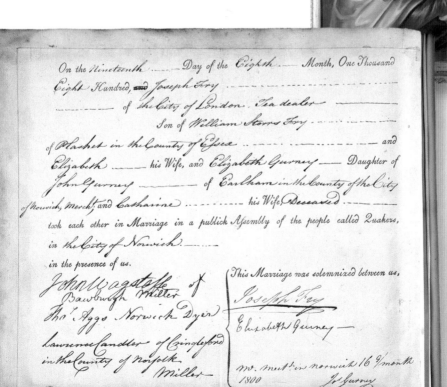

Marriage certificate of Elizabeth Fry, Norwich, 18 August 1800.

now kept at the National Archives in RG 4 and RG 5 and microfilm copies can be seen at the Family Records Centre, which has an explanatory leaflet.

Quaker burials are sometimes recorded in the parish registers of the Church of England, but the first Quakers were often buried in gardens or orchards rather than the parish churchyard and by the close of the seventeenth century most meeting-houses had a burial ground with unmarked graves. In 1850 headstones were permitted by the yearly meeting, provided they were of a uniform size and character that made no distinction between rich and poor. The Quakers were the first Dissenters to keep registers of all vital events, a practice that was well established by 1670. Records of births, marriages, and burials were sometimes kept by local meetings, but usually they were the responsibility of the monthly meetings which may have been held many miles away. The Society of Friends rejected the names of the days and months because they were derived from heathen gods, so Sunday was referred to as the First Day, January as the First Month, etc. Before the Gregorian calendar was adopted in 1752 March was the First Month, April the Second Month, and so on. From 1776 Quaker registers were kept to a standard format and copies were sent to the quarterly meetings. Some meetings also began to keep lists of members in the late eighteenth century, but this did not become general practice until 1836. The central source of information about the Quaker movement is the Library of the Religious Society of Friends, Friends House, 173–177 Euston Road, London NW1 2BJ.

The Moravians also kept registers, starting with that of the Fetter Lane congregation in London in 1741, but this new sect was soon overshadowed by the Wesleyan Methodists. The first national conference of the Wesleyans was held in 1744, but the formal break with the Church of England did not come for another 40 years. Splits within the Methodist movement occurred when George Whitefield and his fellow Calvinistic Methodists broke away in 1747, when the Methodist New Connexion was founded in 1797, when the Primitive Methodists formed their own organization in 1812, and when the Wesleyan Reform Union was established in 1849. For most of the eighteenth century, Methodists attended the local Anglican church for their baptism, marriage, and burial services and so were recorded in the parish registers. Methodist chapels kept very

36.	Burials.				
Names	Days of Departure	Days of Burial	Where interred and Nº	Minister
281 Benigna Theresia Nyberg. Child Childrens Oeconomy Fulneck	April 6th 1764.	April 7th 1764.	Fulneck Nº 264	Revd Mr LaTrobe
282 Elizabeth Booth Single Sister. Chnr House Fulneck	April 21st 1764.	April 24th 1764.	Fulneck Nº 265.	Revd Mr Charlesw
283 Eleonore Brogden, married Sister. Fulneck.	May 4th 1764.	May 7th 1764	Fulneck Nº 266.	Revd Mr La Trobe
284 Abigail Willy. married Sister. Fulneck	June 23? 1764.	June 25th 1764	Fulneck Nº 267.	Revd Mr Tayl
285 Mary Rouse child 11 Month old. High Town of Gummersall Plan	July 23? 1764.	July 25th 1764.	Fulneck Nº 268.	Revd Mr Mill
286 John Ellis. Youth. Hopton of Mirfield Plan.	August 17th 1764.	August 20th 1764.	Fulneck Nº 269.	Revd Mr Taylo
287 Sarah Robinson,	August	August	Fulneck	Rev

few registers before the 1790s; most of the surviving ones start after 1810 and even then they usually record only baptisms.

At the same time as the various Methodist denominations began to grow, some of the older sects were caught up in the evangelical revival. The Congregationalists and the Baptists (both General and Particular) founded many new chapels in the late eighteenth and nineteenth centuries. Some families were prepared to try chapels other than their own. In the first half of the nineteenth century my West Riding ancestors used the local Particular Baptist and Congregational chapels, and other chapels several miles apart, to record births or baptisms, but they went to the parish church a mile from home for their marriage and burial services.

National records

When civil registration was introduced at the beginning of Victoria's reign, a commission enquiring into the 'state, custody and authenticity of non-parochial registers' asked the various Nonconformist chapels and meeting-houses to send their registers to the Registrar-General, where they might be authenticated and made legal evidence. After the passing of the Non-Parochial Registers Act in 1840, 856 volumes of Nonconformist registers were submitted. The cataloguing of a second deposit of 'non-parochial' registers in 1857 was completed two years later. They may now be consulted at the National Archives under the references RG 4 to RG 6 and RG 8 or on microfilm at the Family Records Centre.

Moravian burial register, Fulneck, Yorkshire, 1764.

The List and Index Society has published lists of the Nonconformist registers in RG 4, 6 and 8. These are also searchable on the online catalogue. Some local record offices have microfilm copies of the registers for their district and the entries have been included in the Mormon International Genealogical Index. Many later registers have since been deposited in local record offices, but others were lost or destroyed when chapels closed. The National Library of Wales is the main repository for Welsh Nonconformist registers, especially those of the Calvinistic Methodists; Welsh Quaker records are held at the Glamorgan Record Office. In searching for the vital events of members of later bodies, such as the Salvation Army (founded 1865), it is usually best to use the indexes of civil registration.

Membership of the various Nonconformist denominations expanded enormously during the second quarter of the nineteenth century. When a national census of attendance at religious services was taken on Sunday, 30 March 1851 (for the first and only time) it was revealed that less than half the population of England and Wales went to any form of service and that about half of those who did attend preferred a chapel to the Church of England. In some districts the Nonconformists were more numerous than the Anglicans and in every county they accounted for at least a third of the worshippers. About 80 per cent of the Welsh were Nonconformists, particularly Calvinistic Methodists, Baptists and Independents. Clearly, family historians need to be well aware that ancestors who do not appear in parish registers may be found in the records of a chapel or meeting-house.

Roman Catholicism

When Elizabeth I came to the throne the celebration of a Catholic mass was made illegal. Until the nineteenth century English Catholics were a persecuted minority who frequently appear as 'popish recusants' or 'papists' in the records of archdeacons' courts and quarter sessions. In some parishes, however, private chapels in gentry houses were quietly tolerated. Most Catholics used the parish church for their burial services and, after Lord Hardwicke's Act (1753), for their weddings, but some opted for private baptism and marriage services in Catholic chapels. Few Catholic registers were kept before the middle of the eighteenth century because of the risk of persecution, though retrospective entries were sometimes inserted into later registers. Priests often assumed personal responsibility for these registers and kept them when they moved. Many Catholic registers do not start until the early nineteenth century.

🖝 When civil registration began in 1837, some Catholic authorities declined to deposit their registers because they were required for religious purposes. However, registers from the north of England were deposited and these can now be consulted in the National Archives in RG 4 or on microfilm at the Family Records Centre.

🖝 A National Archives information leaflet on 'Catholic Recusants' is available at <www.catalogue.nationalarchives. gov.uk>.

🖝 Many Catholic registers and other records have since been deposited in county record offices.

🖝 M. Gandy, *Catholic Missions and Registers, 1700–1880* (6 vols, 1993) provides full details of all the surviving Catholic baptism, confirmation, marriage and burial registers, and the copies that may be consulted.

🖝 Documents published by the Catholic Record Society include many baptism registers, records of convents abroad, recusant rolls, and the national returns of papists in 1767. See M. B. Rowlands, ed., *Catholics of Parish and Town, 1558–1778* (CRS, 1999) for the national background.

🖝 Much genealogical material is held by the Catholic Central Library, Lancing Street, London NW1.

The website of the Catholic Family History Society is at <www.catholic-history.org.uk/cfhs/index.htm>.

Very few Catholic families can trace their descent in the male line from English Catholics who were living during the time of persecution. In the more tolerant period between 1791 and 1814 large numbers of Catholic chapels were opened, mainly in the north of England, and the total number of English Catholics increased to about a quarter of a million. The majority were immigrants from Ireland, with some from France and other parts of continental Europe. The Catholic Emancipation Act of 1829 allowed Catholics to worship as they pleased and led to the building of more churches and cathedrals. The large numbers of Irish people who crossed the sea to escape the potato famine in the 1840s established Catholic congregations in many of the industrial districts of England and Wales. By the middle of the nineteenth century three-quarters of the Catholic population in England were Irish in origin.

A page from the Papist Returns for Middlesex, 1767.

ROMAN CATHOLICISM

Jewish records

European Jews belong to one of two main groups: the Sephardim, who were originally based in Spain, and the Ashkenazim, who inhabited the Rhine valley and later moved across Germany and into Poland and Russia. Small groups of Sephardic Jews were the first to settle in English towns, starting with those financiers who accompanied William the Conqueror. They numbered fewer than 3,000 when they were expelled by Edward I in 1290. Though some wealthy Sephardic merchants, who came mainly from Portugal, settled in London from 1541, Jews were not formally readmitted into the country until 1656. Other Sephardic Jews came from Mediterranean countries and joined the Portuguese synagogue in London. Perhaps half of the estimated 6,000 English Jews in 1734, however, were Ashkenazim from central Europe. Their native language was Yiddish, a form of German written in Hebrew characters. Some of these immigrants were skilled craftsmen, such as engravers, but most were poor men who hawked jewellery and haberdashery until they had saved enough to become shopkeepers. During the middle and later years of the nineteenth century large numbers of Ashkenazic Jews fled to England to escape persecution in Central and Eastern Europe. Thousands of poor Jews left the Russian Empire to escape from Tsar Alexander III's pogroms in the 1880s. They settled mostly in the East End of London and certain districts of Manchester

Certificate of naturalization of Noé Meyer Baum, 1874, giving his address, place of birth, age, occupation and information about other members of his family.

Plate 62.

and Leeds until the British government brought this immigration to an end in 1905.

In tracing Jewish ancestors, it is best to start with the usual civil registration indexes and census returns at the Family Records Centre. One of the greatest difficulties is that Jewish names were often spelt in a variety of ways and were sometimes changed into forms that the English would recognise. For example, people named Davis, Harris and Moss sometimes have ancestors whose Jewish names have been altered. Some Jews deliberately adopted English names that had little or no connection with their Jewish one.

Jews were recorded in the parish registers of the Church of England, though Jewish marriages were exempt from the provisions of Lord Hardwicke's Act (1753). Early

View of the Great Synagogue, Duke's Place, Houndsditch, with congregation, by Charles Augustus Pugin and Thomas Rowlandson, from Ackermann's Microcosm of London, *1809, long before the arrival of poor Jews in the East End.*

synagogues usually kept an accurate record of marriages and burials, but they were less concerned with recording births. Specialist - guidance is needed when consulting the records of Ashkenazic synagogues, for not only were they written in Hebrew or Yiddish in a cursive script but they used Hebrew or synagogue names, which were not always the same as the English names which they used every day, and they do not record surnames. Synagogue records have generally been deposited in local record offices. A good starting point is the website of the Jewish Genealogical Society of Great Britain at <www.jgsgb.org.uk>.

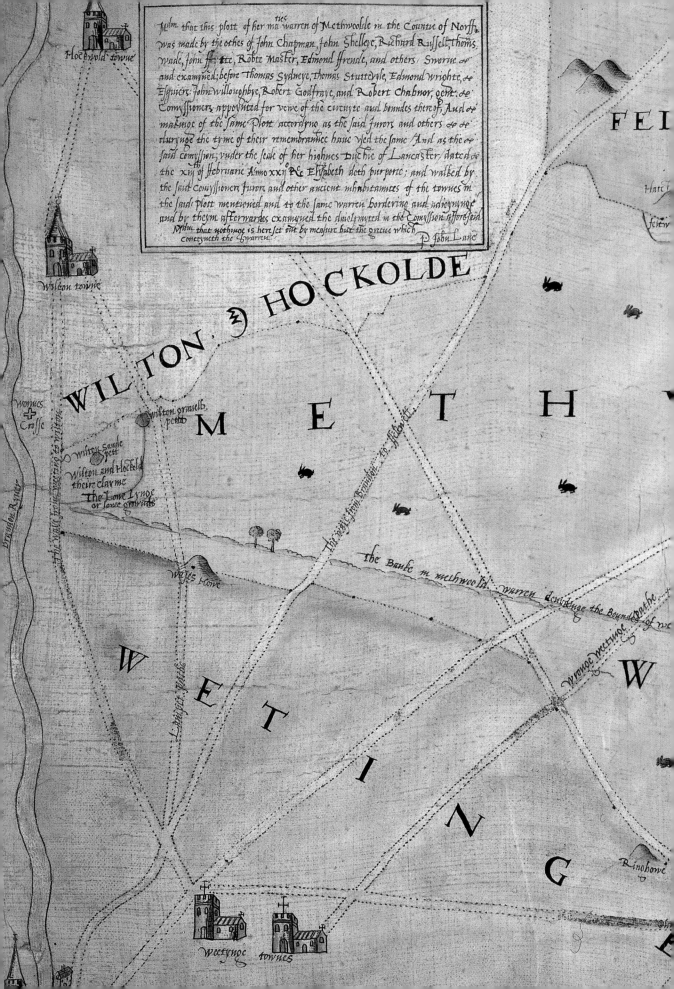

Hockwold towne

Wilton towne

Wormes + Crosse

WILTON ⅋ HOCKOLDE

Wilton ormesth pettr

Wilton Sande pett
Wilton and Hockold their clayme
The Lowe Lynge or lowe groundes

Brandon Ryver

METH

Wakes Howe

The Banke in methwoold warren devidinge the Boundes pathe of me

The way from Brandon to Feltwell

WETING

Wronge meetinge

W

G

Ringhowe

FEI

Hatch fellow

Weetynge townes

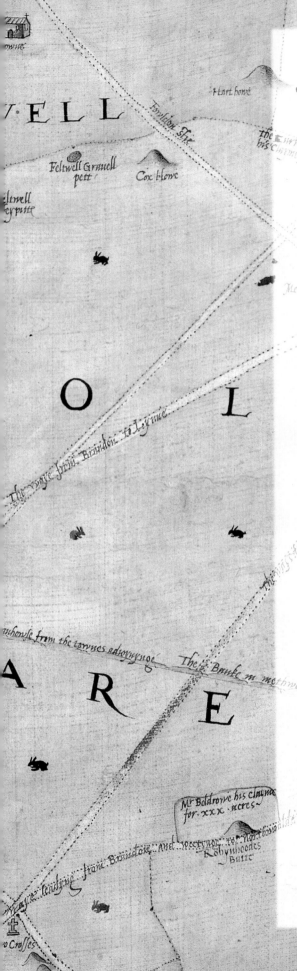

3 Making Early Connections (1550–1800)

As to his ancestors, we have searched with great diligence, but little success: being unable to trace them farther than his great grandfather, who, as an elderly person in the parish remembers to have heard his father say, was an excellent cudgel-player. Whether he had any ancestors before this, we must leave to the opinion of the curious reader, finding nothing of sufficient certainty to rely on.

Henry Fielding, *Joseph Andrew* (1742)

EXPLORING YOUR PAST

Introduction	156
Urban and rural	158
Families	161
Houses	166
Rich and poor	169
Core families and 'country'	173
Kinship and inheritance	178
Servants and apprentices	180
Migration	182
Work	185

FINDING YOUR ANCESTORS

Parish registers	190
The Old Poor Law	204
Wills and other probate records	211
Apprentice and freeman records	222
Land tax assessments	227
Hearth tax returns	229
Protestation returns, 1641–2	234
Muster rolls and militia returns	236
Courts of Chancery, Exchequer, Star Chamber, and Requests	239
The legal profession	241
Title deeds	242

Introduction

Family memories were longer in the Tudor and Stuart period than they are now. Perhaps this was because most people lived in small communities in the countryside and did not move far. They knew all their neighbours well and were familiar with everybody's family histories. When Richard Gough wrote his history of the Shropshire parish of Myddle in 1701–2 he was able to trace his own family back about 200 years and to give long accounts of all the other families. He examined the parish register, the manor court rolls, and deeds and leases, but much of his knowledge was obtained from talking to his neighbours. He noted that, 'We have a tradition', 'I have heard by antient persons' and 'I have been credibly informed by antient persons'. He knew that he was descended from Richard Gough who died in 1538 in the adjoining parish of Wem and from five other Richard Goughs who had successively farmed the property that he had inherited at Newton on the Hill, a mile or so from the parish church. Gough was an exceptionally able man, but he was not alone in placing family history at the heart of an interest in everything to do with his locality. Most people's lives were lived at an intensely local level, their mental horizons bounded by the nearest market towns. The histories of local families were known to everyone.

Gough's stories show that human nature has not changed since his time. He wrote about virtuous neighbours such as Thomas Ash, who was 'a proper comely person', of boastful characters such as Thomas Newans, who 'was unskilled in husbandry, though hee would talke much of it', and of Elizabeth Tyler who was 'more commendable for her beauty than her chastity, and was the ruin of the family'. Alas, Gough's parish history is unique. We can rarely find stories about our seventeenth-century ancestors that bring them to life. All we usually have are names and dates found in parish registers or taxation returns. We are lucky to find a will or a mention in a Poor Law document that

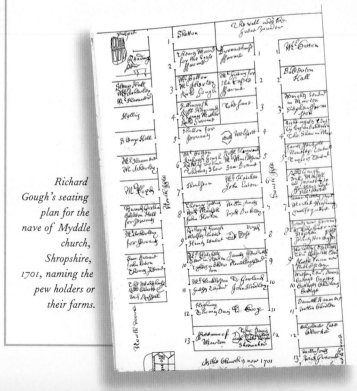

might provide insights into an ancestor's life and exceptionally fortunate to discover that an ancestral home has survived intact since Stuart times. Most of us have to be content with the broad outlines of our family's story. I have found that I am descended from a succession of younger sons, who moved across the West Riding parish of Kirkburton from the ancestral farm at Birk House to a new home taken in from the edge of the common at Thorncliffe, where Joseph Hey was taxed on one hearth in the 1660s and 1670s. His son, William, was churchwarden in 1703 and his grandson, James, was a clothier, but I have found little else about them apart from the usual genealogical information in the parish register.

IN BRIEF

- We can find only basic genealogical information about our Tudor and Stuart ancestors, unless we are lucky enough to come across some exceptionally-rich sources.

- Most people's lives were lived in the localities that they were familiar with, bounded by the nearest market towns.

Urban and rural

The Gloucestershire countryside around Dixton manor house, from an anonymous oil-painting of c.1715. Ridge-and-furrow patterns show that some of the pastures were once ploughed for growing cereals.

During the long reign of Queen Elizabeth the country emerged from its medieval past. From 1538, when parish registers began, we have clear evidence that the population of England and Wales was starting to climb back to the level that had been achieved before the Black Death. The same trend can be seen all over western Europe. Families had more children and did not lose quite so many when they were very young, so the national population rose steadily from about 2.75 million in 1540 to about 5 million 100 years later. Growth seems to have faltered over the next two generations, though it

remained steady in rural counties such as Shropshire which still had space for immigrant cottagers and continued strongly in some of the industrial towns and their neighbourhoods, including the new dockyard towns of Deptford and Greenwich and the coal port of Whitehaven. By 1700 old market towns which had become centres of industry, such as Birmingham, Leeds, Sheffield or Manchester, were growing significantly. Whereas in 1616 the population of the central township of Sheffield was a modest 2,207, by 1736 it had soared to 10,121. From the 1740s onwards the national population began a long period of growth that continues to the present day. It seems that about one-third of this growth was

caused by lower death rates and the other two-thirds by earlier and more frequent marriages that produced more children. When the first national census was held in 1801 the population of England and Wales was counted at 8.9 million, a figure that is usually adjusted because of under-recording to 9.2 million. The kingdom was about to enter an era of rapid and unprecedented change.

Until well into the nineteenth century the national population remained overwhelmingly rural. In 1700 three out of every four people lived in the countryside, either in villages, hamlets or isolated farmsteads. Even most urban families had only 1–2,000 neighbours, often fewer, and they could view the surrounding fields and woods from the central streets and market place. Poole had only 1,357 inhabitants in 1574 and Stafford no more than 1,550 in

1622. London was in a different league to any other English city. During Elizabeth's reign London's population grew from about 120,000 to 200,000, by 1650 it had reached 375,000, and by 1700 about 490,000. Whereas in 1550 its share of the national population was about 4 per cent, by 1700 nearly 10 per cent of the nation were Londoners. All the inhabitants of the provincial cities put together could not match the size of the population of the capital city. In 1700 Norwich had about 30,000 people, Bristol about 20,000, and Exeter, York and Newcastle had fewer. The industrial towns, such as Leeds and Manchester, still lagged a long way behind, though their rate of growth astonished contemporaries. Some of the ancient cities benefited from the growth of the economy – Bristol became an Atlantic port and Norwich a flourishing

IN BRIEF

- In Elizabethan and Stuart times three out of four people still lived in the countryside.

- In 1700 most towns had only 1,000–2,000 inhabitants, but London's population approached half a million.

- From about 1740 the national population began a long period of growth that has lasted to this day.

- By 1801 one person in three lived in a town and the new industrial centres were much larger than the ancient cathedral cities.

centre for the 'new draperies' – and many an old market town grew modestly. The Civil War had disrupted the economy of some towns and disastrous fires had damaged others, but the late seventeenth and eighteenth centuries saw an 'urban renaissance' that improved the quality of life with fine buildings and public spaces. The first leisure towns, notably Tunbridge Wells and Bath, developed as spa centres from the late seventeenth century onwards.

This ancient pattern changed dramatically with the coming of the Industrial Revolution and the great rise in the national population during the second half of the eighteenth century. Birmingham's population rose from 23,688 in 1750 to 73,670 in 1801, that of neighbouring Wolverhampton from 7,454 to 12,565 in the same period, and that of the whole of the Black Country in similar fashion. Between 1664 and 1801 Lancashire's population grew by 360 per cent, more than five times the national figure. Manchester had an estimated 43,448 inhabitants in 1664, and 281,290 in 1801. By then, an enormous shift in the distribution of the national population had taken place, away from the agricultural counties of southern and eastern England and towards the rapidly-developing industrial districts of the Midlands and the north, especially Lancashire, Warwickshire, Staffordshire and the West Riding of Yorkshire. One person in every three now lived in a town. Manchester, Liverpool and Birmingham were the largest places after London, and amongst the old provincial centres only Bristol had stayed in the top six. Leeds and Sheffield had overtaken York, the ancient capital of northern England. Yet the rise of the industrial towns and their neighbourhoods was only just beginning.

'The Naval Dockyard at Deptford', by Samuel Scott (c.1702–72). Deptford had grown considerably as a dockyard town during the late seventeenth and eighteenth centuries.

Families

Most households consisted of parents and children only. Of course, sometimes an elderly grandparent was accommodated, but most widows or widowers lived in their own houses, perhaps with a lodger or an elder grandchild. Newly-married couples might have had to live with parents for a time, but their ambition was always to set up home on their own. The biggest difference with later times was that households often included farm or domestic servants and apprentices. Children were expected to leave home in their early teens to live and work with another family.

The early death of one partner and the subsequent remarriage of the other meant that many households contained step-children. This helps to explain why people sometimes appear in contemporary records with an alias name. Arrangements were more flexible than the idea of the simple, nuclear family might suggest. An average of about 4.75 people per household allows us to estimate the total population of a town or village, but the composition of individual households, and indeed particular communities, ranged far more widely than that. The number of people living together at any one time varied according to the stage that had been reached in the family life cycle. It also varied according to wealth and social standing, for the richer households had greater numbers of living-in servants.

Although aristocratic families often arranged the marriages of their children at a very young age, parish registers show that the great majority of English and Welsh couples were well into their twenties when they married. The median average age was about 26 for a man and 23 for a woman, but this figure hides much variation. Some couples married in their teens, others in their thirties, and we can all find examples of a man in his thirties marrying a girl who was not yet 20. Nevertheless, the average figure does remind us that on the whole people did not marry young. The registers also show that a lot of people never married

IN BRIEF

- The average household contained four or five people, usually just parents and children, like today.

- Children often left home in their early teens to live and work as servants or apprentices.

- The population began to rise, as people married earlier and had more children, while at the same time death rates declined.

- Despite the high rates of infant and child mortality, Tudor and Stuart society was far more youthful than today. Only 6 or 7 per cent lived into their 80s.

at all. Sometimes, the proportion in the early modern period was as high as one in four.

This relatively late age at marriage and the high numbers of people who never married were the major factors in preventing a steep rise in the national population before the middle years of the eighteenth century, when better employment opportunities allowed earlier marriages and thus more children. As death rates declined at the same time, the population began to grow quickly during the early years of the Industrial Revolution. The state of the economy clearly influenced the timing of marriage. In the reign of Queen Elizabeth, for example, the marriage rates fell sharply as real wages dropped in value. By contrast, in 1733 the nailmakers of south Yorkshire tried to enforce seven-year apprenticeships, claiming that many lads were leaving after only two years and setting themselves up in business, so that they 'frequently married very young

'Christening of the Heir', an oil-painting by William Redmore Bigg, c.1799.

and inconsiderately and by that means have often a great charge of children to maintain before they scarce know how to maintain themselves'.

RIGHT
A woodcut from an old ballad depicting a housewife spinning outside her cottage.

Pregnancy might bring a marriage date forward, otherwise couples usually waited until they had sufficient savings to set up home on their own. Parents, then as now, helped if they could, and in some cases the death of a parent allowed a child to inherit the family property. Boys might be provided with land or set up as a master craftsman after completing an apprenticeship; girls were given a 'marriage portion'. Richard Gough's *History of Myddle*, written in 1701–2, mentions marriage portions in his part of Shropshire that ranged from £30 to £100.

We have all read of examples where aristocratic families arranged the marriages of children, long before they were of full age and with no regard for their feelings, in order to further their wealth and social standing. This was not the case with the great majority of ordinary families, however. Young people chose their own marriage partners and few listened to parents who disapproved of their choice of partner. Many of them no longer had a parent alive to offer advice by the time they got married. Youngsters mingled with the opposite sex in the streets or alehouses when they were away from home as servants or apprentices in neighbouring towns and villages, where they were free to meet

whom they wished. While it was common for families to bargain over marriage portions, young couples believed in romantic love.

The peak periods for marriage were when servants were released from their annual contracts, around May Day, Michaelmas or Martinmas. Another popular time for the weddings of country people was just after the harvest had been gathered in. The church had prohibited periods for marriages; Lent remained the main one well into Victorian times, but the restrictions on Advent were lifted in the late seventeenth century. Another practical consideration that determined the date of marriage was pregnancy, for in Elizabethan times one out of every three brides was pregnant before she married. However, this high figure is partly explained by the widely-accepted contemporary belief that marriages could start with witnessed pledges of betrothal before a wedding in church. The number of illegitimate births rose as employment opportunities fell and a series of bad harvests took their toll, but even in the worst period between 1590 and 1610 it never amounted to more than three per cent of recorded baptisms, and this level was not reached again until the middle of the eighteenth century. Illegitimacy rates were particularly low in the 1650s, during the time of the 'godly revolution' following the Civil

War. They long remained at a much lower level than the high rates that were reached in the first decades of the nineteenth century.

Baptism registers show that children succeeded each other at regular intervals of 15–30 months, or on average every two years, which suggests that women were unlikely to conceive while they were breastfeeding. As women married at a later age than their descendants in the nineteenth century, their families were smaller. High rates of infant and child mortality were a severe check on population growth. Across the country, about one in six or seven infants died, but the rates were far lower in the countryside than in the unhealthy suburbs of the capital city, where they reached one in three, even in years when the plague was not virulent.

The cause and nature of an epidemic was often not understood at the time, as is evident from Richard Gough's references to 'violent fevers' or 'violent distempers' and to the death of Andrew Bradocke from 'a sort of rambeling feavourish distemper, which

The burial of plague victims at St Giles without Cripplegate, London, 1665.

raged in that country'. A particular disease can sometimes be identified from the pattern of burials recorded in a parish register. The 'sweating sickness' of the late 1550s, for instance, was probably a virulent form of influenza. Bubonic plague was not understood until about 1900, since when it has been usually accepted as the killer disease which remained endemic from the Black Death of 1348–50 until the Great Plague of London in 1665, and later in the Mediterranean basin. But neither the speed by which the disease spread nor the high death rates were typical of the modern epidemics caused by bubonic plague and there is little evidence that rats (which were supposed to transmit the disease) were a problem in medieval England; nobody mentioned them at the time. In western Europe plague behaved as if it spread through the air. It is now known that although true bubonic plague may have occurred in the Mediterranean from time to time, it was not the culprit in England and most of the rest of Europe. Some other viral disease which is now extinct, but which resembled bubonic plague in its ability to produce buboes in the lymph glands, was spread by human contact. It disappeared as mysteriously as it arrived.

Whatever its exact nature, the threat of plague dwindled and smallpox became the major killer disease of the late seventeenth and eighteenth centuries. However, unpredictable outbreaks of other infectious diseases were usually responsible for the sharp increases in the number of burials that were recorded from time to time in parish registers. These local crises occurred throughout the year, but they were much more frequent in late summer and autumn, particularly in the months of August and September. This pattern suggests that dysentery and other diarrhoeal infections were responsible. Children were especially vulnerable. No less than 82.6 per cent of the 224 people whose burials were recorded in the Sheffield parish register between July and October 1715 were children; during the month of August only one of the 54 recorded deaths there was that of an adult. Famine was rarely the cause of death in early-modern England and Wales. Malnutrition may have made people less resistant, but infectious disease was the real problem.

Despite the high rates of infant and child mortality, Tudor and Stuart society was far more youthful than today. Dependent children formed about 40 per cent of the English and Welsh population. Men and women who reached the age of 30 could expect to live, on average, for another 30 years, but sudden death was an ever-present threat for people in middle age. Many children never knew their grandparents.

Lists of households that survive for parishes scattered across the land show that between 1550 and 1800 about 20 per cent were headed by widows, or to a far less extent by widowers. Elderly widows feature regularly in parish payments for poor relief. Only 6 or 7 per cent of the population lived beyond 80, compared with a proportion that is three or four times higher today.

Printed notice of Common Prayer and Fasting at the time of the Great Plague of London, 1665.

Houses

In Elizabethan England and Wales most of the houses of ordinary families were built of wood and infilled with more humble materials, such as mud, cobbles and flints, just as they had been in previous centuries. In his *Description of England* (1577) William Harrison wrote that 'the greatest part of our building in the cities and good towns … consisteth only of timber'. This ancient tradition petered out during the seventeenth century, partly because of fashion and partly because it became more economical to build

in stone and brick. At the same time, thatched roofs were replaced in districts where tiles or stone flags could be obtained at reasonable prices. The experience of disastrous fires persuaded many town authorities to ban thatched roofs and to insist that new buildings did not have wooden frames. In the countryside the gentry led the way and they were soon followed by the yeomen and then the husbandmen. The fact that relatively few cottages were substantial enough to survive from this period, however, shows that the poorest sections of society did not share this new-found prosperity. Even by the end of the eighteenth century, farm labourers and industrial workers commonly lived in one-storey cottages that were open to their thatched roofs.

One of the most appealing characteristics of vernacular architecture is the use of local building materials. The picturesque appearance of so many of the houses that survive from the Tudor and Stuart period is the result of the remarkably varied geology of England and Wales and the high cost of moving building materials overland before the construction of canals and railways. The use of traditional building materials helps to define the many different 'countries' that a traveller passed through in a week's journey. Yet the outward appearance of farmhouses

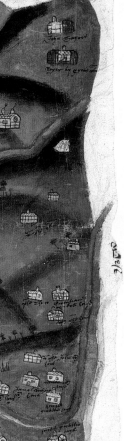

An Elizabethan map of the manor of Grosmont, Monmouthshire, 1588, showing scattered timber-framed houses and cottages of various sizes, all of them with new-fangled chimneys. The names of many of the owners are written alongside their properties.

IN BRIEF

- The old tradition of timber-framed houses roofed with thatch declined in the seventeenth century as people began to build in stone and brick.

- Houses and cottages were built in local materials, which gave each district its special character, but their plans were similar across the country.

- Living conditions improved from Elizabethan times onwards, with hearths, comfortable beds, better furniture, and more pots and pans.

- But standards of hygiene remained low in the sixteenth and seventeenth centuries.

disguises their common internal arrangement throughout much of England and Wales, for most were based on three units in a line – one for cooking, one for living in, and one for sleeping. At first, houses were one-room deep and open to the rafters, but during the seventeenth century many old houses were adapted by the construction of a chimney or two and by inserting ceilings to create upstairs bedrooms and extra storage space. New houses incorporated these features in their design as the fashion began to spread.

These changes helped to bring about higher standards of domestic comfort. In 1577 William Harrison reported that the beneficial changes which old people had observed over their lifetimes were 'a multitude of chimnies latelie erected', 'a great amendment of lodging' whereby comfortable beds had replaced straw pallets, and a remarkable increase in the amount and quality of tableware. He was quick to add that these improvements were not yet general, but the comments of later writers show that they were adopted in northern and western districts during the course of the seventeenth century. Their observations are confirmed by the evidence of thousands of probate inventories and by studies of the pedlars and petty chapmen who sold cheap consumer goods all over the kingdom. Nevertheless, the standards of hygiene in most houses during the sixteenth and seventeenth centuries remained low. People did not wash their bodies, and they did not replace their rush-strewn, earthen floors with stone flags or bricks until the late seventeenth or early eighteenth century. The insanitary conditions in which people lived help to explain the high levels of infant and child mortality. Improved standards of building and comfort were introduced in south-eastern and eastern England much earlier than elsewhere, but even in the more prosperous parts of England some parishes were poorer than their neighbours and their inhabitants were slow to improve the quality of their housing. Datestones on new buildings demonstrate that what had become standard in one region or neighbourhood during the late sixteenth century was not introduced into others until two or three generations later.

During the eighteenth century the better-off farmers and townsmen turned to a new style of building with a central door and symmetrical windows. These houses were usually double-depth in plan, which helped to make them warm and comfortable, and often three storeys high. As they used stones and roofing slates from local quarries or hand-made bricks and tiles, they remained intensely local in appearance. Each house had its own character, despite its standard basic design. The widespread use of machine-made bricks and Welsh blue slates came later.

The south front of East Riddlesden Hall, Yorkshire, built for James Murgatroyd, a wealthy clothier, in the 1640s. The rows of mullioned and transomed windows were fashionable before sash windows were invented. The combination of Gothic battlements, rose-window and Renaissance porch is typical of the better houses in and around Halifax at this period.

Rich and poor

Group portrait of a squire with his wife and children on the edge of the New Forest, 1817, an oil-painting by W. Allison.

In 1577 the Essex parson, William Harrison, divided people into four social groups, ranging from 'the first degree' of gentleman to the 'last sort', formed by day labourers, poor husbandmen and 'all artificers'. None of these groups could be defined precisely. At the top were peers, knights, esquires and 'they that are simplie called gentlemen'. Although the heralds insisted at their visitations that a gentleman must bear a coat of arms, in practice many families that were

not armigerous were thought of as gentry in their own communities and were recorded as Mr or Mrs in the parish registers. Hard-and-fast definitions were made more difficult by the rise and fall of individual families over the generations. By the nineteenth century few gentlemen could prove descent from the Normans, though that did not prevent many of them from claiming such a pedigree. As titles descended only in the eldest male line, younger members of a family often did not retain their nobility and the frequent failure of male lines meant that many peerages became extinct. Other titles and estates passed to distant cousins, many of whom were prepared to change their surname in order to inherit. The continuity of an aristocratic line is often illusory. On the other hand, it was never easy for the newly rich to enter the top levels of society and it usually took three generations to become accepted. Some of those who did rise rapidly, notably the Cavendishes at Chatsworth, seized their chance at the dissolution of the monasteries. At the same time, well-established aristocratic families, such as the Talbots, earls of Shrewsbury, added to their possessions at bargain prices. The dissolution led to the greatest redistribution of land since the Norman Conquest.

The opportunities for enrichment that were provided by industry and trade were also gratefully accepted by the aristocracy. The Talbots and Cavendishes, together with the Manners family at Haddon Hall and gentry families such as the Eyres of Hassop or the Gells of Hopton, dominated the prosperous Derbyshire lead industry, benefiting both from royalties and tolls and from investments in smelting mills. Such industries also enabled local farming families to rise to minor gentry status and a considerable number of younger sons earned fortunes as merchants in London before they or their descendants retired to a country estate as gentlemen. Josias Wordsworth of Penistone, for instance, acquired so much wealth from trade with the Baltic countries that he was able to return to his native Yorkshire at a splendid new seat at Wadworth, that was designed for

him in the late 1740s by the leading architect James Paine. In the early modern period parish gentry were not sharply divided from the rest of local society, as their nineteenth-century successors were; the numerous junior members of the Wordsworths who were to be found amongst the yeomen or even the husbandmen of their native parish were typical of such poorer relations.

The yeomen were prosperous farmers who worked their own land. They held their farms by a variety of tenures – freehold, leasehold, copyhold – and sometimes combined all three methods. The term yeoman had no precise definition but was used in wills and other local documents to signify a status that was superior to that of the average husbandman. It is common to find that a man might describe himself as a yeoman in his will, but that his neighbours downgraded him to husbandman in the inventory of his personal estate that they appraised upon his death. More rarely, the appraisers upgraded a modest man. When Henry Yellott of Totley (Derbyshire) made his will in 1608 he was content with 'husbandman', but when he died ten years later he was designated 'yeoman'. Perhaps his fortunes had improved in his last decade? Both terms were gradually replaced by farmer from the eighteenth century onwards. Together with the craftsmen (many of whom were part-time farmers) the yeomen and husbandmen formed the stable core of rural communities throughout the sixteenth, seventeenth and eighteenth centuries.

The 'chief men of the parish' or 'the principal inhabitants' were differentiated

A view of a 'coal works' near Neath, Glamorganshire, by John Hassell (1767–1825). Note the horse-drawn windlass and the water wheel on the river.

from the 'other inhabitants', 'poor inhabitants', the 'meaner sort' or 'poorer sort', those who formed Harrison's 'fourth and last sort of people'. During the sixteenth and early seventeenth centuries the number of poor people rose considerably as job opportunities failed to match the rapid growth of the national population. The problem of the poor was exacerbated by the Dissolution of the Monasteries, which cut off a major source of regular charity. The bequests that were commonly made in wills and the charity boards that survive in many a parish church bear witness to much generosity at a local level, but this was insufficient to meet the growing need. The state had to create a system of poor relief that was based on parishes and townships,

under the supervision of the Justices of the Peace at the quarter sessions. By 1660 at least a third of the parishes of England and Wales were well accustomed to raising poor rates to spend as cash doles to the poor, especially to widows. The parish overseers of the poor reacted in practical ways to meet individual cases of hardship, so rents were paid, children cared for, and orphans apprenticed. Parish ratepayers looked after their own 'deserving poor', but were quick to remove others to the places where they were legally settled. Those who were regarded as 'undeserving' were treated roughly, often with the whip.

The desperate poor took to the road in search of a livelihood. We know little about

The London Bridewell, unattributed engraving. It was named after Bride Well, where Henry VIII had a lodging. Edward VI granted the site to the City of London in 1552 to erect a house of correction for vagabonds.

them, but they seem to have been mostly young and single. Some became squatters and day-labourers in parts of the countryside that were still thinly populated, others sought a living in the new industrial districts, such as the Northumberland and Durham coalfield or the parts of the Pennines where lead was mined. Many more headed for the towns, often moving on from one to another until they arrived in the suburbs of London. Wages were better there and mortality rates were so high that the chances of stepping into a dead man's shoes and finding employment were greater. But

vagrants were not welcomed by the respectable classes. The London Bridewell was erected in 1552 as a house of correction for vagabonds, and later for prisoners, who were set to hard labour. By the 1630s every county in England and Wales had a similar institution.

In the later seventeenth century, when population levels became more stable and the general standard of living was improved by better farming methods and the growth of industry, the number of tramps on the road declined considerably. The Act of Settlement of 1662 encouraged the poor to stay in or near the parish where they had a legal right to relief and deterred them from venturing into places where they would be rejected. But once the population started to grow again, so the expenditure on the poor rose to new levels. By the end of the eighteenth century parishes were spending record amounts on their poor and the demand for a new system of relief was expressed stridently.

IN BRIEF

- ☞ Parish gentry were recorded as Mr or Mrs in parish registers, everybody else by their personal name and surname.
- ☞ In local records the 'principal inhabitants' were differentiated from 'the meaner sort' or 'the poorer sort'.
- ☞ Prosperous farmers were known as 'yeomen', ordinary farmers as 'husbandmen'.
- ☞ Parish ratepayers looked after their 'deserving poor' but were quick to remove others to the places where they were legally settled.

Core families and 'country'

The study of parish registers, occasional lists of inhabitants that have survived for communities scattered across England, apprenticeship records, depositions before quarter sessions and ecclesiastical courts, and the few surviving diaries from the sixteenth, seventeenth and eighteenth centuries has shown that although people often moved away from their native parish most of them did not venture beyond their immediate neighbourhood, unless they had decided to try their luck in London or one of the provincial cities such as Bristol or Norwich. Family historians are well aware that an ancestor who was born in one parish may have died in another, but that usually the place of burial was not far removed from the place of birth.

Much of this turnover of names at the level of the parish was caused by the movement of young people, some of whom returned in later life to inherit the family farm or workshop. Unless they were trained to follow their father's trade, the young knew from an early age that one day they would move to a neighbouring parish or market town, the girls working as domestic servants, the boys as farm servants or apprentices. Once he had served his term,

an apprentice usually settled in the district where he had learned his trade. Most apprentices had not moved far from their native parishes to the homes of their new masters, but those that had journeyed long distances brought new surnames, which sometimes became as well established as those which had been formed locally in the Middle Ages. In Hallamshire, for example, the Derbyshire surnames Heathcote, Memmott and Ollerenshaw appear in the apprenticeship records of the Cutlers Company in the eighteenth century.

Although people were strongly attached to their own parish, they also felt that they belonged to a wider, more loosely-defined district, which they thought of as their 'country', the neighbourhood that was bounded by the nearest market towns. One of the definitions of 'country' in the *Oxford English Dictionary* is 'A tract or district having more or less definite limits in relation to human occupation, e.g. owned by the same lord or proprietor, or inhabited by people of the same race, dialect, occupation, etc.'. This old usage is a useful term for local and family historians, for it reminds us that people had a sense of belonging to a neighbourhood in which they had friends and relations who spoke like they did and who earned their living in the same, familiar ways, whether on a farm or in a craft. The potters of north Staffordshire, the cutlers of Hallamshire and the metalworkers of the Black Country worked in well-defined industrial 'countries', Warwickshire was split between the corn-growing 'feldon' country in the south and the wood-pastures of the Forest of Arden in the north, and rural Wiltshire was divided into the 'cheese country' of the claylands and the 'chalk country' of the downs. Elsewhere, the divisions between 'countries' were not as

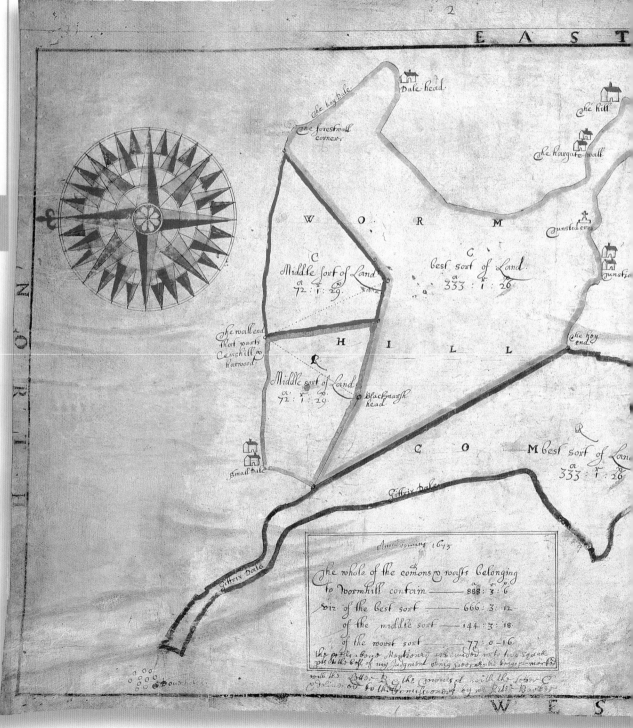

The former school and market hall at Market Harborough, Leicestershire, founded in 1614 by Robert Smyth, a local man who had made his fortune in London.

obvious, but a market town or a county boundary formed a psychological barrier that few ventured across. When Robert Smyth, a successful London merchant tailor, founded a grammar school in his native town of Market Harborough in the early seventeenth century, he explained that he remembered that 'I came out of my country and from my father's house with my cuppe empty' and that 'with my staff I came over the Welland', the river that formed the Leicestershire–Northamptonshire boundary, before heading for the capital city.

Although the gentry often went beyond their immediate neighbourhood to find their marriage partners, ordinary men and women generally married someone from their own

A map of the Peak District township of Wormhill in 1675 showing the two 'Gittrix' farmsteads (now Great Rocks Farm) that are the source of the local name Greatorex. The place-name means 'the great valley', outlined in red and blue on the map.

'country'. Every time that parish registers have been used to determine the geographical origins of husbands and wives the conclusion has been that partners were overwhelmingly chosen from within a radius of about 20 miles. The limited range of most movement is confirmed by other studies, such as that of the 'Dade registers' for parishes in the Vale of York which traced the movements of 2,268 individuals between 1777 and 1822. This showed that only 18 per cent migrated more than 10 miles and that more than four in every five of those who ventured further did not leave Yorkshire.

Each 'country' was partly defined by its own set of distinctive surnames which had been formed locally during the Middle Ages. As the population grew during the sixteenth and seventeenth centuries, so these names spread. Their distribution patterns in the reign of Charles II can be traced from the various hearth tax returns that survive in the National Archives. These patterns are immediately obvious where a surname has been derived from a local farmstead or a hamlet. For example, the Armisteads took their surname from a farmstead in the parish of Giggleswick, where they were recorded in 1379. By the time of the Yorkshire hearth tax returns of Lady Day 1672 the Armisteads had increased to 72 households, but nearly all of them lived close together in Ribblesdale, including 26 who were taxed in the parish of

- People were strongly attached to their own parish but also felt that they belonged to a wider district that they knew as their 'country'.
- They often moved across parish boundaries but usually stayed within a neighbourhood bounded by the nearest market towns, unless they were attracted by London.
- Most people found their marriage partners within their 'country'.
- Each 'country' had its set of distinctive surnames which had been formed locally during the Middle Ages.

Engraving of Crowder House, Ecclesfield, Yorkshire, the home of the Wilkinson family by direct inheritance between 1402 and 1859.

Giggleswick. Surnames from every category of origin had similar distribution patterns in the Yorkshire returns. For instance, families with surnames that were derived from nicknames such as Beever, Senior and Shillitoe were mostly found in their original 'countries' in the West Riding; even the Seniors, who were recorded in 28 different townships mostly lived within a few miles of each other. The rarer occupational names had similar restricted distributions. One example is Jagger, which was derived from a northern word for a packman who carried heavy loads, such as coal. All the Jaggers in England were probably descended from the John Jagger who paid poll tax in Stainland, high in the Calder valley, in 1379. Three centuries later, 23 of the 30 householders who shared this name still lived in the same wapentake. A final example is provided by Alderson, a name that was so common in Swaledale that each individual formerly had to have a distinctive by-name. In the hearth tax returns of Lady Day 1672 Swaledale was the home of 70 households of Aldersons; another four families had moved into the northern Vale of York and two had arrived in York, but no Aldersons lived anywhere else in Yorkshire.

Even at parish level, it is obvious from a perusal of the register that certain 'core families' stayed in the same place for several generations. In Ecclesfield parish, to the north of Sheffield, it was not just the families with distinctive local surnames such as Creswick, Hartley or Shirtcliffe that were long resident; the Wilkinson family farmed at Crowder House from 1402 to 1859. In the Shropshire parish of Myddle a stable group of small farmers and craftsmen continued for five, six, or seven generations during the sixteenth and seventeenth centuries. When a male line failed, the property often passed to a daughter, so that continuity in a direct line was even more common than the surnames suggest. These 'core families' were the ones who dominated local affairs as jurors of the manor court and as churchwardens and overseers of the poor and the highways. They preserved the distinctive dialects and accents of each 'country' and passed on the local culture from one generation to the next. Linked as they were by frequent inter-marriage, they provided local societies with a sense of continuity amongst all the coming and going of the young.

This underlying structural continuity needs to be emphasized, for much of the work of demographic historians has stressed what has seemed to be constant movement in and out of a parish. When tracing a family tree in the seventeenth and eighteenth centuries, it is common to find that the great majority of the members of a family stayed within a day or two's journey of their birthplace. Even Londoners, who were always looking for better accommodation, often stayed within the same network of streets and thought twice about crossing the Thames.

Kinship and inheritance

Families appealed for help from their distant relatives only in certain circumstances, such as finding a job, moving to a nearby town or London, or perhaps obtaining a loan. Friends and neighbours could be just as important in these situations. The executors of wills were normally the widow or children of the testator, though brothers or brothers-in-law were sometimes called upon. People were rarely chosen from beyond this immediate circle. Extended kinship links were more important in business and amongst the gentry, whose property would pass to a collateral in the absence of a descendant. The importance of title and property helps to explain the gentry's keen interest in genealogy from Tudor times onwards.

In some parts of the country, such as Kent, where the custom was known as gavelkind, all sons (and in the absence of male heirs all daughters) were entitled to a share of the paternal estate under a system of partible inheritance. In other districts, the primogeniture system, by which the property passed to the eldest male child, was usually diluted in practice so that all children were provided for. Children were often given their share of the patrimony upon marriage or had their education or apprenticeship paid for. Widows were usually entitled to at least a third of the estate during their lifetime or perhaps until the eldest son came of age, and wills often specified how they were to be provided with rooms, furniture, and income.

Copyhold tenure, by which a large entry fine was paid at the beginning of a tenancy and a heriot (often the best beast) at the end, with low rents at Lady Day and Michaelmas, long remained the normal

IN BRIEF

- Whatever the legal system of inheritance in different parts of the country, in practice all children received a share of the family's estate, often at the time of their marriage.

- The ways in which people held land varied from manor to manor. Many farmers rented some of their land from the lord and owned other acres as freeholders.

- In the eastern half of England leases were usually held for 21 years; in the western half they lasted for three lives.

- Whatever the method of holding land, farming families often stayed put for generations.

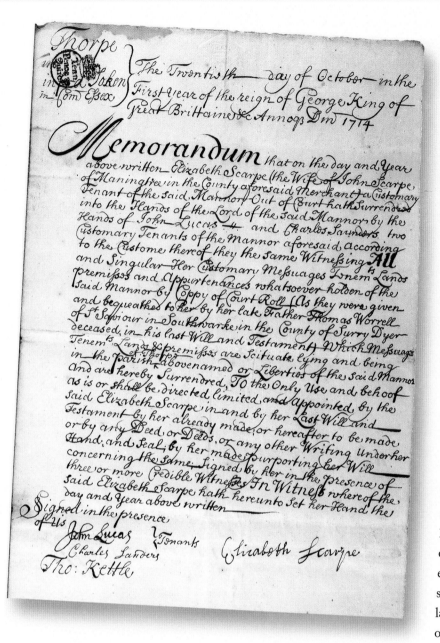

considerably. The entry fines on the Bridgewater estate in north Shropshire, for example, rose 30-fold between 1600 and 1641.

From the middle of the seventeenth century onwards the old copyhold method of tenure was gradually replaced by leases. As a broad generalization, we can say that in the eastern half of England leases were usually for 21 years, whereas in the western half they were for three lives, but of course some estates had different policies from those of their neighbours. In midland England rents were commonly agreed one year at a time. Elsewhere, this method was often used for smallholdings, especially when they were sub-let. The terms by which land was held were significant only when disputes arose, but then they were crucially important. Yeomen and husbandmen often held their farms by a combination of tenures, ranging from copyhold and leasehold to freehold. The general security of possession in the Tudor, Stuart and Georgian period, whatever the form of tenure, is revealed by the common finding that farming and craft families stayed in the same locality, often on the same property, down the generations.

A formal transfer of property through the manor court of Thorpe-le-Soken, Essex, 1714. Elizabeth Scarpe passes on her copyhold lands and buildings as directed in her will.

form of tenure. Local practice varied according to the customs of a manor. Where the level of fines and rents was guaranteed by law, copyhold tenants benefited from the high inflation of the sixteenth century. Elsewhere, however, many landlords were able to prove to the satisfaction of the Court of Chancery that entry fines and rents were 'arbitrary' at the will of the lord, and were therefore able to raise their levels

Servants and apprentices

Children expected to leave home in their early teens to serve an apprenticeship or to become a farm or domestic servant. They became part of the household of their master and might not see their own family for considerable lengths of time. Apprentices were bound to a master for seven years or more and so stayed in the same place, but farm servants often changed their situations at the annual hiring fairs and gradually moved further away, within the bounds of their 'country'. They moved around much more than the average adult. Some men never married and remained farm servants all their lives, but most rented a cottage upon marriage and became farm labourers, who were paid by the job, unless they were lucky enough to inherit a farm of their own. Some left farming altogether and moved to the towns.

IN BRIEF

- Teenage apprentices and servants became part of their master's household and often did not see their own family for considerable lengths of time.
- Servants were hired at traditional fairs, at Michaelmas, Martinmas or May Day.
- Apprentices served a fixed term, usually of seven years, but servants commonly moved on at the end of each year.
- At any one time, three out of every five youngsters were either servants or apprentices.

Apprenticeship records survive in bulk, but few documents provide information about farm service. Most of our knowledge of the annual hiring fairs comes from the nineteenth century. When a boy became a farm servant in earlier times, he usually agreed to work for a year in return for board and lodging and the common wage that was set by the JPs at quarter sessions. Verbal contracts might be entered at any time, through personal connection, but most were made at the local hiring fairs, which were held at customary times. In the corn-growing regions of southern and eastern England Michaelmas was favoured, in the arable parts of the north Martinmas

Proverbs Chap:23.Ve:21.
The Drunkard shall come to
Poverty, & drowsiness shall
cloath a Man in rags.

Proverbs Ch:10.Ver:4.
The hand of the diligent
maketh rich.

Design'd & Engrav'd by W.m Hogarth.   Plate I   Publish'd according to Act of Parliament 30 Sep. 1747.

William Hogarth's engraving of apprentices at their looms in a Spitalfields silk-weaving shop to illustrate 'Industry and Idleness', with suitable quotations from the Book of Proverbs, *1747.*

was usual, and in pastoral areas, especially in the west and the north, May Day was the suitable time. Poor Law settlement examinations show that over 90 per cent of hirings took place on these three occasions and that lads commonly moved a few miles at the end of every year, without ever leaving the neighbourhood, or 'country', with which they were familiar. In Hertfordshire, for example, farm servants moved on average only three or four miles at a time.

The various settlement laws, especially those which were passed in the 1690s, contributed to this restricted movement of servants through the hiring fairs. Of course, far greater distances were covered by the

seasonal migrants who helped to gather in the harvest. Farm service suited both masters and lads in an age when most work was performed at home. One man might not be able to provide employment for his own children, while another might need a boy to help with his work when his own children were not yet old enough, or after they had married. The institution of service solved the labour problems of farmers with small- and medium-sized holdings and of urban craftsmen and tradesmen. At any one time, three out of every five youngsters were employed either as servants or apprentices. A study of 63 parish censuses taken in various parts of England between 1574 and 1821 has shown that servants of all kinds formed 13.4 per cent of the population.

Migration

Though movement was generally restricted to the 'country' where a person was born and bred, the more adventurous travelled far beyond these limits. London was the great exception to the rule that people moved only within the restricted neighbourhood of their 'country', for the city was the destination of migrants from all parts of England and Wales. London's prodigious growth can be explained only by immigration, for the number of burials far exceeded those of baptisms in the city's numerous parishes. The capital city's astonishing rate of advance from about 120,000 inhabitants in 1550 to 960,000 or so in 1800 was the direct consequence of the natural increase of population throughout the land. In 1680 Sir John Reresby, a Yorkshire squire, made the accurate observation that London 'drained

'A Stage Coach on a Country Road', by Julius Caesar Ibbetson, 1792.

all England of its people'. A hundred years earlier a London clergyman had commented that every 12 years or so 'the most part of the parish changeth, as I by experience know, some going and some coming', though of course much of this movement was to a neighbouring parish within the city.

Five major outbreaks of plague occurred in London between 1563 and 1665, but plague was not the only scourge. The evidence of London's parish registers shows that between 1604 and 1659 burials exceeded baptisms by an average of about 3,500 every year. It has been estimated that between 1650 and 1750 an annual minimum number of 8,000 migrants were needed to account for the astonishing rise of London's population. Unlike the rest of England and Wales, where the inhabitants were mostly the descendants of the medieval families of each 'country', the capital city was inhabited by a mix of people from all over the kingdom, with a significant minority from different parts of continental Europe. Surnames which originated in every part of England could be found in the capital city and immigrants outnumbered those who had been born there. As today, Londoners formed a relatively youthful society, for most of the migrants arrived before they were married. Some came to sample city life before moving on or returning to their native 'countries'. It has been estimated that as many as one in every six English people either visited or lived in London at some stage in their lives during the early modern period. They either walked there or arrived by carrier's cart. John Taylor's *Carriers' Cosmographie* shows that by 1637, and probably long before, every part of England and Wales was connected to the capital by weekly carrying services. A typical entry reads, 'The Carriers of Derby, and other parts of Derbyshire, doe lodge at the Axe in St. Mary Axe, neare Aldermanbury, they are to be heard of there on Fridaies'. Other Derby carriers arrived at the Castle in Woodstreet every Thursday or Friday.

These migrants included the younger sons of gentry or yeoman families who hoped to make their fortunes in trade, others of more modest means who had heard that wages were high and life was more exciting than in the provinces, and of course the desperate

IN BRIEF

☛ London's astonishing growth can be explained only by immigration from all corners of the land.

☛ In most parts of England and Wales the inhabitants were descended from local families, but London contained a mix of people, including many migrants from Europe.

☛ Ulster was the first destination for migrating families under James I's plantation policy.

☛ Over half a million people crossed the Atlantic to North America and the West Indies between 1630 and 1700.

poor. Apprenticeship records from the city of London name large numbers of lads from all over England, with one-third travelling from beyond the eastern and south-eastern counties. Poor vagrants often walked over 100 miles to get there. London was the place to head for if you wanted to 'get on' in life.

London was also the chief destination for migrants from the continent. In the second half of the sixteenth century over 50,000 Protestant refugees fled from France and the Low Countries to settle in London and other towns in southern and eastern England. The Government welcomed them, for they brought craft skills that fostered new trades, such as glass making or the 'new draperies'. By the middle years of Elizabeth's reign, the refugees had built their own churches in London and 'alien settlements' had been established in Canterbury, Colchester, Maidstone, Norwich, Sandwich, Stamford and Southampton; the immigrants formed a third of the total population of Canterbury and Norwich. Refugees arrived in even greater numbers after 1680, when Louis XIV re-started the persecution of French Protestants (Huguenots). Most settled in Soho and the East End of London, but some preferred other suburbs or settled in the towns of south-east and south-western England.

Although the names of the immigrants were soon adapted to the English tongue, most remained distinctive enough to allow us to identify them and trace their movements. For example, the Lorraine ironworkers who migrated to the Weald were amongst the 'aliens' whose names are recorded in sixteenth-century subsidy rolls. A few of these men, with names such as Dupre, Hussey, Gelly, Maryan, Perigoe, Valyance and Vintin, appear later in the registers of Sheffield and neighbouring parishes, for

Return of Strangers (i.e. a list of foreign immigrants) in the City and Liberties of London, addressed to the Privy Council and showing entries for St Bride's parish, 1571.

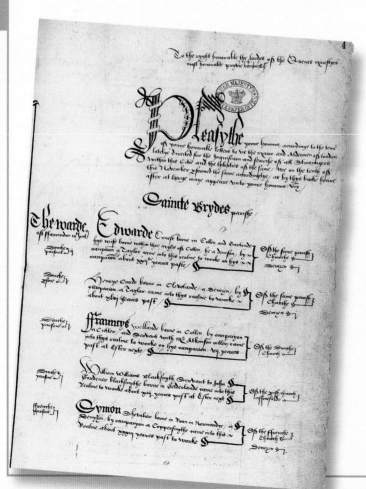

they were invited there by George, sixth Earl of Shrewsbury, to build forges and charcoal blast furnaces. Foreign glassworkers were even more mobile.

Meanwhile, the first destination for people who left England and Wales to settle elsewhere was northern Ireland, under James I's plantation policy which was designed to suppress resistance. Many more emigrants moved into Ulster during the second half of the seventeenth century. The English settlers went mostly from the western parts of the country, ranging from Devon to Lancashire, but they were outnumbered by the Scots by five to one. During the reign of Charles I settlers embarked on much longer and more hazardous voyages to the new colonies in North America and the West Indies. About 380,000 of the estimated 540,000 people who left England between 1630 and 1700 chose the Atlantic crossing. Although many were inspired by the desire for religious freedom, the main motive was the hope of a better standard of living. Many of the young went as indentured servants from lowly backgrounds and others had no choice; over 30,000 convicts were transported there from England between 1615 and 1775. For the first hundred years most prisoners were sent to the West Indian sugar plantations, but from 1718 Maryland and Virginia were the usual destinations. After the War of Independence convicts were transported to Australia instead. This emigration across the Atlantic is of great historic interest, but it accounted for less than half of one per cent of the English population, and hundreds of those who made the long and often hazardous journey eventually returned home.

Work

Before the Industrial Revolution most families earned their living off the land, but they did it in ways that varied from region to region and often between 'countries'. In Derbyshire, for instance, the farmers who lived in the villages of the Midland Plain in the south of the county or on the fertile, corn-growing soils of the magnesian limestone in the north-east pursued a different type of husbandry from those who inhabited the dispersed settlements in the wood-pastures of the coal-measure sandstones or who lived on the edges of the moors in the wild terrain of the Peak District. Within these broad regions, a thriving community of yeomen and husbandmen might be found in the next parish to one that had few or no inhabitants. In neighbouring Leicestershire, Wigston, the most populous rural parish in the county, shared a border with the deserted village of Foston. The process of gradual desertion, which had started with the Black Death, was often not completed until the seventeenth or eighteenth century. The hearth tax returns of the 1660s and 1670s

Richard Arkwright's water frame, shown in his application for a patent, which was granted in July 1769. The frame enabled him to spin cotton in a continuous process by machines that were operated by water power in the world's first cotton mills.

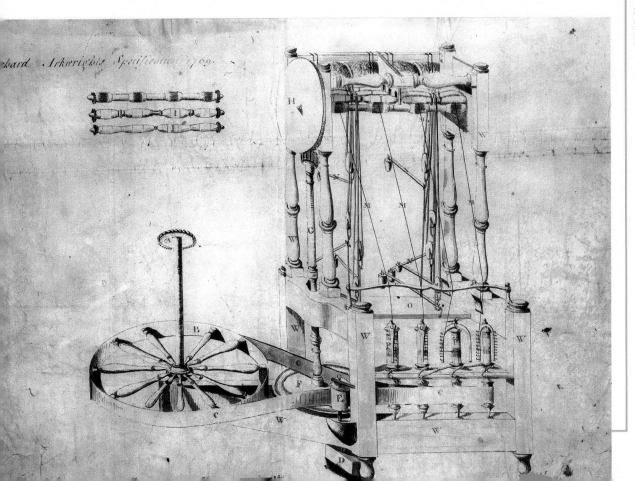

reveal the structural differences that existed between local societies up and down the land. Many parishes were dominated by a squire, others had several farmhouses with three to five hearths, but in the Staffordshire parish of Eccleshall, where numerous poor families squatted on the edge of the commons, 83 per cent of households paid tax on one hearth only.

The transport improvements of the early modern period enabled some farmers to specialize. They could now obtain their corn and malt from dealers who came to the local markets and thus abandon their strips to concentrate on what they could do most profitably. The dairymen of Cheshire and north Shropshire produced cheese for a national market and market gardeners flourished in the neighbourhoods of towns, especially in the vicinity of London. In the mid-sixteenth century responsibility for the maintenance of highways and byways was placed on civil parishes or townships. Elected overseers of the highways were empowered to raise local rates and to see that every able-bodied householder joined them in the six days of labour, filling in ruts with stones and maintaining drainage ditches, as demanded by an Act of 1563. The system worked in a rough-and-ready way. Carriers could reckon on travelling 30 miles a day to provide a direct link to London and connecting services between all

the market towns. In 1787, for example, Sheffield had 42 services linking the town directly or through connections to most parts of the country. By that time, turnpike roads were offering substantial improvements for wheeled vehicles and it was possible to reach London from Sheffield in just 26 hours by 'flying coach'. Most journeys, however, were relatively short, and men on horseback or farm vehicles pulled by a team of horses, oxen or bullocks were a more common sight on the highways than the waggons and packhorses of the carriers who were heading for London or the major ports and market towns. The highways were far busier in the summer months, when they were reasonably firm and dry, than in winter. Many travellers had to walk instead of ride.

During the early modern period private agreements between farmers removed the small open fields that had once been used for growing cereals on the edges of the Pennines, in the south-west and the Welsh border counties, and in Kent, Essex, Suffolk and Hertfordshire. Even in Leicestershire, at the heart of the classic open-field belt in central England, half of the parishes were enclosed between 1607 and 1730 and many of the fields converted to pasture. Where no agreement could be reached, a private Act of Parliament had to be obtained. Some early examples can be quoted, but in general this was the method that was favoured after 1750. By 1830 over 85 per cent of the eventual 4,000 or so Acts had been passed and within the next 40 years the process was completed. The first main period, from 1755 to 1780 (which accounted for 38 per cent of the Acts), was mostly concerned with the heavy soils of the midland clay belts – Northamptonshire, Warwickshire, Leicestershire – and adjoining parts, and with the lighter clays of Lincolnshire and the East Riding. This was the time when hawthorn hedges were planted to create the square or rectangular fields that characterized the landscape of these regions (before many were removed in the late twentieth century) and red-brick farmhouses were built in the new fields away from the villages. The second main period, from the 1790s to the mid 1830s, especially during the Napoleonic wars, when grain prices were high and farming was prosperous, included the extensive moors and commons.

LEFT
Colour engraving of Upper Works at Coalbrookdale, engraved by F. Vivares, published in 1758. Abraham Darby's upper blast furnace and its surrounding foundry buildings are to the left. A team of horses haul an engine cylinder and heaps of coal are being converted into coke by the pool. Ironmasters' houses and workers' cottages are seen in the background.

IN BRIEF

✏ Most families earned their living off the land, but farming practices varied considerably. The dairymen who made Cheshire cheese had a different way of life from the farmers who grew cereals.

✏ The old common fields, divided into strips, were often enclosed by private agreements. The rest disappeared in the era of parliamentary enclosure after 1750.

✏ By 1800 Britain had become the most industrialized country in the world, but improved farming practices meant that the rapidly-growing population could be fed.

✏ Some districts were industrialized long before the Industrial Revolution, but the most significant changes came in the later eighteenth century.

The seventeenth and eighteenth centuries saw a dramatic improvement in the quality of livestock and in better yields from crops, especially wheat, the main bread grain, as English farming became the most advanced in Europe. At the same time, a huge amount of new land was ploughed, especially when the fens of Lincolnshire and East Anglia were drained and brought into cultivation. By the 1830s a third of all English grain was produced in just six eastern counties. Increased output meant that the rapidly-growing population, which included large numbers of industrial workers, could be fed. By 1800 Britain had become the most industrialized country in the world, but only about one-sixth of its grain was imported from Ireland and the European continent.

Long before the classic period of the Industrial Revolution, some towns and rural parishes had been industrialized to a remarkable extent. During the reign of Elizabeth the moderately-prosperous agricultural parish of Whickham, on the south bank of the Tyne, was utterly transformed into an industrial society by coal mining. The 93 households of 1563 grew to 367 by 1666, when 78.8 per cent were exempted from the hearth tax. Meanwhile, three out of every five men in the parish of Sheffield earned their living as cutlers or in associated trades. Probably no other contemporary town had such a specialized workforce, though it was soon to be joined by dockyard towns such as Chatham, Plymouth and Portsmouth.

It is now hard to imagine that the Peak District National Park was once one of the most industrialized districts in England, but when the ancient lead industry began to recover in the 1570s from a long period of stagnation the Derbyshire lead field soon became the most important in Europe. By 1583 mining was said to be the 'onelie livings' of 'many poor people' and by 1641 it had become either the prime or the only source of income for a majority of the Peak's households. In the 1580s and 1590s large numbers of poor immigrants moved into the High Peak from other parts of Derbyshire and neighbouring counties, with a few specialists moving from much further afield. In 1593 an estimated 3,000 people were dependent upon lead mining in Wirksworth wapentake. Between 1563 and 1664 Derbyshire's population probably increased by about a half, and most of the change occurred in the industrial and pastoral north-west of the county. The hamlets of 1563 had become heavily populated industrial villages by 1664, with the 'free miners' outnumbered by the numerous poor 'cavers' who scavenged among the rubbish tips for lead ore. Much of the population of the Peak was unusually poor and landless. Only two of Sheldon's 53 householders dwelt in houses with more than one hearth, while in Wardlow 38 of the

Illustrations from Elements and Practice of Agriculture, *an unpublished work by a leading agricultural writer, Arthur Young (1741–1820). The top picture shows an 'earth scuffer' invented by a farmer named Ducket, whom Young admired. The bottom picture depicts a labourer with a Flemish scythe.*

39 householders and in Castleton 98 out of the 106 householders, were either exempted from the tax or paid for a single hearth. In Little Hucklow the exempted poor amounted to 74 per cent of the householders and in Great Hucklow to 84 per cent.

The lead seams of Derbyshire were eventually exhausted and some other industrial districts, such as the textile manufacturing districts of the Weald of Kent, faded from view. But in many parts of the country, notably the West Midlands, Lancashire and the West Riding of Yorkshire, industries went from strength to strength until they reached a point at which we may speak of an Industrial Revolution.

By the seventeenth century the Shropshire coalfield, for example, ranked second only to that of Northumberland and Durham and by the early eighteenth century the same district was a major producer of iron. Coalbrookdale was attracting visitors by the 1750s, long before its iron bridge made it famous. Soon, travellers in search of the 'Wonders of the Peak' were calling at Cromford to see Arkwright's cotton mills and the rows of workers' houses that were necessary to attract a workforce. A new form of society was being forged. The ports of Liverpool and Bristol grew mightily at this time, yet London remained the most thriving centre of industry and trade and its population rose to record heights. The late eighteenth and early nineteenth centuries are difficult times for family historians who are searching for ancestors in the parish registers. The population was expanding, towns and industrial villages were growing, many people were mobile, and Methodism and other forms of Nonconformity were attracting people away from the Church of England. Bridging the gap between the early years of Victoria's reign, when civil registration records and census enumerators' books become available, and the middle decades of the eighteenth century can be a time-consuming exercise and one which often ends in defeat.

Parish registers

For the three centuries before the introduction of civil registration in 1837, parish registers are the family historian's most important source. In 1538, late in the reign of Henry VIII, Thomas Cromwell ordered all the parishes of England and Wales to keep a record of baptisms, marriages and burials. Few parishes have registers that go back as far as that, for in the early years events were often recorded on loose sheets and, of course, many of these have not survived. An Act of 1597 ordered that from the following year a bound register should be used and that any surviving records should be copied into it, with the signatures of the minister and churchwardens attesting that each page was a true transcript. The instruction was often misinterpreted to mean that records should be copied only as far back as the beginning of the reign of Queen Elizabeth, so that many surviving registers begin in 1558, or shortly afterwards, rather than 20 years earlier. The same Act ordered that from 1598 a copy of the events that had been registered during the past year should be sent to the diocesan office. These bishop's transcripts, as they are known, are now kept at various county record offices or specialist archives such as the Borthwick Institute of Historical Research, York. These are the repositories of the records of the ancient dioceses, such as Lichfield or Lincoln, that were in existence long before new dioceses

were created in the late nineteenth or twentieth centuries. Bishop's transcripts may provide a second chance when a parish register has been lost or is difficult to read, but many of the early ones have not been well preserved.

Parishes

The 11,000 or so ancient parishes in England and Wales were all sorts of shapes and sizes. The West Riding parish of Penistone, which contained numerous small settlements and much wild moorland, covered 22,773 acres, whereas the parish of Warmsworth, 25 miles further east, was only 1,074 acres in extent and served a compact village. Cities such as Norwich and York once had numerous parishes within their walls; London had 101 parishes in the seventeenth century. Finding an ancestor in the registers of London (at the London Metropolitan Archives or at the Guildhall Library) or in an ancient provincial city can be a time-consuming task. Large parishes were divided into chapelries, or chapels-of-ease, many of which had the right to conduct their own baptism, marriage and burial services. The chapelry of Bradfield, within the parish of Ecclesfield, kept its own registers from 1559, yet in neighbouring Sheffield the records of events within the chapelries of Attercliffe

The entry in the Stratford-upon-Avon parish register recording the baptism of William Shakespeare on 26 April 1564. It is pure guesswork to say that he was born three days earlier, but people like to think that the national bard was born on St George's day. The Latin entry reads: 'Gulielmus filius Johannes Shakspere'.

and Ecclesall were copied at the end of each year into the parish register. It takes time for a family historian to become familiar with such administrative arrangements, for there is no consistency across the country, civil parishes were not necessarily the same as ecclesiastical ones, and in Victorian times new parishes were created in populous districts. Towns that are now well known may not have existed or have been mere hamlets when the parish system was created a thousand years or more ago and so they formed part of parishes that were named after settlements that are now much smaller than they are. Market Harborough lay in the parish of Great Bowden, Barnsley in the

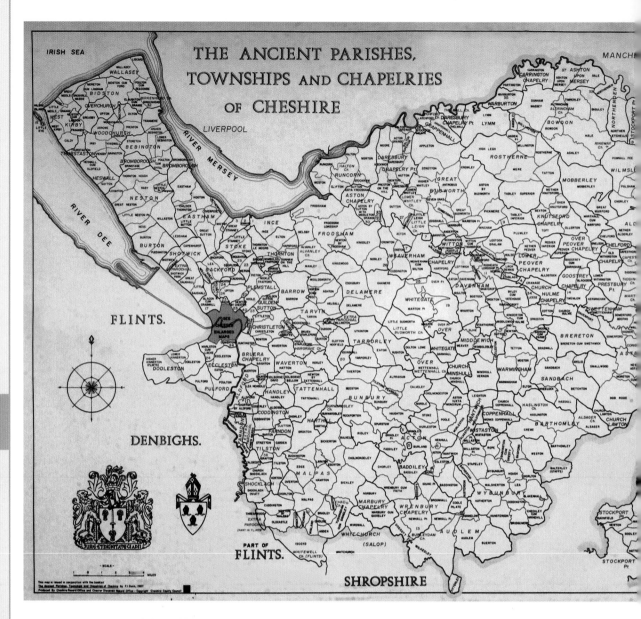

parish of Silkstone, and Hull in the parish of Hessle.

☞ Maps which depict the ancient parish system within a county are usually available at county record offices.

☞ A series of maps covering the whole of England and Wales, county by county, with the starting date of every surviving register has been published by the Institute of Heraldic and Genealogical Studies, Canterbury. These are printed

on a reduced scale in C. Humphery-Smith, ed., *The Phillimore Atlas and Index of Parish Registers* (Chichester, third edn, 2003).

☞ The standard reference works are F. A. Youngs, Jr., *Guide to the Local Administrative Units of England* (Royal Historical Society, 2 vols, 1980–91) and R. J. P. Kain and R. R. Oliver, *Historic Parishes of England and Wales: An Electronic Map of Boundaries Before 1850*

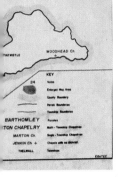

Map of the ancient parishes, townships and chapelries of Cheshire, obtainable from the Cheshire Record Office. Such maps are indispensable aids to the study of local records.

with a Gazetteer and Metadata (Historic Data Service, UK Data Archive, University of Essex, 2001).

🖎 Lists of parishes can be accessed on the internet from the search facility of <www.genuki.org.uk/big/parloc>.

Finding a register

🖎 Few registers are still kept in the parish chest or vestry, for since 1979 churches have had to prove that they have proper facilities for keeping their records.

🖎 Most registers are now deposited with the appropriate county or city record office, where they are usually available only on microfilm or microfiche. It is usually necessary to book a microfilm reader before making a visit.

🖎 Some local record offices and reference libraries also have microfilm copies of bishop's transcripts. The archivists at such record offices can advise on the whereabouts of registers and as to which have been transcribed and published.

🖎 Some county societies have been printing registers since Victorian times and now have a considerable run of them for the early years. Other registers have been published privately by clergymen or local antiquarians, and in recent years family history societies have increasingly transcribed registers and made them available on microfiche or as booklets.

🖎 The Society of Genealogists has a large collection and has published county

volumes of the *National Index of Parish Registers* since 1966. This locates surviving parish registers (or copies, or indexes, of registers) up to at least 1837, and for many parishes up to 1900.

The International Genealogical Index (IGI)

Members of the Church of Jesus Christ of Latter-day Saints (LDS), known also as the Mormon Church, have a duty to trace their ancestors so that they may be baptized by proxy. A vast amount of genealogical information has therefore been collected by amateurs, from parish registers, bishop's transcripts and the registers of other denominations. These have been collated as the International Genealogical Index, or the IGI as it is known to all family historians. This is freely available in three formats: online at <www.familysearch.org>; on CD-ROM at Mormon Family History Centres, larger record offices and libraries, and the Family Records Centre; on microfiche (as above plus smaller record offices and libraries and some family history societies). The British Isles Vital Records Index, on five CD-ROMs, which collates about 5 million entries from parish and other British records between 1538 and 1888, can be used at the Family Records Centre, at the Society of Genealogists, or at the LDS Church's various Family History Centres; it can also be bought from the LDS Distribution Centre, 399 Garretts Green Lane, Birmingham B33 0UH.

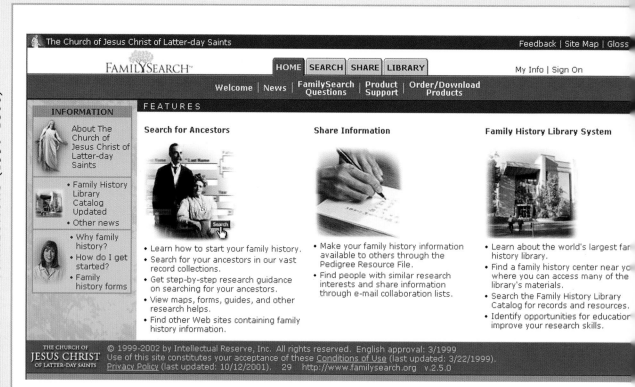

The home page of <www. familysearch.org>.

The IGI's entries for English counties on the microfiche version are arranged alphabetically by surname, including variant spellings for similar names (which may or may not be connected), and then by first name. As some Welsh surnames were not formed until the nineteenth century, Welsh entries are grouped both in alphabetical order of surnames and of first names. The next columns give the date and place of a baptism or marriage (burials are not recorded in the IGI). We must always bear in mind that the entries in the IGI have been made by amateurs, many of whom were beginners who made mistakes. The information must always be checked against the original register. The entries include those that say, for example, 'about 1720'. These are guesswork, based on estimated ages at marriages, and should be ignored. We also need to be aware that the index is far from complete. Some clergymen have objected to the LDS

Church baptizing by proxy ancestors whose parents chose to baptize them according to the rites of the Church of England. Cambridgeshire, for example, has relatively few entries in the IGI. You can check whether a parish register has been searched, and which years have been covered, by looking at the microfiche section of the IGI that is headed 'Parish and Vital Records List'. Nevertheless, the IGI is a most useful source of information, which prevents many a fruitless search and guides the family historian to the original records.

The software program *GenMap UK* can be used with the internet version of the IGI to map the references to surnames. This can be done by county in order to gain an overview of the distribution of the name (remembering the incompleteness and imperfections of the data), or by parish to pinpoint where and when a name was recorded. An example of the latter technique is provided by the rare name Simmonite, which was confined to south Yorkshire and north Derbyshire in entries on the IGI dating from 1616 to 1869.

Problems

Having found a parish register, we need to be aware of some of the difficulties that we are likely to encounter in making sense of the information. In the first place, the earliest registers are very difficult to read as the style of handwriting is so different from today's. There is no easy way round this,

except to turn to books of guidance and to remember the old adage 'practice makes perfect'. Photo-copies will give you more time to make sense of what you read. Fortunately, by the time that we have worked back to the 'Secretary hand' of the sixteenth or seventeenth centuries we will have become used to the ways in which registers were arranged. It helps to know the various formats. From 1813 registration was standardized, but in earlier times entries are often disappointingly brief. A typical record of baptism gives just the date of the event, the name of the child, and the name of the father. The style of entries varies not only from register to register but over time

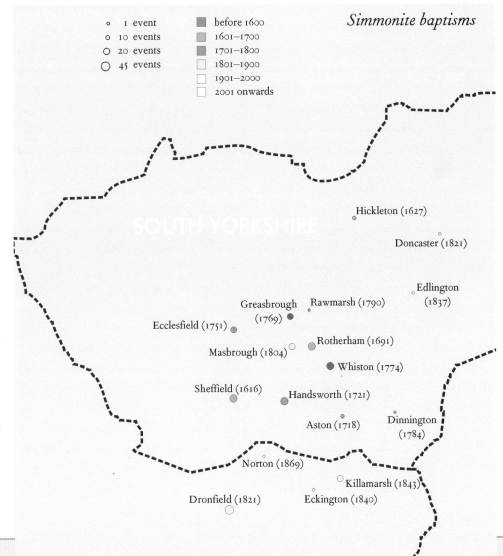

Simmonite baptisms

○	1 event		before 1600
○	10 events		1601–1700
○	20 events		1701–1800
○	45 events		1801–1900
			1901–2000
			2001 onwards

SOUTH YORKSHIRE

Hickleton (1627)

Doncaster (1821)

Edlington (1837)

Greasbrough (1769)   Rawmarsh (1790)

Ecclesfield (1751)

Masbrough (1804)   Rotherham (1691)

Whiston (1774)

Sheffield (1616)   Handsworth (1721)

Aston (1718)   Dinnington (1784)

Norton (1869)

Dronfield (1821)   Eckington (1840)

Killamarsh (1843)

Map based on entries in the International Genealogical Index showing the places where children named Simmonite were baptized. The local concentration of the name suggests that they all shared a common ancestor.

DERBYSHIRE

in the same register. It depended on who was writing the entries and, sometimes, on directives from the bishop. The information does not necessarily get fuller as time passes.

The registers of some parishes were kept well from the beginning, but where entries were not made immediately names may have been forgotten or misremembered. So, the Chesterfield parish register notes that on 16 January 1575/6 'Humphrey Garett's mother was buried at Brampton' (a chapel-of-ease); it also records the burial on 10 January 1561/2 of 'A little female pauper, a stranger, whose name we do not know'. It seems to have been a common practice for clergymen to keep rough notebooks of events and to copy them into the register later. This inevitably led to errors of transcription and mistakes because of faulty memories. A notebook that survives for the parish of Mitcham (Surrey), when compared with the parish register, reveals omissions, inclusions and discrepancies over forenames, surnames and relationships. A comparison between the register of the parish of Worsbrough (Yorkshire) and the bishop's transcripts over a period of 160 years showed that about 1 per cent of the entries in the transcripts were not in the parish register, and that 1–3 per cent of the entries in the register were not transcribed for the bishop. The comparison revealed numerous differences of spelling and of recorded occupations, 19 changes in surname and 15 in forename. It is common to find gaps in parish registers that bring a family tree to an end. The burial of my ancestor, John Hey, is recorded in 1633, but there is no record of his baptism or marriage even though his family were living in the same farmhouse during the previous century. On the other

hand, the quirks of the clergymen who were responsible for compiling the registers sometimes enliven a search. When John Woodhead, labourer, was buried at Worsbrough in 1756 the minister added, 'a true miser'.

Once we have acquired sufficient skill to read the earliest registers, we have other problems to confront. The Latin that was used until 1733 does not cause too much difficulty, for surnames were recorded in English and first names such as Ricardus or Johannes are quickly recognizable as Richard and John. The few common phrases that occur can soon be interpreted, for many English words come from Latin; *baptizatus erat, nupti. erat, sepultus erat*, refer to baptisms, marriages and burials, *natus* to a birth, *conj.* to a wedding, *obit.* to a death. Other terms include *rel*[*icta*] for a widow, *aet* for aged, *eodem die* for 'on the same day', and *filius populi* for an illegitimate birth. We need to be aware of other conventions. Only the gentry were addressed as Mr or Mrs and before the eighteenth century clergymen were recorded as clerk, not as Reverend. The great majority of entries note only the Christian name and surname.

The most confusing problem with the early registers is that the official year started not on 1 January but on 25 March (Lady Day). This means that the entries for each year continue past 31 December to the following Lady Day. An extra year must therefore be added to all dates between 1 January and 25 March. Someone whose baptism was recorded on, say, 12 February 1592 must therefore be noted as 12 February 1592/3, otherwise false assumptions might be made.

A page from the baptism register of St Mary's church, Sandbach, Cheshire, showing the old system of starting the official year on Lady Day, 25 March.

We might, for instance, think that a baptism recorded on 4 March 1623 was before the marriage of the parents on 18 April 1623, though the baptism was in fact 11 months later in 1623/4. This system of reckoning came to an end on 1 January 1752. At the same time the Gregorian calendar that was used in the rest of Europe was adopted in place of the old Julian calendar, which, having no leap year, was eleven days out. That year, 3 September was followed by 14 September. Some clergymen needed time to adjust their thinking to the new system and made a muddle of their registers, and the adjustment of birthdays to the new calendar causes us minor problems. A curious survival from the old system is that the government's financial year still ends on 6 April, eleven days after Lady Day.

The quality of the information

The general quality of parish registers fell during the Civil War. A memorandum in the register of the Shropshire parish of Myddle states that 'Whereas in the year 1644 but one burial is entered, in the year 1645 but one christening is entered'. It goes on to say that during the last three years of William Holloway's ministry no entries were made, perhaps because of illness leading to his death in 1689. In most parishes, the quality of registration improved during the Commonwealth (1653–60). An Act which came into force at Michaelmas (29 September) 1653 gave responsibility for registering vital events to an elected officer, known as the Parish Register [sic], who in practice was often the minister or the parish clerk. During this brief period, births rather than baptisms were recorded and the name of the mother was added to that of the child and father; some registers noted both events, others carried on as before.

For most of the time, baptism registers did not record actual births, but gave only the date of the church ceremony that followed. There is no truth in the assertion that baptism regularly occurred three days after a birth. William Shakespeare was baptized on 26 April 1564, but it is only guesswork that he was born on St George's Day,

Publick Baptism.
Suffer the little children to come unto me, and forbid them not, for of such is the Kingdom of God.

A Church of England baptism, engraved by an unknown eighteenth-century artist in an Anglican prayer book.

Two and a half centuries of marriage registers from St Mary's church, Sandbach, and the neighbouring parish church at Nantwich: from top left they date from 1584–5, 1754 and 1837.

23 April. The interval between birth and baptism varied considerably. Up to the Restoration of Charles II in 1660 baptism normally followed closely on birth, but by the later eighteenth century the interval was usually much longer, often two or three weeks and sometimes over a month. The 59 entries in the register of the Derbyshire parish of Sutton-cum-Duckmanton between 1662 and 1676 which give the dates of both birth and baptism include only five baptisms that were celebrated on the third day after the birth. The median average gap was eight days and in 17 cases it stretched over a fortnight, including one that was 60 days. The Sheffield parish register recorded the dates of both birth and baptism on 43 occasions between 1687 and 1695. The interval between the two events ranged from

1 to 45 days and the median average gap was 20 days. Between 1706 and 1735 the ages of 15 people who were baptized late ranged from an eight-year-old child to a weaver's wife who was baptized on her deathbed when she was about 40. Such cases are exceptional.

When two or more children were baptized on the same day they may not necessarily have been twins or triplets. Their parents may not have baptized the elder ones at the parish church when they were born, either through neglect or because they were Nonconformists. The early Nonconformists used the Church of England for marriages and burials, but not always for baptisms. A return to the Anglican fold may explain a late baptism, such as that at Crowle (Lincolnshire) in February 1751 of 'Mrs Mary Stovin of ripe years born of quaker pairants'. Another complication is that children were sometimes baptized not where they were born but in the parish of the mother's parents. However, the fashion for private baptism at home that began in the late seventeenth and eighteenth centuries, amongst the gentry and in London, did not affect registration, for these private events were normally recorded as such in the parish register. If the private baptism was not followed by a church ceremony, then was child was recorded as 'half baptized'.

The records of marriages and burials are more reliable than those of baptisms. Most marriages were performed in a parish

Left page

Matrimony   October   Day. 4

Thomas Orsom and Margery Hassall — 23

November

William Brooke and Dorothy Morrey — 22

William Housford Minister entered the

January

Richard Knight and Margery Willson — 1
Richard Baxter and Jane Masterson — 16
Richard Blaugg and Ellen Clowes — 23
Thomas Sparrowe and Elizabeth Wotton — 25

February

Thomas Mainwaring married Margret Lea of Lea — 15
Roger Slao and Anne Snead — 21
William Barber and Elizabeth Smithe — 28

Marche 1585

Rowland Sandors and Anne Mainwaringe — 27

June

Homnett Barbott and Margery Reade — 3

October

John Walthall butcher and Elizabeth Deny — 13
Thomas Topcliff and Elizabeth Dale — 17
Richard Morrey and Elizabeth Hassall — 19

November

William Masse and Elizabeth Blaggs — 2
Robert Meadow and Elizabeth Wright — 28
... wright of the Bell and Kathren Browne gent — 30

December

William Corsfey and Ellen Dodd — 6

January

Thomas Milliam and Cissly Blossom — 1
William Watson and Margret Mainings — 30

February

William Dowche and Elizabeth Moyle — 8

Right page

(4)

No 11

Charles Edwards of [this] Parish Gardiner
and Ann Barnett — of [this] Parish Spinster
were married in this [Church] by [Banns] [ ] this third
Day of December in the Year one thousand seven hundred fifty four
By me T Adderley
This Marriage was solemnized between us Charles Edwards
the mark of Ann Barnett
In the Presence of John Gilbert, Samuel Rowen

No 12

Peter Barrow — of [this] Parish Labourer
and Catherine Bibbington of [this] Parish Spinster
were married in this [Church] by [Banns] — this ninth
Day of December in the Year one thousand seven hundred fifty four
By me T Adderley
This Marriage was solemnized between us the mark of Peter Barrow
the mark of Catherine Bibbington
In the Presence of Thomas Chirby, Thomas Church

No 13

William Heath — of [this] Parish Shoemaker
and Mary Hancock — of [this] Parish Spinster
were married in this [Church] by [Banns] this thirtieth
Day of December in the Year one thousand seven hundred & fifty four
By me Ralph Markham officiating Minister
This Marriage was solemnized between us the Mark of William Heath
the Mark of Mary Hancock
In the Presence of Pearce and Nathan Astope

No 14

Simon Cooper — of [this] Parish Corkcutter
and Mary Brow — — of [this] Parish Spinster
were married in this [Church] by [Banns] — this thirtieth
Day of December in the Year one thousand seven hundred & fifty four
By me Ralph Markham officiating Minister
This Marriage was solemnized between us Simon Cooper
the Mark of Mary Brow
In the Presence of Tho Becket, John Harding

Page 3

1837. Marriage solemnized at Nantwich in the Parish of Nantwich in the County of Chester

No.	When Married.	Name and Surname.	Age.	Condition.	Rank or Profession.	Residence at the Time of Marriage.	Father's Name and Surname.	Rank or Profession of Father.
5	20th November	Joseph Lloyd	59	Widower	Clockmaker	Nantwich	John Lloyd	Clockmaker
		Sarah Newhall	56	Spinster	Cook	Nantwich	not known	not known

Married in the Parish Church of Nantwich according to the Rites and Ceremonies of the United Church of England and Ireland by me, W. H. Grillon Rector.
This Marriage was solemnized between us, Joseph Lloyd, Sarah Newhall X her mark
In the Presence of us, Elizabeth Palin, Thomas Compton

1837. Marriage solemnized at Nantwich in the Parish of Nantwich in the County of Chester

No.	When Married.	Name and Surname.	Age.	Condition.	Rank or Profession.	Residence at the Time of Marriage.	Father's Name and Surname.	Rank or Profession of Father.
6	24th November	Thomas Harding	41	Bachelor	Cordwainer	Nantwich	Robert Harding	Cordwainer
		Sarah Galley	38	Spinster	Servant Woman	Nantwich	Thomas Galley	Farmer

Married in the Parish Church of Nantwich according to the Rites and Ceremonies of the Church of England by me, Rd Yonge Curate.
This Marriage was solemnized between us, Thomas Harding, Sarah Galley X her mark
In the Presence of us, Thos Wright, Robert Harding

church after the calling of banns. Entries in the registers usually give no more than the names of the partners, but in the Commonwealth period fuller information is recorded. In Sheffield, for example, the marriage entries from November 1653 to the end of 1660 note the dates of the calling of banns, the place of residence of both partners and the occupation of the bridegroom. Where marriage registers state that one or both partners were 'of this parish', we must not assume that they were born there; they may have arrived recently.

Other couples preferred to marry by licence. These were issued by a diocesan consistory court and recorded in the bishop's register or in the records of certain peculiar jurisdictions, together with the formal allegation and bond. The discovery of an allegation in the court records may be a vital piece of evidence if the parish register does not survive. If the bride and groom lived in different dioceses, they had to apply to the Vicar-General of the Archbishop of Canterbury or York. See J.S.W. Gibson, *Bishops' Transcripts and Marriage Licences, Bonds and Allegations: A Guide to their Location and Indexes* (FFHS, 1997). The Guildhall Library has an information leaflet

about the overlapping jurisdictions in London. As marriage licences were valid for three months, they may have been issued quite a time before the wedding took place. The diocesan court required a written allegation of intention to marry, made by both partners or their representatives. The allegations name their parishes and their approximate ages and declare that no legal impediment to the marriage existed. A bond guaranteed the fine that would be imposed if such an impediment was proved.

Before Lord Hardwicke's Marriage Act came into force in 1754 some couples, from all ranks of society, married without banns or a licence. Certain clergymen got the reputation of being willing to officiate at clandestine marriages. The Fleet Prison chapel, St James Duke's Place, and Holy Trinity Minories were the major centres in London. T. Benton, *Irregular Marriages in London before 1754* (Society of Genealogists, 1993) lists the whereabouts of surviving registers, but many are missing. At the Fleet alone the records of as many as 250,000 marriages survive, despite many gaps; 217 marriages were made on the day before Hardwicke's Act came into force. See M. Herber, *Clandestine Marriages in the Chapel*

↪ Boyd's Marriage Index, which is held at the Society of Genealogists and is available online at <www.englishorigins.com>, records about 7 million names from 12 per cent of all English marriages between 1538 and 1637.

↪ *London Marriage Licences, 1521–1869* is available commercially on CD, with over 1,500 pages of entries.

↪ The Society of Genealogists has published surname indexes to the Vicar-General of the Archbishop of Canterbury's records, 1751–1850, on microfiche; calendars indexed by the names of both parties, 1597–1700, have been published in the British Record Society's *Index Library*, vols 62 and 66.

and Rules of the Fleet Prison, 1680–1754 (Boutle, 3 vols, 1998–2000). The National Archives holds about 300 registers of clandestine marriages in RG 7. Few of these records have been transcribed or indexed.

Hardwicke's Act ordered that every marriage must be preceded by the calling of banns or the issuing of a licence, that the wedding ceremony could be performed only in a parish where at least one of the parties resided, and that a record must be made on a printed form that was bound into a register. The entries henceforth had to be signed by both bride and groom and by witnesses.

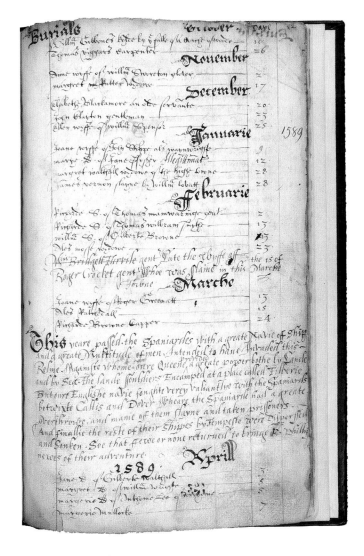

A page from the burial register of St Mary's church, Sandbach, with a note recording the defeat of the Spanish Armada, 1588.

From 1754 to 1813 marriages were the only events to be registered in a standard manner.

The registration of burials was more complete than that of baptisms or marriages, but some events were nevertheless unrecorded because of carelessness. 'Interred' in a burial register might indicate excommunicates and suicides who were buried without Christian rites on the north side of the church, but it usually referred to a Roman Catholic whose family did not use the Anglican service. Suicide was relatively rare, but was sometimes made plain from an entry in the burial registers. At Cantley (Yorkshire) in 1651 the minister noted, 'Sara wife of John Moulson who was found felo de se & Buryed on the north side of the church'. In 1750 the clergyman at Misterton (Lincolnshire) put it more bluntly: 'George Taylor hanged himself and was Inter'd like a Dog'. Acts of 1666 and 1678 insisted that shrouds should be made of woollen cloth (in order to protect an important and widespread industry), and registers sometimes name the relatives who had to pay for an affidavit sworn before a JP. An entry recording non-compliance with the Act was made at Hatfield (Yorkshire) in 1682: 'Thomas Outebridge was buryed the 30th day of July & was wrapt in linnen contrary to the Act for burying in woollen'.

Most entries in the burial registers, even in the Commonwealth period, simply record a name, or in the case of a child the father and perhaps the mother. On occasion, especially from the late eighteenth century onwards, the cause of death was given, but the information is often too vague to be trustworthy. The Sutton-cum-Duckmanton (Derbyshire) register for 1800–6 refers to eight cases of consumption and eight of dropsy, but is less precise with fevers, rheumatism and cramp, inflammatory rheumatism, convulsions, and fits; eight old people aged 73–84 were said to have died from 'decay of nature'. Burials are not recorded on the LDS Church's International Genealogical Index, but the Federation of Family History Societies is overseeing a National Burials Index; a first edition of some 5 million entries from parish, Nonconformist and cemetery burial registers is available on CD-ROM.

As the registration process was left to parish clergy or clerks, individuals sometimes provided extra information. Some noted a man's occupation when he was married or buried or when his children were baptized.

From Lady Day 1698 Joseph Jollie, the new clerk at Sheffield, took his duties seriously, distinguishing men by their occupations and their residence in one or other of the six townships of the parish. His appointment coincided with the passing of an 'Act for preventing Frauds and Abuses in the charging collecting and paying the Duties upon Marriages Births Burials Batchelors and Widowers'. Such pressures from the central government were rarely effective, however. Clerks soon tired of providing lengthy information.

From 1813

The passing of Rose's Act in 1812, which came into effect on 1 January 1813, standardized the entries in parish registers. Henceforth, the registers of the Church of

DADE REGISTERS

Named after William Dade, a Yorkshire clergyman whose idea was taken up by the Archbishop of York, these registers provide an astonishing amount of genealogical information from 1777, sometimes up to the end of 1812. Over 200 of this type of register are known, most of them in Yorkshire, but the quality is very variable and in many the system was soon abandoned. The fullest baptism registers note the infant's name, his or her order of seniority in the family, the father's name and occupation, the names, occupations and places of residence of the paternal and maternal grandparents (and sometimes even a great-grandparent), the date of birth and the date of baptism.

The most complete burial registers provide similar information and give the date and cause of death and the age of the deceased. See Roger Bellingham's article 'Dade Parish Registers – An Exceptional Source' in *Ancestors* 15 (Aug/Sep, 2003).

England are bound volumes of printed forms that provide a great deal of information. Entries of baptisms name the child, state the date of the baptism, give the Christian names, surnames and abode of the parents, and the father's occupation. The record of marriages notes the names of both partners, their parishes, the date and place of the wedding, and the names of the witnesses, as it had done since 1754. The burial register records the name of the deceased, his or her abode, the date of the burial, and his or her age. If a family lived in the same district for much of the nineteenth century and attended church rather than chapel, a family historian may find it easier and cheaper to trace them through parish registers than through the records of civil registration.

Identifying ancestors

From 1813 parish registers are informative, but in earlier centuries the terse entries often leave us doubtful as to whether or not we have found the right person. Even if we are looking for a distinctive surname we may find a cousin with the same first name as our ancestor and discover that he chose the same name for his son as well. If the mother's name was not recorded, there may be no way of identifying the right father. Guesses are often wrong and if we are uncertain about the evidence we must take the position of 'the devil's advocate' and put the case against our identification. 'Negative proof' means that no other solution is reasonable. The problem cannot always be solved, but sometimes we are able to find an answer through a search of other records, such as wills or manor court rolls.

A fine example of a Dade register, recording baptisms in the parish of Selby, Yorkshire, in 1782 and supplying a great deal of genealogical information.

The common practice of using the same Christian names down the generations helps us to identify members of our family. If an ancestor's baptism is not recorded in a parish register but he is known from other evidence to have had brothers and sisters whose distinctive first names were those of their grandparents or uncles and aunts, we may reasonably infer his place in the family. Proof of this nature becomes easier in the nineteenth century, when the use of two forenames became more common; the second name was sometimes a surname from the maternal side of the family. The role of godparents in choosing the Christian name of a child is evident in the earliest parish registers, but during the seventeenth century the fashion for naming the eldest boys and girls after their parents spread from the south across the whole of England and Wales.

The use of an alias can sometimes frustrate the genealogist but on other occasions it solves a problem. Aliases might arise through illegitimacy, from a step-father, perhaps as a nickname, or for less obvious reasons. Between 1562 and 1576 the Chesterfield parish register notes 14 cases, including John Hodgekinsone alias Alattson (1572) and John Alattson alias Hodgkinson (1576). Sometimes, an alias became hereditary and both forms of the name were used for several generations. In other cases, the alias might be dropped for a time in a parish register but continue in wills or other records, only to re-emerge in the register later on. See G. Redmonds, *Surnames and Genealogy: A New Approach* (FFHS, 2002) on the ways that aliases provide proof of a link between two surnames, which would otherwise be very difficult to establish.

The Old Poor Law

Overseers of the poor

In the sixteenth century the old ecclesiastical parishes (or their subdivisions, the townships) were given responsibility for relieving the poor. The Poor Law Acts of 1597–1601, which were passed in the final years of the reign of Queen Elizabeth I, provided the framework for the Old Poor Law. This survived until the Poor Law Amendment Act of 1834 created the New Poor Law, based on unions of parishes and 'Union Workhouses'. Every year, about Easter time, an unpaid overseer of the poor was chosen by a meeting of the parishioners. He was normally chosen from the ranks of the local farmers and craftsmen on a rotation basis; thus the poor law records of Attercliffe township, in the parish of Sheffield, record the election in 1690 of William Steer 'for the house hee purchased of John Rose' and in 1704 of Abijah Ashton 'for the house he lives in'. During his year of office the overseer raised local rates (or 'assessments'), dealt with the everyday problems of relieving the poor, and kept accounts which he presented at the close of his period of office. He was responsible not only to the parish meeting but to the Justices of the Peace, meeting in quarter sessions. In 1686, for example, the West Riding of Yorkshire JPs ordered Joseph Loy, the overseer of the poor for Attercliffe, to attend the quarter sessions to answer the charge of 'misbehaving himself in his office'. Five years later, Joseph Wild, the officer of a neighbouring township, was called before the justices to explain his 'misbehaviour in his late office of Overseer of Poor of Hallam by collecting more money than he accounted for'.

Such cases were untypical, however. Most overseers did their job to the best of their ability and some regarded the holding of parish office as an honour. In his history of the Shropshire parish of Myddle, written in 1701–2, Richard Gough says disdainfully that William Parker of Myddlewood 'was a person that affected to be accompted somebody in this parish', who actively sought the office of churchwarden and who afterwards 'made that year the epoch of his computation of all accidents, and would usually say such a thing was done soe many yeares before or after the yeare that I was Churchwarden'. The office of the constable or of the overseer of the poor or of the highways carried a similar local prestige which compensated for the onerous nature of some of the duties.

The money that was collected from the poor rates was supplemented by that which was donated from charity. People commonly left something for the poor when they made a

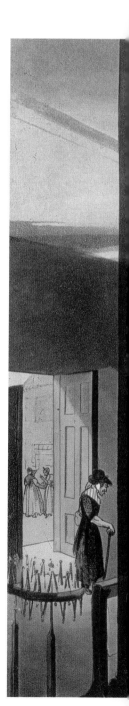

The workhouse of St James's parish, London, shown in a lithograph by Thomas Rowlandson (1756–1827) and Augustus Charles Pugin (1762–1832), published in Ackermann's Microcosm of London.

will and charity boards inside the towers of parish churches record the substantial bequests that were doled out every year. Some towns had public bodies – perhaps derived from a dissolved medieval guild or chantry – whose income came from rents and went a long way towards alleviating the burden of the poor. The situation varied considerably from parish to parish. The most important source of information – where the records survive – is the collection of overseers' accounts, which were once kept in the parish chest but which are now held in local record offices. These can be supplemented by the quarter sessions records, which are often housed in the same record office as order books, indictment books and petitions.

The 'deserving poor'

The Old Poor Law was designed to relieve the 'deserving poor', to provide work for the unemployed and to discipline the idle. Beggars were whipped unless they had a licence from the JPs. The difficulty, of course, was in deciding who were 'deserving poor' and who were not. The old and the sick were treated charitably but the overseer had to balance the demands for relief against the pressure to keep down the rates. He frequently found himself in a difficult face-to-face situation, for he knew that a person who was denied relief would use his or her right to appeal to the JPs and that he would have to explain his decision. If he were too lenient, however, he would face the wrath of his rate-paying neighbours and might not have the expense allowed when he submitted his accounts to their scrutiny.

In some cases the JPs decided that the overseers had neglected their duties. In 1671, for example, the Hallam overseer was ordered by the West Riding justices to relieve Thomas Machon, 'a very poore man and not able to take any paines as towards getting him a lively hood' and in 1686 the overseers of Sheffield township were ordered to pay a weekly allowance to Martha Cartwright, who was 'very old and Lame and hath nothing to Live upon, nor is able to work'. But in other cases the JPs ruled in favour of the overseer's decision, even when presented with a petition that was designed to move them to tears. In 1698, for instance, the West Riding JPs heard that Helen Wigfall of Sheffield was

an aged woman who for the time past whilst she had strength was a very laborious and great painstaker for a Lively hood and always ready and willing to work at any imployment … towards the maintenance of her self and family … [and who] is now by reason of old age and Lameness brought into great want and poverty.

They decided in favour of the overseer's judgement that her existing allowance of 9d. a week was sufficient for her needs.

A particularly difficult task for an overseer was the finding of a home for a poor orphan or the child of parents who were in receipt of poor relief. The Elizabethan Acts gave overseers the power to bind poor children as apprentices and to pay premiums to their masters out of the parish rates. A typical entry from the overseers' accounts at Repton (Derbyshire) notes that John Bull, aged 13, a poor boy of the parish, was apprenticed to Edward Best of Repton, basket maker, until

The account of the Overseers of the Poor for Worsbrough, Yorkshire, 1707–8, itemizing payments for clothes, coals and food and sums of money given to the 'deserving poor' of the township.

he was 21 and that Best was to be paid £5 to take him. An Act of 1697 imposed a £10 penalty on anyone who refused, without good reason, to accept a pauper child. Those who felt aggrieved at having a poor child sent to live and work with them often appealed to the quarter sessions if they thought they had good reason to protest. In 1675 William Greaves of Fulwood claimed that the overseers of Hallam

of malice and evil will put Mary Sykes a poore child of the said Towne apprentice to the said petitioner hee not being capable by estate to take one and there being many substantiall inhabitants in Hallam who are fitt to take Such apprentices and have none at this time.

The JPs agreed with him and ordered that the child should be placed elsewhere.

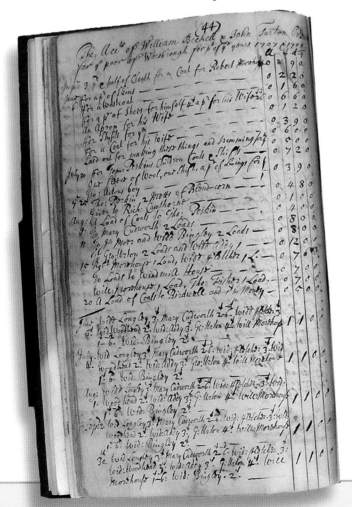

Local tax payers were certainly willing to help those whom they regarded as their 'deserving poor', but they were hard-nosed about paying for others. In 1681, for instance, the overseer of the poor for the south Yorkshire parish of Ecclesfield gave Isabell Kirkby 10d. to help her in times of difficulty and a further 2s.0d. 'towards Repayring her house'. He also paid 5s.6d. to 'Widd. Birley for Reliefe of her children being in the Small pox', and in the same year the accounts record 3s. 0d. spent on 'a payr of shooes for Hellin Carr'. At first sight this seems another typical payment, but subsequent entries reveal that Hellin did not come into the same category as Isabell Kirkby and Widdow Birley. They read: 'charges about remo[ving] Hellin Carr, 2s.8d., payd for an Order for Removeing her, 2s.0d., Charges of a horse to cary her away, 1s.6d'. She was not one of the parish's poor, but was the responsibility of others and the charges of getting rid of her were thought to be worthwhile compared with the potential burden of allowing her to stay. Even so, the overseer ends his record with 'Given to Hellin Carr, 6d'. He was not stony hearted even if he and the parishioners were sticking to the strict letter of the law.

Settlement disputes

Much of the business of quarter sessions was concerned with settlement disputes. The Act of Settlement of 1662 formed the basis of the law, though in fact it merely placed on the statute book a practice that had been common in many parishes for some time previously.

- The poor were made the responsibility of the parish where they were last legally settled.

- The Act defined the various ways in which a settlement could be acquired, starting with the place of birth.

- If someone worked in another parish for over a year, or if a boy served an apprenticeship beyond his native place, or if a family moved to a new residence and were unchallenged by the overseer for more than a year, then their new parish became the legal place of settlement.

- Upon marriage, a woman became the responsibility of her husband's parish.

Parishes were naturally reluctant to allow immigrants within their boundaries if they felt they were likely to become a burden on the poor rates, perhaps for generations to come. Concern about the cost of maintaining poor families who had gained a settlement is evident in parish agreements not to hire outsiders for more than 50 weeks. In 1681 the Ecclesfield overseer allowed himself 1s.0d. expenses 'for Goeing to the Storrs to Ed. Bramall to Give him Notis that the parish was not Willing but against him to let his Land to such a man as may becom chargible'. The custom grew up for parishes to demand that newcomers should bring a certificate from the parish where they were legally settled, whereby that parish accepted responsibility. In 1697 an Act defined the various ways in which such certificates might be obtained.

Many such 'settlement certificates' survive among parish records which have been deposited at local record offices. They are standard printed forms with spaces in which to write the details of individual cases. For example, Sarah Stewart, widow, 'a rogue and vagabond' apprehended in the parish of Saint Mary White Chapel was examined before a JP for the county of Middlesex on 14 February 1767.

This Examinant on her oath saith that she hath heard her parents say and believes she was born at Barlow in the County of Derby and that her parents also belonged to the same place and she never was a yearly servant nor an apprentice and saith that her husband was an Irishman, but what part of Ireland he belonged to she never heard, nor that he gained any settlement in England, and since her husband's death she hath wandered from place to place being in distress not able to maintain her three children Mary, George and Augustus.

She signed the record of her examination with a mark and she and her children were conveyed to the constable of Barlow twelve days later.

The diary of the Revd F. E. Witts, parson and magistrate of Upper Slaughter, for 27 April 1821, records:

The overseer of Halling brought up two gipsies, casual poor in their parish in order to their being examined to their settlement. Merach Lock the husband swore that he was born under an oak on Halling down as he had heard from his mother, being an illegitimate child and knowing nothing of his father; also that he was recently married to his wife Mary with whom he had cohabited twenty years, having by her six children.

It seems that the parish of Halling had little or no chance of proving him settled elsewhere. When the woman was examined, she swore all the children to be Merach Lock's – Lucas and Adam being born like their father in the parish of Halling, Eve at Cold Ashton, Sara at Brimpsfield, Temperance at Hawkesbury, Joanna at Cranham. The law was strictly interpreted and removal orders were made in respect of the last four children, sending them to their respective birthplaces.

At the quarter sessions disputing parishes found it worth their while to go to the expense of employing learned counsel to argue their case, based on information obtained from parish records. Such records were kept under lock and key in the parish chest in the church. Richard Gough remembered that his parish of Myddle had lost their first settlement contest because they could not find an old warrant from a JP, but they learned their lesson and 'thanks be to God', wrote Gough, 'we never lost any afterwards'. Potential paupers were also keen to preserve written and oral evidence of their legal rights to settlement. Where they survive, the records of settlement disputes are a mine of information about the poorest class of society. They often record places of births and all the subsequent movements which might have led to a legal settlement.

Concern about incoming poor was also expressed in manor courts. On 19 April 1665, for example, the constable and sworn men of Shelley at the Kirkburton (Yorkshire) court leet presented John Hey for taking John Naylor and his family 'into such houseing of his as formerly hath bene no dwelling house', contrary to the Act of 1589, which tried to restrict new building and to insist that every cottage should have at least four acres of land attached.

A settlement certificate of 1769 whereby the overseers of Peper Harrow, Surrey, acknowledge that William and Ann Mayes and their infant daughter were legally settled in their parish and accept their removal from the parish of Elstead.

BASTARDY

Overseers were also keen to identify the fathers of illegitimate children and make them pay for maintenance. A typical entry from the accounts of the township of Wilne and Shardlow (Derbyshire) on 26 January 1830 notes that Esther Wall, singlewoman, had given birth to a child that was now chargeable to the parish and that David Garner of Elvaston, servant, the father, was to pay £1.7s.0d. and then two shillings a week. The mother was to pay one shilling a week if she did not nurse and take care of the child herself. Likewise, when Mary Kemp had 'a female bastard child' in the township of Bradfield (Yorkshire) in 1827, the father, Joseph Bettany of Stannington, 'servant in husbandry', was ordered to pay £2 and then two shillings a week 'as long as the bastard child is chargeable to the township', plus the 2s.6d. cost of the order, and the mother had to pay sixpence a week as long as the child was chargeable.

Workhouses

Some parishes also took a firm line by adopting the provision of an Act of 1697 which said that those in receipt of poor relief should have the letter P and the initial of the parish sewn on to their clothes, but many took a more charitable view towards their 'deserving poor'.

☞ A few parishes had built workhouses in the late seventeenth century and these became more common after 1722 when parishes were allowed to farm out their responsibility for the poor to a contractor for a fixed fee.

☞ In 1782 Gilbert's Act encouraged the erection of workhouses by unions of parishes, with each parish paying the costs of its own poor. The able-bodied inmates were to be employed outside, but no pauper was to be sent to a workhouse more than ten miles away, badging was abandoned, and children under the age of seven were not separated from their parents.

The Old Poor Law worked adequately for the best part of two centuries, but it felt the strain of the great increase of population in the late eighteenth and early nineteenth centuries and was replaced by a new system in 1834.

An unattributed wash and ink view of the workhouse at Bow, Poplar, London, c.1796.

Wills and other probate records

Where to find a will

After 1858

Since 12 January 1858 the State has been responsible for proving wills. These may be seen at the Principal Registry of the Family Division, First Avenue House, 42–49 High Holborn London, WC1V 6NP, which is open to the public (without prior appointment) between 10 a.m. and 4.30 p.m., Monday to Friday. Here you may consult yearly indexes, or 'calendars', arranged alphabetically, which name everyone for whom grants of probate or letters of administration ('admons') have been made. Copies of the calendars to wills proved and admons granted between 1858 and 1943 can be

The National Probate Calendar entry for Benjamin Disraeli, Earl of Beaconsfield, 1881, with his portrait taken three years earlier.

1881.

BEACHCROFT Sarah.

Personal Estate £21,280 1s. 1d.

15 November. The Will of Sarah Beachcroft formerly of Westbourne-street Hyde-Park-gardens but late of Talbot-square Hyde Park both in the County of **Middlesex** Spinster who died 6 August 1881 at 11 Talbot-square was proved at the **Principal Registry** by Matthews Beachcroft of 11 Talbot-square a Retired Lieutenant-Colonel in Her Majesty's Indian Army the Brother and Richard Melvill Beachcroft of 9 Theobald's-road Bedford-row in the said County Esquire and Thomas Seward Beachcroft of 24 Maitland-Park-villas Haverstock Hill in the said County Esquire the Nephews the Executors.

BEACHELL James Esq.

Personal Estate £2,542 0s. 4d.

14 September. Administration of the Personal Estate of James Beachell late of Rawcliffe in the Parish of Snaith in the County of **York** Esquire who died 10 June 1881 at Rawcliffe was granted at **Wakefield** to Lucilla Beachell of Rawcliffe Widow the Relict.

The Right Honourable DISRAELI Benjamin Earl of BEACONSFIELD and Viscount HUGHENDEN K.G.

Personal Estate £76,687 4s. 7d.
Resworn April 1882 £84,019 18s. 7d.

29 June. The Will of the Right Honourable Benjamin Disraeli Earl of Beaconsfield and Viscount Hughenden late of Hughenden Manor in the County of **Buckingham** K.G. who died 19 April 1881 at 19 Curzon-street in the County of Middlesex was proved at the **Principal Registry** by Sir Nathaniel Mayer de Rothschild of Tring Park in the County of Buckingham and Sir Philip Rose of Rayner's Penn in the County of Buckingham Baronets the Executors.

consulted at the Family Records Centre and the National Archives. The calendars record the name of the testator, his or her address, the date and sometimes the place of death, the date of probate, the names of the executors or administrators, the value of the estate, and the name of the district office in which the will was proved. As it could take a couple of years or more for the administrative process to be completed, a search in the calendars might need to go beyond the year of death.

☛ Once you have found the reference to the required person, a copy of a will, or a grant of probate (which may tell you no more than the calendar), or letters of administration can be obtained upon completing a form and paying a fee; last orders are taken at 3 p.m., but it may take an hour for them to be delivered.

☛ The Postal Searches & Copies Department, York Probate Sub-Registry, Duncombe Place, York YO1 7EA will search a name in the calendars over three years if you enclose a cheque for £5 payable to HM Paymaster General.

☛ Copies of Welsh wills may also be seen at the National Library of Wales.

☛ Some of the larger municipal libraries have printed copies of the indexes, and microfilm copies of calendars from 1858 to 1935 are available at the Society of Genealogists and some record offices.

☛ Otherwise, copies of wills might survive in solicitors' collections which have been deposited at local record offices and in registries of deeds or, of course, in family papers.

Before 1858

Before 12 January 1858 the Church was responsible for proving wills. These are kept at the record offices which house the records of the ancient dioceses. For example, the probate records of the diocese of York are housed at the Borthwick Institute of Historical Research at the University of York; wills proved there before 1689 have been indexed in several volumes of the Yorkshire Archaeological Society Record Series and a typescript index at the institute is available for the later ones. Welsh wills are kept at the National Library, Aberystwyth. The wills of the Exeter diocese were mostly destroyed by bombs in the Second World War. It can be quite a problem to find the whereabouts of a will.

☛ The standard guidebook is J. Gibson and B. Langston, *Probate Jurisdiction: Where to Look for Wills* (FFHS, 5th edition, 2002).

☛ Before searching for London wills it is advisable to read the London Metropolitan Archives' information leaflet no. 6: 'Wills in London Metropolitan Archives and Elsewhere'.

☛ Most people had property in only one archdeaconry and so used the archdeacon's court, those with land in two archdeaconries had to go to the bishop's courts, those with property in two bishoprics went to the Archbishop's

*Illustrated title page from Prerogative Court of
Canterbury Wills Register 'Chayre', 1562.*

Prerogative Court, and in the minority of cases where a testator had property in the two provinces of Canterbury and York his executors went to the senior court at Canterbury.

🖙 The probate records of the Prerogative Court at Canterbury (PCC) consist mainly of the wills of the wealthier members of the province, but the great prestige of the court attracted other business. During the Commonwealth (1653–60) all wills throughout England and Wales were proved at the PCC.

The probate records for the PCC between 1383 and 1858 are now housed at the National Archives and can be seen on microfilm there and at the Family Records Centre. Before searching for a will, you need to have a good idea of when and where the person you are looking for died, unless you are searching for an unusual surname.

🖙 An index of all the PCC wills from 1383 to 1858 is now available online at <www.documentsonline. nationalarchives.gov.uk>. Digital images of the wills can be seen for a fee of £3.00 per will.

🖙 Indexes of all PCC wills from 1383 to 1858 and of administrations from 1559 to 1858 are available in the bookcases in the General Reference Area at Kew, either in printed or typescript form.

Portrait of Isaac Newton by Edward Scriven, with Prerogative Court of Canterbury administration act book showing Newton's administration, 1728.

☞ To find a will at the FRC, convert the reference number in the index to a microfilm number, by using one of the three copies of a burgundy-coloured binder in Bookcase 4 entitled 'PCC Wills Reference Book'. This involves finding the year (under the heading 'Date') and the range of 'Quire'

numbers that includes yours. The microfilm number is in the column headed PROB11 on the left of the page.

☞ To find a grant of administration, turn to one of the three copies of a burgundy-coloured binder in Bookcase 4 entitled 'PCC Administrations Reference Book' and convert your reference to a microfilm number.

Further information is supplied in the FRC leaflet, 'How to Use PCC Wills and Administrations'.

The wills that were proved in the ancient dioceses are usually arranged by deaneries, so that those for the southern half of Yorkshire, for example, are in bundles for the deaneries of Pontefract and Doncaster, but some parishes (or scattered properties within a parish) belonged to peculiar jurisdictions, whose records are kept separately. As the parish of Laughton en le Morthen (Yorkshire) was a peculiar jurisdiction of the Dean and Chapter of York, its probate records are kept in different bundles from those in the deanery of Doncaster. The records of peculiar jurisdictions are normally kept at the same record offices as other wills, but some peculiars were formed from properties whose tithes had once belonged to the Knights Templar or the Knights Hospitaller, or from special liberties, and their records might now be found in a solicitor's deposit at a local record office. Archivists will be able to advise on their whereabouts.

Making a will

The custom of making a will goes back to Anglo-Saxon times, but most of the wills that survive from before the fifteenth century were made by aristocrats, gentlemen, or prosperous townsmen. In the later Middle Ages the fashion began to spread down the social scale, but few farmers and craftsmen made wills before the sixteenth century and labourers' wills are not very common at any time. Widows and spinsters often made wills, but until the Married Women's Property Act (1882) a wife needed the consent of her husband. The majority of people did not make a will,

for they had other methods of passing on their property. Various studies have shown that wills were made only by one in three or one in four of the adult males whose burials are recorded in a parish register. A will was needed only when the descent of property was uncertain. Children often received their share of the patrimony when they married. Those who were left only a nominal sum – a shilling in early wills, £5 by the nineteenth century – had normally already had their share of the estate. Clauses that disinherited a wife if she remarried were inserted to protect the interests of under-age children, for her new husband would otherwise own her property during her lifetime.

Wills follow common formats, for they were written by clerks who had books to guide them. A usual beginning is 'In the name of God, Amen'. The testator then gave his name, parish, occupation or standing, and said that although he was 'sick of body' he was 'of full and perfect memory'; in other words he knew what he was doing when he made his will. This is followed by a standard formula whereby the testator committed his soul to Almighty God and his body to burial in the parish churchyard, or inside the church if he were rich and influential. A Catholic formula before the Reformation might read: 'I bequeath my soul to Almighty God, our Lady Saint Mary and all the Holy Company of Heaven, to pray for me and my body'. Typical Protestant forms are: 'I commend my soul unto Almighty God my Maker and Redeemer by whose abundant and great mercy I hope to be saved' or

Prerogative Court of Canterbury index of wills and administrations, 1825.

'I commend my soul unto Almighty God my Maker and Redeemer trusting to be saved by the merits of his blessed passion'. Most speak of the uncertainty of life, of salvation through Christ and of the hope of immortality. In some wills a Calvinist tone is unmistakable; testators disposed of estates that God had 'bestowed' on them, a sure sign of being one of God's Elect and Chosen. Expressions of penitence for sin and requests for forgiveness are commonly made in seventeenth- and eighteenth-century wills and in some cases over half the will consists of a lengthy, repetitive preamble in phrases chosen from formula books. This makes it difficult to determine how far the preambles were conventional sentiments and how much was an expression of individual belief.

A typical will proceeds to arrange for the payment of debts and the funeral expenses and to annul any previous will before making specific bequests. Although wills were written by professional scribes, they did express the wishes of the testator. Occasionally, they include a human touch, as in 1594, when Thomas Woodhouse of Dore (Derbyshire) said:

I do desire of God and wyshe with all my harte a loveinge and Frendly agreemente betwyxte my wieff and my daughter after my death.

The executors or 'supervisors' of the will were friends or relations; a wife was often named as executrix. She was entitled to a third of her husband's property during her lifetime, as long as she did not remarry. The will of Thomas Bright of Dore (1579) makes a common arrangement clear:

Item I will that all the reste of my goods to be devided into three equall parts wherof I will that my wyfe shall have one parte and the other two parts to be equally devided amongst my three children That ys to saye Thomas Bright Ellen Bright and Ales Bright and the rest of my children to be excluded from gaininge any part or parcell of my sayd goods consideringe that they have had thear porcions alredye.

Last wills were normally made shortly before death, as is evident from shaky signatures or the use of marks by people who signed their names on earlier documents. If a final illness was short and a written will could not be made, then a nuncupative will (an oral statement attested by sworn witnesses) was accepted by the church court. A good example is that of Grace Woodhouse of Totley (Derbyshire) in 1679:

Memorandum that uppon or aboute the Fifth day of November in the yeare of o[ur] Lorde Christ one thousand sixe hundred Seaventy and Nyne: Grace Woodhouse of Totley in the County of derby spinster beinge weake in body & lyeing sicke at Mary Woodhouses of the Last sickness of w[hic]h shee dyed beinge the place of her residence her mothers house in Totley aforesaid but was of good & sound & disposseinge minde & memory desiered us whose names are hereunto subscribed to beare witnesse of her Will nuncupative w[hic]h shee then uttered & declared in manner Followeinge Item it is my will and I leave unto Ralph Woodhouse my brother Five

Prerogative Court of Canterbury original wills:
the will of Frances Dodkin, spinster of the parish of
St Leonard's, Shoreditch, Middlesex, 1689.

poundes I leave to Robert Woodhouse my Brother Five pounds I leave to Alice Brelsford my Sister Five pounds To Anthony Woodhouse my Brother Fower yowes three hogg sheepe & one greate chest with all that is in it standinge in the great Parlour & one newe Fether bedd I leave my Brother Anthony & my Couzen Alice Woodhouse all my hives and bees wheresoever I leave unto my three Godchildren George Newbold Alice Woodhouse & Elizabeth North two shillinges six pence apeece I leave my Godchild Alice Woodhouse daughter of Francis Woodhouse one bed hilleing I make & appoynt my Mother & my Brother Anthony my Executo[rs] & give them all the rest of my goods payeing my legacyes afores[ai]d All w[hic]h wordes or the like in effecte were uttered & spoken before us whose names are hereunto subscribed. Witnesses: Mary Woodhouse her + marke, Mary Glossop Widow her + marke, Alice Woodhouse her + marke, Raphe Woodhouse his + m[a]rk.

From 1837 nuncupative wills were no longer valid, except for members of the armed forces who died in action.

Wills are particularly important in naming children and confirming relationships. We need to remember, however, that father, mother, brother, sister, son, and daughter were terms that were also used for in-laws and that cousin could refer to a wide range of kin. The wills of people who were not direct ancestors can also provide important genealogical information, for brothers, sisters and cousins might be named as beneficiaries or called upon to act as witnesses or executors. On the other hand, older children from an earlier marriage, who had already been provided for, might not be

mentioned in a will, and if a will was proved long after it was made a child or kinsman who was left a bequest might have died in the meantime.

A couple of probate records provided important information about where my maternal ancestors had lived before Richard Batty settled in Coxwold, north of York, in the first part of the eighteenth century. The will of Richard's son, James Batty of Coxwold, yeoman, proved in 1814, mentions his properties in Bishop Thornton, Clint and the Forest of Knaresborough, some 20 miles to the west. In 1758 Richard Batty of Coxwold, farmer, was one of the administrators of the estate of Thomas Batty of Dale Bank, Bishop Thornton, yeoman, the other being Thomas's widow, Mary. It seems likely that Richard was Thomas and Mary's son, but I have not been able to prove this beyond reasonable doubt.

Probate inventories

From the second quarter of the sixteenth century until well into the eighteenth century (and in some parts of the country much later) church courts insisted that the executors of a will should appoint three or four local men to make 'a true and perfect inventory' of the personal estate of the deceased, in order that disputes over wills might be settled more easily. Tens of thousands of these probate inventories survive for most parts of England and Wales, filed with the will or the letters of administration when a person died intestate. The appraisers, as the valuers were usually known, were friends and neighbours of the deceased. They did their best to make an accurate list, for they acted under solemn oath and executors, widows, heirs and creditors had the legal right to query their accuracy. The appraisers went from room to room, listing the furniture and every pot and pan, and then they went outside to value the livestock and crops, the contents of a workshop, and other moveable goods. Probate inventories are the major source for the study of houses, farming and the numerous crafts of Tudor, Stuart, and early-Georgian times. They provide vivid insights into the living conditions of our ancestors. Family historians who find an inventory for a house that still stands are fortunate indeed.

One such building is Barlow Lees Hall (Derbyshire), the home of John Lobley, the

Death or estate duty registers show what actually happened to a person's estate after death and provide information about next of kin and those who received bequests. The registers from 1796 to 1903 are held at the National Archives in IR 26 and are currently being indexed by the Friends of the National Archives and the Family Records Centre. The registers from all the probate courts in England and Wales up to 1858 are on microfilm at the Family Records Centre. The FRC also has indexes on microfilm, up to 1903, of IR 27, which provide the name of the deceased, or of executors or administrators, and of the probate court. Copies of indexes up to 1858 are also held on microfilm at the Society of Genealogists.

vicar of Chesterfield, whose inventory was appraised on 4 June 1695. Sash windows have since been inserted, but enough architectural detail survives to prove that the house is essentially that which Lobley knew. After valuing 'Purse and apparrell' at £20, the appraisers listed everything they saw in the hall (meaning the main living room), dining room and little parlour on the ground floor. They then climbed the stairs to the best chamber and five smaller ones before descending to the pantry, buttery and dairy. The outbuildings included a brewhouse, malt house, stable, wain house, corn chamber, and barn. The livestock and crops were then recorded, including a debt for barley that had been sold. 'Debts upon Security', worth £500, brought the total valuation of the personal estate to £917.15s.4d.

Probate inventories do not provide a complete picture of an individual's wealth, however. The appraisers were asked to record personal estate, but not the value of buildings, land or other real estate. They regularly listed the debts due to the deceased, but they often did not record the debts that he owed. Even the list of personal estate might not be complete. The apparent absence of a bed in a chamber might be explained by the appraisers not noting goods to which a husband was entitled through his wife, and the contradiction between a man being described as a yeoman and his meagre possessions in a single room might mask comfortable retirement after he had passed on most of his estate to his children.

The inventories are often difficult to read, not only because of unfamiliar styles of handwriting but because they use dialect or technical words which are now obsolete. Fortunately, a number of glossaries have been published and are usually available in record offices. These archaic words were spelt in a variety of ingenious ways, for spelling was not yet standardized and the same word was sometimes spelt differently on the same line. In the collection of sixteenth-century Chesterfield inventories, for example, saucer was spelt sosar, sawcar, sauster, and sossare, and cushions was spelt in about twenty different ways, ranging from cussions to quisshions and quoshines. As in the wills, punctuation was almost completely disregarded and capital letters were used indiscriminately. Nor did the appraisers' skills extend to simple mathematics; total valuations cannot be trusted and are especially incorrect where the prices of individual items were expressed in roman numerals in the early inventories.

Barlow Lees Hall, Derbyshire.

INSET
The probate inventory of John Lobley of Barlow Lees Hall, 1695.

Apprentice and freeman records

Apprentices

The medieval practice of binding boys (and occasionally girls) as an apprentice to a master if they wished to learn a trade was made compulsory by the Statute of Artificers (1563). This followed the custom of the City of London in binding apprentices by indenture for a term of at least seven years. A premium was paid to the master by the boy's parents (or, in the case of paupers, by the overseer of the poor). In return, the boy received board and lodging and was taught his trade. During his term, he was forbidden to marry or to set up his own business. The apprenticeship system was enforced by JPs and so the records of quarter sessions in county record offices include cases of ill-treatment or abscondment and disputes over the placing of pauper apprentices.

Thousands of apprenticeship indentures survive in miscellaneous collections throughout England and Wales, but there is no national collection apart from *Crisp's Apprenticeship Indentures* at the library of the Society of Genealogists. An Act of 1710 imposed stamp duty on apprenticeship indentures, but boys who worked for their father, and pauper children, were exempt, and many industries were excluded by the ruling that the Statute of Artificers did not extend to trades which did not exist when the Act was passed in 1563. Thus, although the manufacture of knives goes back at least 700 years in Sheffield, local cutlers evaded payment, presumably on the grounds that the Company of Cutlers in Hallamshire was not founded until 1624.

- The registers of duties received are kept in the Inland Revenue records (IR 17) at the National Archives for the period 1710–1811.

- They record the name, place of residence, and trade of the master, the name of the apprentice, and, until 1752, the name of the apprentice's father.

- Indexes compiled for the Society of Genealogists (which are also on microfiche at the National Archives and the Guildhall Library) cover apprentices up to 1774 and masters up to 1762.

- Some local indexes have been published by record societies, e.g. C. Dale, ed., *Wiltshire Apprentices and Their Masters, 1710–1760* (1961) in the Wiltshire Archaeological & Natural History

*Indenture whereby Abraham Parkins, the son of
a weaver, was apprenticed to Thomas Sutton,
woolcomber, of Burbage, Leicestershire, 1769.*

This Indenture Witnesseth That Abraham parkins son,
of Thomas parkins of Burbage in the County of Leicester Weaver
doth put himself Apprentice to Thomas Sutton of Burbage in the County
of Leicester aforesaid Woolcomber
to learn his Art, and with him after the manner of an Apprentice to serve from the
Day of the Date hereof unto the full end and
Term of Seven Years from thence next ensuing and fully to be compleat and ended
during which Term the said Apprentice his Master faithfully shall and will serve,
his Secrets keep, his lawful Commands every where gladly do, he shall do no Damage
to his said Master nor see it to be done of others, but to his Power shall let or forth-
with give Notice to his said Master of the same. The Goods of his said Master he shall not waste,
nor the same without Licence of his to any give or lend. Hurt to his said Master he shall not do, cause,
or procure to be done, he shall neither buy nor sell without his Masters Licence. Taverns, Inns, or
Ale-houses he shall not haunt. At Cards, Dice, Tables, or any other unlawful Game he shall not play,
nor from the Service of his said Master
Day nor Night absent himself, but in all Things as an honest and faithful Apprentice shall and will demean
and behave himself toward his said Master and all his during all the said Term. And the said

Thomas Sutton the said Master the said Apprentice in the Art
of a woolcomber which he now useth shall teach and instruct, or cause to be taught and instructed
the best Way and Manner that he can, finding and allowing unto his said Apprentice sufficient Meat, Drink,
Washing, Lodging and all other Necessaries during the said Term of seven Years and the said Thomas
parkins shall find provide for his said son the said Apprentice All manner of
wearing apparrel, Linnens and Woollens Hatts and Shoes During the Term
of his apprenticeship
And for the true Performance of all and every the Covenants and Agreements aforesaid, either of the said Parties bindeth
themselves firmly by these Presents. In Witness whereof, the Parties abovesaid to these Indentures inter-
changeably have set their Hands and Seals the third Day of February in the
Second Year of the Reign of our Sovereign Lord George the Third by the Grace of
God of **Great Britain**, France and Ireland **King**, Defender of the Faith, And in the Year of our Lord 1769.

Abraham porkin

Thomas porkins

Thomas Sutton

...livered in the

...W. Attenon

...am wwell

Society Records Series, XVII, which lists 2,759 apprenticeships. A typical entry (for a boy with a distinctive Wiltshire surname) reads: 'Neate, William, of Chicklade: to William Cooke, joiner, of Pewsey: 1 Nov. 1743'.

Although most boys served an apprenticeship for at least seven years, until they were 21 or more years old, much longer terms are recorded, especially during the seventeenth and early eighteenth centuries. The archives of the Cutlers' Company of Hallamshire contain records of some 28,500 apprenticeships and freedoms between 1624 and 1814. As many as 1,354 of these boys served at least ten years, and three of them each served 16 years. Ten-year apprenticeships were entered as late as 1814. Some of these boys started young, though in 1712 a minimum age of 12 was set for entry into an apprenticeship. No less than 2,774 of these apprentices served more than one master during their term, usually because the master had died, but sometimes because he had left the trade or district, or had grown too old to work. The boys who changed masters were recorded as 'turnovers'.

Apprenticeship records are useful in tracing the movements of families. They may explain how a surname that had originated in the countryside came to be established in a town. For example, the surname Glossop comes from a settlement in north-west Derbyshire that was small in the Middle Ages. In 1381 the poll tax returns for the High Peak of Derbyshire name just two Glossops – John and Thomas – in the township of Bowden, eight miles to the south. The surname spread slowly to various parts of north Derbyshire and by the second quarter of the seventeenth century a branch was settled at Offerton, eight miles to the east of Bowden. In 1628 it made its first appearance in Sheffield, ten miles further to the east, when Edmund, the son of Robert Glossop of Offerton, yeoman, deceased, was apprenticed to

THE PEPYS BALLADS

A Warning and good Counsel to the WEAVERS.

Tune of, *The Country Farmer.* Or, *The Devonshire Damosels.*

This may be Printed, R. P.

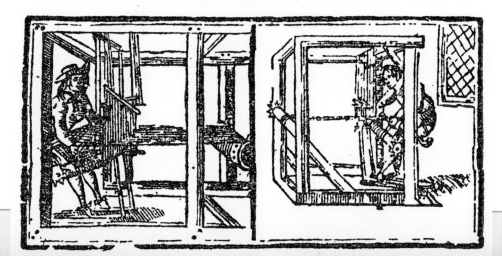

Thomas Skargell, a Sheffield cutler. Other Glossops moved from Derbyshire villages into Sheffield as apprentices when the cutlery trades expanded during the eighteenth century, so that the surname is now concentrated in and around the city.

When he had finished his apprenticeship, a man could become a freeman of his company and start business as a master in his trade. The sons of freemen did not need to complete a formal apprenticeship if they were trained by their fathers. Many young men did not take their freedom, however, but remained journeymen, who worked for other masters. Throughout the country, apprentices commonly failed to complete their training or did not enter their trade once they had served their time. During the sixteenth and seventeenth centuries about half the apprentices in London did not become freemen of the City. In Bristol, during the same period, only about a third of the apprentices eventually enjoyed the privilege of citizenship, despite the fact that no more than 5 per cent were legally discharged and only 10 per cent died. Many seem to have left Bristol, often for the New World. In Hallamshire 47 per cent of apprentices between 1624 and 1814 became freemen upon completing their terms. Some of the boys who failed to stay the course are known to have run away to London or to have joined the Army. The great expansion of industry and the remarkable growth of the national population from the second half of the eighteenth century onwards led to the collapse of the apprenticeship system.

Most apprentices came from places that were within walking distance of their master's home and workshop. A. J. Willis and A. L.

Illustration of a seventeenth-century weaver and his apprentice, from Samuel Pepys's collection of ballads.

Merson, *A Calendar of Southampton Apprenticeship Registers, 1609–1740* (1968) shows that about a third of the first 650 apprentices in the early and middle decades of the seventeenth century came from the town itself, that most of the others came from rural Hampshire, and nearly all the rest had travelled from the neighbouring counties of Wiltshire, Dorset and Somerset. A high proportion were yeomen and husbandmen's sons. Likewise, in Hallamshire in the second quarter of the seventeenth century 83.7 per cent of the apprentices came from within 21 miles of Sheffield.

Freemen

In London and the provincial cities the transition from apprentice to freeman meant that a man could set up as a master in his trade and enjoy the privileges of citizenship. The municipal authorities kept a register (or a series of rolls) of those who had been admitted into freedom. The most complete lists record the date of admission, the freeman's name, the name and residence of his father, and (if he had served an apprenticeship) the name and trade of his master. Historians have queried the reliability of freemen's rolls and, of course, they cover only a proportion of the local population, but family historians should certainly look at any that have been deposited at their local record offices or which have been published. *The Register of the Freemen of the City of York*, for example, has been printed in volumes XCVI and CII of the Publications of the Surtees Society, covering the years 1272–1558 and 1559–1759. The York registers were simple lists of

List of maltsters, swalers, badgers and drovers licensed at the quarter sessions held at Knutsford, Cheshire, in 1725.

1439, or of 'Johannes de Mounser, vynter', who achieved his freedom in 1444? The 'de' form of the vintner's name suggests a derivation from Monceaux (Calvados). The Monsieurs did come from France, but they arrived more than three centuries before the revolution and had no aristocratic connections.

The early records of the freemen of the City of London were destroyed by the Great Fire of 1666. Surviving records of freedom are held at the Corporation of London Record Office. The Manuscripts Section of the Guildhall Library holds records of the individual guilds. The trade guilds of the City of London are known as Livery Companies because of their distinctive dress or livery. An outline of the records available there is given in *City Livery Companies & Related Organisations: A Guide to their Archives in the Guildhall Library*.

The lists of members and apprentices of 75 livery companies or Related Organizations are extensive but unindexed, and so time-consuming to search. Before the late eighteenth century most men (and some women) who practised a trade or craft in or around the City of London almost certainly belonged to the appropriate livery company. Records of the binding of apprentices and the admission of members up to 1800 have been extracted and indexed by Cliff Webb for about 40 companies and more volumes are planned. These have been published by the Society of Genealogists and may also be consulted at the Guildhall Library.

names and trade, arranged by year of admission, but they provide vital information about individuals. Descendants of John Monsieur, a stable groom at Woolley Hall (Yorkshire) in the late eighteenth century, cling to the romantic belief that their ancestors were French aristocrats who fled from the impending revolution, but this surname is found, under a variety of spellings, much earlier in Yorkshire. In 1672 Arthur Mounser was taxed at Clifton, a York suburb. Was he descended from 'Thomas Mounseux, yoman', who became a freeman of York in

Land tax assessments

Land tax was first levied in England and Wales in 1693. Assessment was organized on a county, hundred or wapentake, and parish basis, so returns may be found either amongst quarter sessions records, or at local record offices in estate and family archives. Relatively few records survive before the period 1780–1832, when annual copies or 'duplicates' of the assessments were lodged at quarter sessions, in order to determine who had the right to vote. The only record that covers almost the whole of England and Wales in a uniform way is that for the year 1798, which is contained in 121 volumes in IR 23 at the National Archives. J. Gibson, M. Medlycott and D. Mills, *Land and Window Tax Assessments* (FFHS, 1993) lists the various holdings, and a good idea of the appearance and use of returns for a whole county can be gained from the two volumes of the Sussex land tax assessment for 1785 that were published by the Sussex Record Society in 1991 and 2001.

The duplicates of 1780–1832 are arranged in columns that record the name of each proprietor within a township, the names of the occupiers, and the amount of tax that was due. Despite this simple arrangement, the information is not always what it seems. Some returns are just copies of previous years and may be out of date. More disturbingly, a high proportion of

Land tax assessment for the High Street, Borough of Portsmouth, 1798.

WINDOW TAX

Window tax was levied from 1696 to 1851 on the occupiers of property (rather than owners). Returns usually note the name and address of a taxpayer, the number of windows in the house, and the amount of tax paid. Those householders who were excused by poverty from paying the church or poor rates were exempt. On the whole, the survival rate of returns is poor. They are generally found in county record offices, although a few are housed in the National Library of Wales, the National Archives, and elsewhere.

smallholders (in some cases up to 80 per cent) was unrecorded and cottagers disappeared altogether in some assessments after 1798, but reappeared briefly when new arrangements for collecting the tax were made. In practice, it is often difficult to identify farms because land was scattered,

and both owners and tenants often had land in other townships.

Family historians will nevertheless find land tax assessments a useful source for the period immediately before civil registration and the census returns. They may suggest which parish registers to search. By looking at a series of assessments, we might be able to spot the year when the name of a head of household was replaced by a different one. D. E. Ginter, *A Measure of Wealth: The English Land Tax in Historical Analysis* (Hambledon, 1992) is a comprehensive account that identifies the problems and shows how the returns can be used for the study of agricultural history.

Land tax assessment for the parish of Steventon, Hampshire, 1798, headed by the father of Jane Austen.

Hearth tax returns

The hearth tax returns of the 1660s and 1670s can be of great assistance to anyone searching for an elusive ancestor in the second half of the seventeenth century. They suggest which parish registers to turn to and they show the distribution of family names halfway between the period of surname formation in the Middle Ages and the present day. They also give a good idea of a person's social standing in a local community, for the size and comfort of the house was reflected by the number of hearths on which tax was paid, and the poorest householders were exempted from payment.

- The hearth tax was the government's chief source of revenue during the reigns of Charles II and James II. It was introduced in 1662, 'it being easy to tell the number of hearths, which remove not as heads or polls do', and was abolished after the Glorious Revolution of 1688.

- Each hearth was taxed at the rate of 2 shillings a year, payable in two instalments at Lady Day and Michaelmas.

- Householders were exempt if they were too poor to pay church or poor rates, if they occupied premises worth less than 20 shillings a year, or if their annual income was less than £10.

- Some returns add the marginal comment 'Poor' or 'Ced' (for those who had received a certificate of exemption from a JP) and others list the poor at the end of the roll.

- Collections of exemption certificates, covering most counties, in E 179/324–359 at the National Archives have recently become better known. Those for Norwich, Great Yarmouth, King's Lynn and Thetford have been published in P. Seaman, ed., *Norfolk Hearth Tax Exemption Certificates, 1670–74* (British Records Society, 2001).

Hearth tax was assessed and collected in the various townships or 'constablewicks' that formed the basic units of local government until the nineteenth century, with the assistance of the local constable. The money was taken to the high constable of the hundred or wapentake, who forwarded it to the sheriff of the county. This administrative structure explains the layout of the returns that were sent to the Exchequer. Surviving returns in the National Archives relate only to 1662–6 and 1669–74, for at other times the collection of the tax was farmed out to speculators, whose records do not survive. The family historian needs to have some understanding of the administrative structure of the county that he is interested in. This can be gained from Samuel Lewis,

A list of those claiming exemption from payment of the hearth tax, approved by the minister, churchwardens and overseers of the poor of the parish of Frettenham, Norfolk, 27 January 1671/2.

A Topographical Dictionary of England (seventh edition, 1848–9) and *A Topographical Dictionary of Wales* (third edition, 1849), from the various volumes of the *Victoria History of the Counties of England* and old county histories, or perhaps from nineteenth-century trade directories. In some parts of the country townships were often identical with the ecclesiastical parishes, but in moorland, fenland or woodland districts where settlements were scattered, parishes were divided into numerous townships, quarters or hamlets.

Returns such as that for Lady Day 1672 for the West Riding of Yorkshire occasionally survive as copies in county record offices or libraries, but the bulk of the returns are to be found in the National Archives in the Exchequer division, under the call number E 179. Their reference numbers can be obtained from the website <www.nationalarchives.gov.uk>, which highlights E 179 on its home page. Type in a place-name and the type of record that you require, then make a choice of date. The reference is accompanied by brief information about the tax and any local problems. You can gauge the completeness of the various returns for your county by their length and so judge which is the best one to see. The fullest returns for many counties have been published, with indexes of names and places, by a record society or a family history society. A current project of the University of Surrey Roehampton and the British Record Society aims to publish

the best return for each of the remaining counties of England and Wales in cooperation with local record societies. Volumes for Cambridgeshire and Kent have already appeared.

In estate villages, the name of the squire headed the list. He lived in a house with many hearths and was recorded as 'Mr' if he did not possess a title. The rest of the inhabitants were listed by their Christian name and their surname. Only the name of the head of household was noted; if a man had died his widow was usually recorded as such, instead of by her first name. The number of hearths in the house was noted alongside the name. Collectors and constables had the power to enter houses to count the hearths, but they did not always succeed. The return for Curry Mallet (Somerset) in Michaelmas 1665 has a marginal comment after the record of Richard Collier's three hearths: 'Shutts the door and refuses entrance'. The returns for London are particularly suspect because many families shared a house (by living on just one floor) and the number of people who evaded the tax was greater there than anywhere else. Sharing is implied where two or three names are joined in the same entry. The best guide to these problems is K. Schürer and T. Arkell, eds., *Surveying the People* (Leopard's Head Press, 1992).

Generally speaking, the number of hearths reflected the size of the building and thus the wealth and standing of the household.

The Great Fire of London, 1666, with hearth tax return for part of the City of London. Halfway down the right-hand column is the entry for Thomas Farrinor, baker, and his oven in Pudding Lane where the fire began.

However, some large, old houses might have contained unheated rooms that had not yet been improved, whereas smaller, modern houses would have been provided with chimneys, and in the towns some of the buildings with a large number of hearths might have been inns. Occasionally, a house was noted as being extended or demolished. Owners paid the tax on empty houses.

The hearth tax returns show that every county in England had a large group of surnames that were not found, or appeared only rarely, in other counties. If we look at the Dorset returns we will find such names as Gallop, Samways, Snook, Squab and Sturmy; if we turn to Derbyshire we find different names such as Bagshaw, Greatorex, Kinder and Ollerenshaw. Greatorex comes from Great Rocks farm, Wormhill, high in

Welsh Surnames in the Staffordshire Hearth Tax, 1666*

	Seisdon	Offlow	Cuttlestone	Totmanslow	Pirehill	Total
Jones	13	6	8	1	11	39
Evans	15	3	4	8	6	36
Griffen	6	14	0	0	9	29
Price	7	7	1	0	5	20
Powell	11	0	0	0	4	15
Onyons	6	6	1	0	1	14
Gough	5	0	6	0	2	13
Welch	3	0	4	2	2	11
Lloyd, Floyd	11	5	1	2	1	2
Morgan	1	4	0	0	4	9
Craddock	0	1	1	1	4	7
Meredith	3	0	2	0	2	7
Flint	0	3	0	0	2	5
Bevan	0	0	3	0	0	3
Griffiths	0	0	0	0	2	2
Davyes	0	0	2	0	0	2
Owen	1	0	0	0	0	1
Rice	0	0	0	1	0	1
Binnion	0	0	1	0	0	1
Gettinges	0	0	0	0	1	0
Vaughan	0	0	0	0	1	1
Mould	1	0	0	0	0	1
Howell	0	1	0	0	0	1
Conway	0	0	0	0	1	1
Evan Rogers	1	0	0	0	0	1
Evan ap Omfre	1	0	0	0	0	1
Total	**79**	**46**	**35**	**14**	**59**	**233**

* *Not included*: Edwards, Phillips, Roberts and Williams, some of which may have originated on the Welsh side of the border. Griffin Ap Evan (Bilsdon) and John Appeaven (Rocester) have been included under Evans.

Swynnerton Constablewicke adew

Acton adew / Hearthes Chargeable

Widdow Hawton	Two
Anne Hammond	One
Richard Holland	One
John Sharpley	One

Beech

Mr Ralph Broston	Sixe
George Walton	One
John Walton	One
Thomas Lawnder	ffoure
William Palyn	One
Stephen Playnt	Two
William Beere	Three
Ralph Watkin	One
Walter Collyer	Three
Richard Pea	One
William Wotton	One

Yearnfeild

Anne Swynnorton	One
Richard Swynnorton	One
Thomas Harde	One
William Tayar	Two
John Playnt	One
Thomas Playnt	One
Thomas Beeabridge	One
John Hitcrofte	Foure
William Palyn	Three
Thomas Underwood	One
Widdow Gerue	Two
Richard Hanssley	Two

Betley Constablewicke

Landes Egerton Esqr	Sixe
Mrs Elizabeth Egerton	ffive

These followinge are Listed for not to be Chargeable accordinge to the Acte as aforesaid viz:

Hearth tax return for Swynnerton and Betley constablewicks, Pirehill hundred, north-west Staffordshire, 1666.

the Peak District; the place-name means 'great valley' and it was recorded in 1251 as Greatrackes. Twenty households of Greatorexes (various spellings) were taxed in Derbyshire in 1670, but none was recorded in the neighbouring counties of Nottinghamshire or Yorkshire. Nor did those counties have any Bowdens, whereas Derbyshire had 26, mostly in High Peak hundred; Mr Bowden was taxed on eight hearths in Bowden Chapel (or Chapel-en-le-Frith) and two other Bowdens were assessed in the same township. Most of the other Bowdens lived nearby. Such patterns and their implications for discovering where a family name originated are discussed in detail in D. Hey and G. Redmonds, *Yorkshire Surnames and the Hearth Tax Returns of 1672–73* (York: Borthwick Paper, No. 102, 2002).

Protestation returns, 1641–2

An engraving of a minister and his parishioners taking the Oath of Protestation.

The protestation returns of 1641–2, which are kept in the library of the House of Lords, list all males aged 18 and over who subscribed to an oath 'to live and die for the true Protestant religion, the liberties and rights of subjects, and the privilege of Parliaments'. The oath was read out in parish churches after services, and lists of those who signed (and the Catholics who did not) were made by churchwardens and constables. Unfortunately, the returns for several counties such as Leicestershire and Norfolk are missing and others are incomplete. For instance, the returns for the Yorkshire wapentake of Agbrigg survive, but those for its southern neighbours do not. A full list of surviving returns is given in J. Gibson and A. Dell, *The Protestation Returns, 1641–2* (FFHS, 1995). The returns for some counties, such as Durham, Nottinghamshire or Lincolnshire, have been published with indexes.

The protestation return for the parish of Callington, Cornwall, 1641, with the signatures and marks of the male parishioners aged 18 and above.

The surviving lists appear to be remarkably comprehensive and so are a great aid to family historians who are trying to locate an ancestor just before the Civil War. Those for Lincolnshire, for example, contain about 33,000 names. The returns are not a complete record of families, however, for a father might have died before his sons reached the age of 18. My ancestors do not appear in the Kirkburton parish list in Agbrigg wapentake for that reason. Protestation returns do not provide as full a record of local surnames as do the hearth tax returns, which name widows who were heads of households, but they are full enough to give an idea of the distribution of a name over a county. As Lincolnshire does not have a published hearth tax return, the printed protestation list is a valuable source for this exercise. It allows us to see, for example, that the Brumbys lived within a few miles of the village that had produced their name, in the north-western part of Lindsey, whereas the Lusbys had moved north from their village and had clustered near Grimsby. The Jeckills were neighbours of the Lusbys; the Crusts and Farmerys knew the Brumbys; but the Ancells, Gambles and Peppers lived in the south of the county, many miles away. These distributions suggest the likely range of parish registers that need to be searched in tracing such families and often provide a clue as to where they originated.

Muster rolls and militia lists

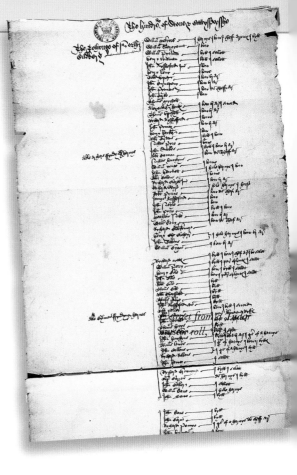

Muster rolls

From ancient times, whenever an invasion was feared, able-bodied men aged between 16 and 60 were liable for service in the local defence force, or militia. The earliest surviving list of names was drawn up in 1522. Most of the Tudor and Stuart muster rolls are kept at the National Archives (within the Exchequer or State Papers Domestic divisions), though some have survived in local record offices amongst the private papers of those local gentry families who served as commissioners of array or deputy lieutenant. Their whereabouts are listed in J. Gibson and A. Dell, *Tudor and Stuart Muster Rolls: A Directory of Holdings in the British Isles* (FFHS, 1991). The National Archives has a leaflet, *Tudor and Stuart Local Soldiery: Militia Muster Rolls*, available through the online catalogue.

Muster rolls list the names of the men who were liable to be called upon and the equipment they had to provide. In 1626, for example, my ancestor John Hey had to bring his musket along. The rolls do not give all the names of local men, for they omit the old and the infirm and those who were too poor to provide their own equipment. Where they survive, early Tudor rolls can prove the existence of a family name within a particular parish or district before the earliest parish register. Some county record societies, including those for Bedfordshire, Buckinghamshire and Rutland, have published their earliest rolls. The best known is J. Smith, *Men and Armour for Gloucestershire in 1608* (Gloucester, Sutton, 1980), which records 19,402 men by name, age, occupation, and parish. The rolls are useful for spotting ancestors and for mapping the distribution of surnames across a county.

Militia lists

Fear of foreign invasion seemed very real in the middle years of the eighteenth century. France was an ever-present threat

Extract from a muster roll of 1539 for the tithing of North Cadbury in the hundred of Stone and Catsash, Somerset.

'City trained bands', a caricature engraved by John Nixon and published by Edward Harding, depicting the militia men who lined the streets of London from Temple Bar to St Paul's Cathedral when George III processed to a thanksgiving service in 1789.

and Bonnie Prince Charlie's Highlanders had got as far south as Derby in 1745, so in 1757 Parliament re-established the militia and ordered that each parish should train a group of able-bodied men aged 18 to 50 (lowered to 45 in 1762). These groups were chosen by ballot from lists drawn up by the constables of each township and forwarded to the lord-lieutenants of the counties. Where they survive, they tend to be found amongst private papers that have been deposited in local record offices. See J. Gibson and M. Medlycott, *Militia Lists and Musters, 1757–1876: A Directory of Holdings in the British Isles* (FFHS, 1994) and W. Spencer, *Records of the Militia and Volunteer Forces, 1757–1945* (Public Record Office, 1997).

Militia lists compiled under the Act of 1757 survive for several counties, including Cumberland, Dorset, Kent and Lincolnshire, or for smaller units such as hundreds or wapentakes or individual parishes or cities

(see Gibson and Medlycott). The returns for Hertfordshire (1758–65) are gradually being published by the Hertfordshire Family and Population History Society, and V. A. Hatley edited *Northamptonshire Militia Lists, 1777* for the Northamptonshire Record Society in 1973. Some militia lists have been published commercially on CD-ROM. The *Posse Comitatus* lists of 1798 and the *Levée en Masse* lists of 1803–4, drawn up at the time of war with France, are similar in appearance to the militia ballot lists, but Buckinghamshire is the only county with a complete return. This list of 23,500 men has been published as F. W. Beckett, *The Buckinghamshire Posse Comitatus, 1798* (Buckinghamshire Record Society, 1973). Occasionally, lists turn up amongst parish records. The chapelry of Bradfield (Yorkshire), for instance, has a set for each year between 1819 and 1831; they record the name, occupation, age, and residence of each man and state the grounds for all exemptions.

FINDING YOUR ANCESTORS

An Act of 1802 divided the able-bodied poor into four classes, who would be called upon in order if the occasion arose: (1) men under 30 having no children; (2) men above 30 having no children; (3) men aged between 18 and 45 with no children under 14; (4) men aged between 18 and 45 having children under 14. The best lists include the men who were exempted from service: peers, clergymen, Quakers, articled clerks, apprentices, seamen, soldiers, and parish constables, and in some ballots judges, medical practitioners, and licensed teachers. Exemption from service was also granted on the grounds of poverty, for it was not considered sensible to force a poor man to serve in the militia only to find that his wife and children had then to be kept on the parish rates. Precise definitions of 'poor' and 'infirm' were not provided by the various Acts, but the constables were supposed to write their reasons for allowing exemptions, e.g. 'Blind of 1 eye', 'Lame', 'both legs broke', and 'lost a finger & 2 bad legs'. Many other men were recorded as having already served by ballot or as volunteers, or as substitutes for others who had been chosen by ballot. Of the 3,322 men listed in the 1806 returns for Staincross wapentake (Yorkshire), 1,763 were exempt from service. Those whose names were selected by ballot had the option of paying someone else to serve in their place. Those exempted on grounds of poverty were not always recorded. The overall impression is that most of the township returns were reasonably accurate, but standards varied according to the diligence of the constable.

As militia returns note the occupations of the men, they show how very different in character neighbouring townships could be, with neat estate villages alongside sprawling industrial communities. We can see how family names were distributed within a hundred or a county and sometimes we can identify an ancestor. My great-great-grandfather, John Hey, was listed as a young weaver in Thurlstone township in the Staincross wapentake returns in both 1804 and 1806. These were my first records of his having moved from his birthplace in the neighbouring township of Shelley, some five miles to the north.

Militia list for Thurlstone township, Staincross wapentake, Yorkshire, 1806; the entry for John Hey is highlighted.

Courts of Chancery, Exchequer, Star Chamber, and Requests

Interior view of Lincoln's Inn showing the Court of Chancery in session, by Augustus Charles Pugin and Thomas Rowlandson, published by Rudolph Ackermann, 1808.

The indexes to several series in the copious records of legal disputes in the Court of Chancery, held at the National Archives, are now much more accessible through the catalogue at <www.nationalarchives.gov.uk>. This has transformed searching from the laborious task that it used to be. Simple name or place-name searches bring up many references to lawsuits in 'C'. In particular, the catalogue has revealed the wealth of information in the suits in C 1, covering the period *c.* 1386 to *c.* 1558, which are well catalogued. The catalogue also allows the search of C 3, covering 1484 to 1690, and part of C 4, which ranges from the reign of Edward I to *c.* 1790. It provides

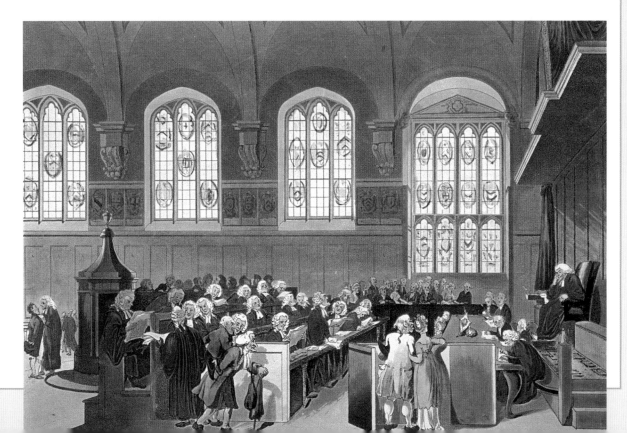

the names of plaintiffs and defendants and the witnesses that were called. Forenames have been standardized, surnames are recorded as written.

A. Hanson, 'A Litigant in the Family', *Ancestors*, 13 (April–May, 2003) explains the progress of a case through Chancery. The procedure involved the gathering of written pleadings and evidence. The arguments of the parties were set out at length and the witnesses drew on their long memories to make 'depositions' which are the equivalent to the oral history of recent times. Over the centuries the Lord Chancellor or his deputies heard thousands of disputes over a wide range of matters, including inheritance and wills, lands, trusts, debts, marriage settlements, apprenticeships, and so on. The documents provide vivid insights into the daily lives and concerns of ordinary families and sometimes record descents over the generations. Women were as litigious as men. Most Chancery records are in English. The early ones are neat, but many are in the difficult Secretary hand of the sixteenth century.

Indexes to the 43,000 or so documents in C 6/1 to C 6/359, dating from 1625 to 1714 can be searched through the catalogue at <www.nationalarchives.gov.uk>. These provide the names of the parties, the date, the subject, and the county, but they do not name witnesses. Much fuller information is given in the indexes for C 6/360 to C 6/419, dating from about 1680 to 1714. See D. Gerhold, 'Searching for Justice: Chancery Records on the Internet', *Ancestors* 13 (Apr/May 2003), which looks at 67 cases from Putney between 1580 and 1735, and H. Horwitz, *Chancery Equity*

Records and Proceedings, 1600–1800 (Public Record Office, 1995).

In the mid-sixteenth century the Court of Exchequer developed an equity jurisdiction to rival that of Chancery. Its business included disputes over titles of land, manorial rights, tithes, mineral rights, ex-monastic land, debts, wills, etc. In practice, any suit that could be brought in Chancery could equally well be brought in the Exchequer, where it was dealt with much more quickly. A keyword search of E 134 on the catalogue lists the documents at the National Archives, but the index is limited to the plaintiffs and defendants and does not include the names of the witnesses.

Star Chamber became a separate court of law in 1485 and its business expanded considerably throughout the sixteenth century. It was abolished in 1641. Cases brought to Star Chamber were shaped as offences against public order, but many of them were actually private disputes about property rights. The procedures were similar to those of Chancery and the Exchequer and the main series of records are in English. Most cases can be searched for on the catalogue.

The Court of Requests, an offshoot of the King's Council, existed over a similar period, 1483–1642. It aimed to give poor people access to royal justice and equity by providing a cheap and simple procedure. It attracted many suitors, especially women, though not all of them were poor. The procedures were like those of the equity courts and the records are in English. The catalogues are not yet searchable online.

The legal profession

BROWNE's
General Law List
For the Year 1799,
WITH THE
NAMES AND RESIDENCES
OF ALL THE

JUDGES and SERJEANTS,
KING'S COUNSEL & BARRISTERS
PROVINCIAL COUNSEL,
JUSTICES under the POLICE ACT,
EQUITY-DRAFTSMEN,
SPECIAL-PLEADERS,
CONVEYANCERS,
BENCHERS of the INNS of COURT
UNDER-SHERIFFS and AGENTS,
ATTORNEYS, from the Rolls,
Register and Certificate Books
PUBLIC NOTARIES,
OFFICERS of the LAW-COURTS,
MASTERS IN CHANCERY, and
Provincial Extra ditto,
COMMISSIONERS of BANKRUPTS

DOCTORS and PROCTORS,
LORD-MAYOR, ALDERMEN,
CITY-COMPANIES, &c.
PEERS, ENGLISH and SCOTS,
HOUSE of COMMONS, shewing
the various Qualifications, and
Number of Votes.
HIGH-STEWARDS, RECORDERS,
TREASURERS, CLERKS of the
PEACE, CORONERS, and TOWN-
CLERKS,
CIVIL and LAW OFFICES, and
Holydays kept at Each,
LAW-STAMPS and LICENCES,
COFFEE-HOUSES, in LONDON,
and by whom Kept,

LONDON NEWS-PAPERS, and where Published, &c. &c.
ENGLISH and WELCH CIRCUITS, with the JUDGES,
SERJEANTS, COUNSEL, &c.
Circuits they go, and the Towns where the Assizes are held.
A LIST of CITIES, BOROUGHS, CINQUE PORTS, TOWNS,
MARKET TOWNS and VILLAGES, in England and Wales,
Market Days; Distances from London, Postage of Letters,
Stage Coaches, with the Times & Places they go from London

THE EIGHTEENTH EDITION,
WITH GREAT IMPROVEMENTS.
Corrected at all the respective OFFICES, to the present Time.

LONDON:
PRINTED and SOLD by the EDITOR, and Sole Proprietor
in BRIDE-LANE.
SOLD ALSO BY
J. BUTTERWORTH, FLEET-STREET.
(Price Four Shillings, Bound in Red, Gilt and Lettered.)

The best recorded profession is that of the law. The admission registers of the major lawyers' inns note a student's age, his father's occupation and address, and the date when he was called to the Bar. They have been published as H. A. C. Sturgess, *Registers of Admissions to the Honourable Society of the Middle Temple from the 15th Century to 1944*, 3 vols (Butterworth, 1949), J. Foster, *The Registers of Admissions to Gray's Inn, 1521–1889, together with the Marriages in Gray's Inn Chapel, 1695–1754* (Hansard Publishing Union, 1889), *The Records of the Honourable Society of Lincoln's Inn: vol. I from 1420 to 1799, vol. II Admissions from 1800 to 1893 and Chapel Registers* (Lincoln's Inn, 1896), and *Students Admitted to the Inner Temple, 1547–1660* (Inner Temple, 1877); the admission books for later periods are at the Inner Temple library.

The names of solicitors (who until 1873 were also known as attorneys at law) appear in published lists from the late eighteenth century onwards, especially as *The Law List*, from 1797 to 1976. Copies are held at the National Archives, the Guildhall Library, and (for records from 1812) at the Society of Genealogists.

Title deeds

Title deeds can be complex documents, as is shown by the contract of sale, indemnity and mortgage of Mr J. H. McClure's property in 1880–81.

Title deeds are legal documents which transfer property or rights from one person (or institution) to another. Huge collections of title deeds that were formerly held by solicitors have been deposited at local record offices, and most of these have been calendared. The enormous numbers of deeds at the National Archives are held in various series and are more difficult to access as they do not form a single collection. In the early eighteenth century voluntary registries of deeds were established in the three ridings of Yorkshire and in Middlesex. The deeds, which were copied into bound volumes and indexed both by personal name and by place-name,

are now available for consultation. The West Riding registered deeds for 1704–1970 are housed at the West Yorkshire Archive Service, Wakefield, the East Riding deeds of 1708–1974 are at the East Yorkshire Record Office, Beverley, and those for the North Riding from 1736 to 1970 are kept at the North Yorkshire Record Office at Northallerton. The deeds that were registered in Middlesex between 1709 and 1938 have been transferred to the London Metropolitan Archives.

Title deeds often begin with the words 'This Indenture' in large, flowing letters, followed by the date of the transaction, the names and places of residence of the vendors and purchasers, the agreed price, some description of the property, and (from 1840) a plan. Under the heading 'abstracts of title', they sometimes summarize previous sales of the property and in so doing may give brief details of family history. The names and signatures of the witnesses come at the end. The best introduction to an understanding of these documents is N. W. Alcock, *Old Title Deeds: A Guide for Local and Family Historians* (Phillimore, 1986).

A 'deed of bargain and sale' was a sixteenth-century method of conveying property by a private agreement that had

been drawn up by a lawyer. From 1614 this method was gradually replaced by 'lease and release', whereby land was transferred from one party to another without the necessity of enrolling a deed in a central court. The purchaser avoided the need to enrol by first taking a one-year lease of the property, then on the following day the vendor conveyed to him the reversion of the lease. The records of the transaction consisted of two documents, the lease and the release. The method remained popular until the 1840s. Large collections of deeds relating to mortgages also survive from the early modern period, when obtaining a loan upon the mortgage of a property was a common form of credit.

Part of a sale indenture of 1753, showing the typically wordy nature of such documents.

iudicia tua

Quoniam

super omne

tis es super

4 Back to the Middle Ages (—1550)

She, for her part, does not hide her opinion that the only kind of superiority she values is that of having ancestors who took part in the Crusades. Money comes only a long way behind.

Stendhal, *Scarlet and Black* (1830)

EXPLORING YOUR PAST

Introduction	246
The Black Death	248
Families	252
Houses	254
The countryside	256
Towns	258
Stability and mobility	262
The origins of surnames	266

FINDING YOUR ANCESTORS

Manor court records	272
Subsidies and poll taxes	280
Other medieval records in print	284
Heraldry	286

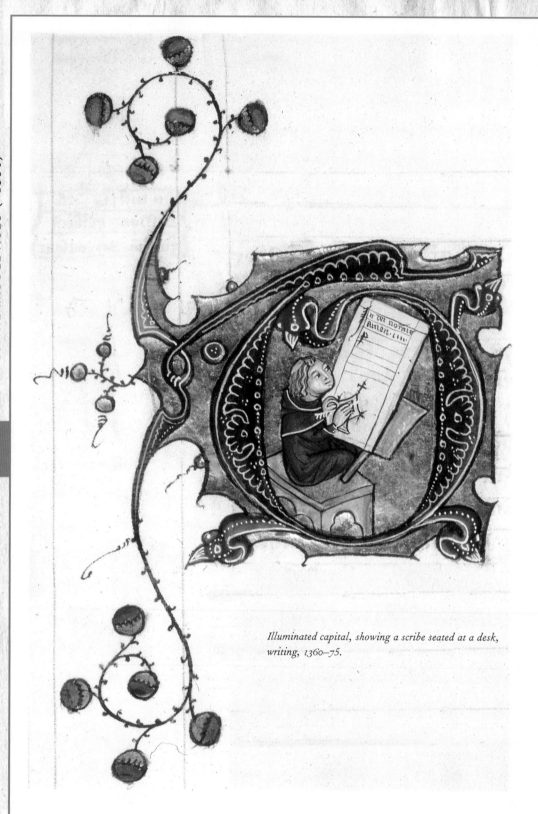

Illuminated capital, showing a scribe seated at a desk, writing, 1360–75.

Introduction

When Edward and Joan Palley of South Croxton, Leicestershire were involved in a case in the Court of Chancery in the 1530s they recited Joan's pedigree going back over seven generations to a Robert Randolf. The accuracy of this claim is supported by the appearance of this Robert as a South Croxton husbandman in the poll tax return for 1377. Other records show that the family were there at least 50 years earlier. The Palleys were not alone in having long memories of their families. Knowing who your ancestors were was a common accomplishment in the late Middle Ages, especially if you were concerned to prove your right to a property through descent from a long line of owners.

These memories were passed down orally. Few people other than clerics had the ability to write before the reign of Queen Elizabeth and even then handwritten family histories are rare. This information that was passed down by word of mouth is lost to us and without it we cannot now prove a descent, step by step back into the Middle Ages, unless our predecessors were great landowners or we are exceptionally fortunate in finding that a long and detailed series of manor court rolls have been preserved. Usually, we have to be content with finding unlinked references to our surname and with deciphering its meaning and its place of origin. Most English surnames were fixed by the end of the fourteenth century, though many have assumed different forms since. The Welsh had their own naming system in the Middle Ages and rarely took English-style surnames until after the Act of Union of 1536. Locating the home of a family name takes us as far back as we can get, but for people with common surnames even this achievement often remains elusive.

IN BRIEF

- In the Middle Ages family memories were passed down orally and went a long way back.
- We can rarely trace a family line step by step back into the Middle Ages unless our ancestors were great landowners.
- But we can often locate the place where our surname originated.

The Black Death

The population of England and Wales during the Middle Ages cannot be measured with certainty, but the general trends are clear. Estimates for the late eleventh century, based on the imprecise figures in the Domesday Book, range from 1.5 to 2.25 million people. During the next two centuries these numbers rose considerably so that by 1300 the national population was at least 4 million and some historians believe it was much higher, at about 5 or even 6 million. This was the time when new towns were founded, old towns and villages expanded, and many new farmsteads were created on the edges of the moors, woods and fens. The majority of the medieval population of England and Wales lived in small family farms, their mental world extending no further than the vague boundaries of their 'country'. This world was shattered in the fourteenth century, first by a series of harvest failures and livestock disasters in the second decade and then by the mysterious, virulent epidemic known to us as the Black Death.

The plague arrived on the Dorset coast in 1348 and spread rapidly through the country during the next two years. By then, it had reduced the national population by at least a third and possibly by a half. The evidence of some manor court rolls is that the proportion of peasant farmers who died was

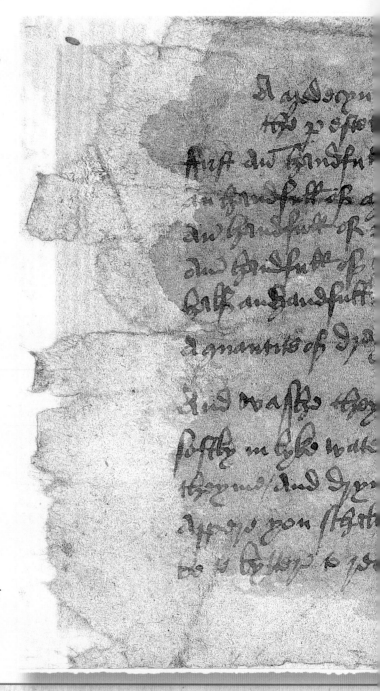

TRANSCRIPTION

First an handful of Rewe
an handful of Maregoldes
an handful of Burnett
an handful of Sorell
half an handful of Fetherfoy
a quantite of drag[enc?] of the Croppys or elles of the rotts And wasshe
theyme Feyer in Rynnyng water, And Seth them softly in lyke water frome a
potell [?] aquart. And then streyne theym, And drynk hit. And if ye drynk
byfore the purpylles appere you schall have remedy. And if the foresaid
medecyn be as bytter to receive then put thereto a little sugar candy to aley hit.

A fifteenth- or sixteenth-century recipe for
'A medecyn ayenst the pestelence'.

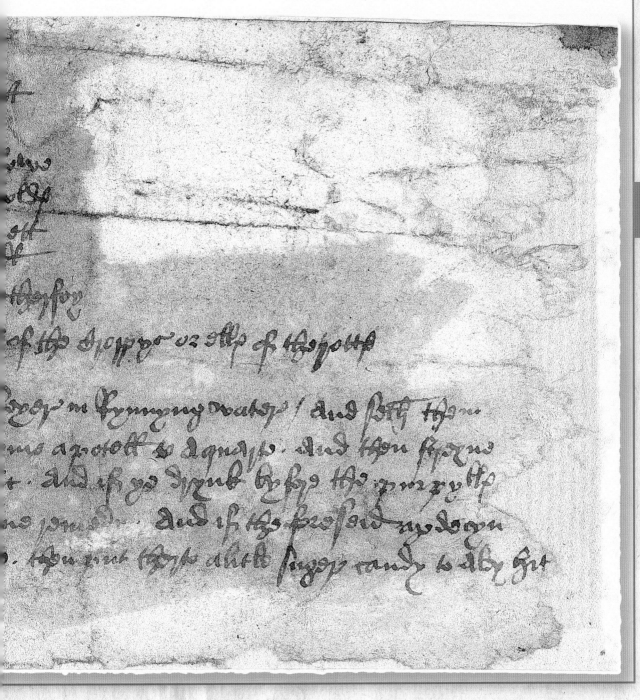

over 40 per cent and in some places it was as high as 70 per cent. Most families lost at least one member and the tradition that 50,000 corpses had to be buried in London may be correct. Decayed farmhouses, cottages and outbuildings became a common sight, though very few villages or hamlets were completely destroyed by the plague. Although the chroniclers at the time do not suggest that society was paralysed by the loss of life, the long-term effects were profound.

The population failed to recover because this new plague became endemic, breaking out again in 1361–2, when it killed another 10–15 per cent of the population, most of whom were too young to have immunity, and again in 1375. Localized outbreaks occurred in most parts of England once in every ten years from the 1390s until well

after 1500. Nor was plague the only killer disease of the time. Tuberculosis was an ever-present threat, dysentery may have been responsible for the high number of deaths in 1473, and the 'sweating sickness', which was perhaps a virulent form of influenza, arrived in 1485 and came back repeatedly until its last and worst outbreak in the late 1550s. People who lived in towns may have suffered worst, but unpredictable epidemics posed an ever-present threat in the countryside as well. By 1380 the national population had fallen to between 2.2 and 3 million. Few records are available on which to estimate levels in the late Middle Ages, but by 1500 England and Wales may have had only about half as many people as they had 200 years earlier.

Manorial court rolls reveal that in the 1350s large numbers of farms lay 'in the lord's

hands', in other words tenants could not be found for them. This novel situation provided the survivors with opportunities for advancement. Younger brothers found that they were now the senior members of a family, or sons came to their inheritance sooner than they had expected. On 18 May 1350 my probable ancestor, Richard son of Alan del Hey, inherited the tenancy of the farm in Scammonden (West Yorkshire) – from which the surname is derived – after the death of his elder brother Thomas del Hey. Men who had once been landless labourers and servants were sometimes able to become farmers, though they had to struggle to raise the money to buy equipment and livestock and pay their rents. The better-off tenants who survived had the resources to take on extra land, perhaps a whole new farm, and so to begin the family's rise from servile status to the ranks of the yeomen. The Elmhirsts of Hound Hill (South Yorkshire), who were parish gentry by the eighteenth century, were descended from Robert of Elmhirst, a serf of the manor in 1340. In lowland England other families rose in status by taking a lease of the lord's demesne or of a monastic grange where lay brothers were no longer available to do the work.

A fourteenth-century engraving of 'The Black Death'.

The dramatic fall in the level of population weakened the grip of lords of the manor on their tenants. In the last two decades of the fourteenth century, in particular, increasing numbers of people moved to better prospects in other manors. Those who remained were usually able to negotiate better deals, in the form of lower entry fines and rents and the abolition or conversion of labour services and other dues into money payments. Wage earners also benefited, for

IN BRIEF

- The plague of 1348–50 reduced the national population by at least a third and possibly by a half.

- Plague remained endemic and other epidemics kept population levels low, so that by 1500 England and Wales may have had only about half as many people as they had 200 years earlier.

- Those who survived found that they had better opportunities to obtain a higher standard of living.

they were no longer tied to yearly contracts but could earn more from short-term employment or from day labour. Real wages rose markedly from 1375, when corn became abundant and grain prices fell. The unemployment and under-employment that had caused so much hardship in the first half of the fourteenth century disappeared. Another consequence of the new situation was that women had the chance to earn more and to establish better rights to property.

These changes were not universal, however. At the end of the fourteenth century tens of thousands of tenants still held their farms by hereditary tenure according to the customs of the manor. Although a higher proportion of farms now measured 30 to 60 acres, farms of 100 acres or more remained quite rare. Peasants probably had difficulty in finding labour, either from within their own families or by hiring workers, to farm such large acreages. Other men were able to combine a craft with a smallholding. In central Essex, for instance, nearly half of the land (both before and after the plagues) was farmed in smallholdings of less than five acres, perhaps because so many tenants were employed in the local textile industry.

Families

Curiously, the average age at which people died seems to have fallen steadily during the fifteenth century, even though the worst of the calamities were over. Studies of Essex manors suggest that in the late fourteenth century peasants could expect to live for another 42 years if they reached the age of 12, but three generations later this average had fallen to 36. Yet cheap bread was widely available, more people enjoyed a balanced diet with a higher proportion of meat and fish, diseases associated with a poor diet, such as leprosy, were in decline, and no great increases in deaths were reported during the last great medieval famine, from 1437 to 1440, except in regions where an outbreak of plague coincided with the food shortages.

The fifteenth century is a difficult period to study, for it has not left abundant records

A man shapes dough into loaves and the baker places them in his oven, from 'The Smithfield Decretals', c. 1340.

IN BRIEF

☞ Medieval people did not usually marry until they were well into their twenties, and many people did not marry at all.

☞ The average family consisted of parents and two children. Households rarely contained more than two generations.

☞ Wealthier households were larger because they had living-in servants and perhaps more children because of earlier marriage.

from which we can obtain firm statistics. Before parish registers began in 1538, we do not have enough evidence to answer basic questions with any certainty. It seems that families were small, often with just parents and two children. High rates of infant and child mortality took their toll, couples did not marry until they were well into their

*'Conversation in Front of the Fire',
painting by an Italian artist, from a
fourteenth-century manuscript.*

twenties and many people did not marry at all. What is certain is that households rarely contained more then two generations, unless an elderly grandparent was being looked after. A census of the inhabitants of the city of Coventry in 1523 revealed that only three of the 1,302 households in the city contained members of more than two generations and that only one per cent of all households contained adult relatives of any sort. Ten years later, a list of about 51,000 people in the archdeaconry of Stafford, arranged in family groups, shows that only about 10 per cent of the families included relatives other than spouses or children. Most of these relatives were the parents of the head, and as many of these were dead (for the list was concerned with souls) this figure should be reduced considerably. The small, nuclear household has long been the usual form in England. The poll tax returns of 1377–81 confirm its ubiquity in an earlier century and we have no evidence that extended family households under the same roof were ever common.

Of course, average figures mask the diversity of experience within local communities. The size of a particular household varied in time, as new children arrived and others left home. It was also affected by the wealth or poverty of the head. Wealthier households were larger because they had greater numbers of living-in servants and perhaps more children through marrying earlier. The composition of late-medieval households seems to have been very similar to what it was in Tudor and Stuart times. By the time that parish registers begin, the pattern was well established.

Houses

The peasant families that had the resources and the opportunities to increase the size of their farms in the decades following the Black Death began to build the fine late-medieval houses that still adorn many parts of the English and Welsh countryside. The new technique of dendrochronology has shown that these farmhouses were erected in growing numbers from 1380, but especially from 1440 onwards. The accommodation that they provided was superior to that which had been available to previous generations. In the wealthy south-east the better-quality houses commonly had a chamber at first-floor level, which enabled families to live away from the dirt of the farmyard. Town houses were also built to a higher standard, and urban authorities carted rubbish to communal middens and provided piped water for household use or for flushing away dirt. The leading peasant families were now able to buy more furnishings and household equipment and better clothes. They also ate wheat bread and more meat and fish. The families for whom these houses were built cannot usually be identified, but the more prosperous ones had started to call themselves franklins and yeomen and some were the owners of small manors.

The quality and the survival rate of late-medieval peasant houses varies considerably across the land. Thousands of examples in Kent, Essex and Suffolk used sophisticated carpentry techniques. Best of all are the 350 or so Wealden houses that date from 1400 to the 1530s and whose standard design is masked by different sizes and a variety of decoration. In contrast, few, if any, medieval farmhouses survive in Cornwall, west Wales, the East Midlands, or the northern counties other than Yorkshire. Within each region, however, there are also marked differences of standard from one 'country' to another and between the various social groups in the same parish. The pattern of surviving peasant houses was largely determined by the distribution of wealth in the late Middle Ages, but it was also influenced by the availability or

---

IN BRIEF

- Large numbers of late-medieval houses survive in the English and Welsh countryside and in some towns.

- But the quality and the survival rate of peasant houses varies considerably across the land. The best ones are in Kent, Essex and East Anglia.

- The use of local materials gives the houses of each district a distinctive appearance, though they were built to the same plan.

- The timber-frame tradition continued into the seventeenth century.

otherwise of suitable timber. Supplies were short in the East Midlands counties, but plentiful on the borders of England and Wales. Cornwall had little timber, but it did have suitable stone, so the lack of surviving medieval farmhouses must be the result of its poverty. Neighbouring Devon was much more prosperous and its numerous medieval farmhouses were built with granite or cob walls, and with massive timber doors and roofs.

The changing appearance of vernacular buildings across the land disguises the similarity of their plans. The larger peasant farmhouses were simplified versions of the homes of the gentry. They were arranged around an open hall of almost standard width but varied length, which was entered from a cross-passage that divided it from the kitchen and perhaps other service rooms. The private quarters, which were situated at the other end of the hall, consisted of an inner room, or parlour, which sometimes had a solar above. The smaller farmhouses just had three rooms in a line – kitchen, hall, parlour – open to the rafters, where a louvre allowed the smoke to escape. Away from the more prosperous south-east, many of these humbler farmhouses were constructed with a cruck frame. The earliest known examples are cottages in the Oxfordshire villages of Harwell, Steventon and Radley, which are thirteenth-century in part, and a complete example survives at Mapledurham in the same county, which is dated 1335. The use of cruck frames continued well into the seventeenth century, but most of the cottages of the poorest section of society have long been demolished.

The Suffolk market town of Lavenham retains a remarkable collection of timber-framed buildings from the late-medieval period. They have a jettied upper storey and their posts are arranged in the 'close-studding' method that was typical of East Anglia.

The countryside

Throughout the Middle Ages, peasant farmers spent much of their time ploughing, sowing, weeding and harvesting cereals and raising small numbers of livestock. Farming techniques did not change fundamentally during the Middle Ages, and although surpluses were produced for the market most produce was consumed on the farm. Millions of acres were cultivated in open fields under communal supervision through the manor courts, especially in the counties that formed the central spine of England, from Yorkshire down to Dorset, but even in the highland and wood-pasture districts, where the corn fields were smaller, few farmers were able to concentrate on sheep- or cattle-rearing or on dairying. Whichever part of the country they were from, medieval farmers practised mixed husbandry. The typical farm was small or medium-sized, and nearly all the labour was provided by members of the family. Although freehold tenure was widespread, much of the land was held by copyholders who paid entry fines on acquiring a holding, a heriot when they died or left, and rents

IN BRIEF

- Most people earned their living from a small or medium-sized farm. Nearly all the labour was provided by members of the family.
- As the population declined, thousands of villages, hamlets and farmsteads shrank or became deserted.
- In pastoral districts many farmers also worked at a craft or in a rural industry.
- The wealth of some communities is demonstrated by England's fine collection of medieval churches.

that had been fixed in the fourteenth century.

A marginal illustration from the Luttrell Psalter, c. 1325–35, showing a horse-drawn harrow. The slinger to the left has missed his target, for his stone passes between the crows.

Thousands of villages, hamlets and farmsteads shrank or became deserted in the late Middle Ages as peasants moved away in search of economic opportunities and better lifestyles. Lords tried to assert the authority of their manor courts to prevent this migration, fearing the loss of regular income from rents, but often their efforts were to no avail. The smaller settlements fared the worst. The villages that were eventually abandoned are now plaintive features of the landscape in Leicestershire, Northamptonshire, Oxfordshire and Warwickshire, and to a lesser extent of other counties in the central belt, but many of the estimated half-million houses that were abandoned between the 1320s and the 1520s were not in villages but in scattered settlements elsewhere.

As the population began to recover, some of the abandoned farms were reclaimed and land was once again taken in from the edges of the woods, moors and fens. Manorial records note the 'assarts', 'intakes' or 'stubbings' that were cleared piecemeal and the new rents that were paid. Some of these clearances were added to existing farms, others formed the nucleus of new farms for younger sons. The right to feed livestock on the common pastures and to collect fuel were essential assets for all farming families. In pastoral districts many were able to combine agriculture with a craft. By the late Middle Ages clothmaking was a flourishing trade in eastern England, the Cotswolds and the West Riding of Yorkshire, the tin industry was prospering in Devon and Cornwall, and by 1540 John Leland could note the many smiths and cutlers of Hallamshire.

The combined wealth of many rural communities in the late Middle Ages, particularly those whose industries continued to flourish, is evident from their magnificent parish churches. Some parishes had rich lords of the manor or local merchants to act as benefactors, but all the parishioners were expected to help raise money by gifts or at church ales and May games. The magnificent church at Lavenham (Suffolk) owes much to the patronage of the Earl of Oxford, its lord of the manor, and to the Spring family, the wealthiest merchants outside London, but at nearby Long Melford an inscription on the church tells us that contributions came from 'all the well-disposed men of this town'. Where insufficient wealth was available for a complete rebuilding, a tower might be added or the nave redesigned with aisles and porches and a range of clerestory windows, while the interior was embellished with screens, images and wall paintings. In all parts of the land we can find splendid examples of Perpendicular Gothic architecture, the last – and uniquely English – medieval style of church building.

Towns

The rapid growth of the national population between the Norman Conquest and the Black Death encouraged trade and the foundation of market towns, especially in lowland England. New towns such as Boston, Chelmsford and Market Harborough were created around their tapering market-places, other towns such as Ripon and Thirsk have retained huge market squares to this day, and the towns that Edward I planted in the shadow of his new castles at Beaumaris, Caernarvon, Conway and Flint still keep their original shape. Kings, barons, bishops and abbots saw that profits were to be made from founding towns on their manors, in establishing markets and fairs, and by attracting merchants, craftsmen and shopkeepers with special privileges. The leading townsmen in places such as Beverley, Doncaster and Nottingham held their land by burgage tenure, which meant that they were free of the labour services and feudal dues of the typical rural manor; they just paid their rent and were able to pass on their property freely. The most privileged urban centres such as Coventry or York were run by a mayor and corporation, but most medieval towns were 'seigneurial boroughs' like Bakewell or Sheffield, whose burgesses had some independence but who were still dominated by the local lord through the authority of his manor court.

By the time of the Black Death perhaps 15 per cent of the English population lived in towns. Most of these inhabitants (or their ancestors) had been drawn from the surrounding countryside. Even in busy modern towns it is possible to trace the medieval street plan on the ground and to find that old names are still in use. In Pontefract the broad street of Micklegate was the original market-place by the castle, and though the market area of the new borough of West Cheap, created in the 1250s, has been much encroached upon, the surrounding streets preserve their medieval names – Market Place, Wool Market, Shoe Market Street, Corn Market, Beast Fair, Horse Fair, Roper Gate, Salter Row and Middle Row. Chesterfield's market-place still has the shape that it was given in Norman times, Derby has its Market Place, Corn Market and Iron Gate, and Barnsley its Market Hill and May Day Green. In many places, the long, narrow burgage plots of the leading families that stretch back from the central streets are well defined on old maps and are sometimes still evident on the ground.

The plans of some medieval towns are so evident that we must conclude that they were planted on new sites sometime between the Norman Conquest and the Black Death. A famous example is

Salisbury, a new town that was laid out in 1225 on a grid pattern by the cathedral to replace Old Sarum, two miles to the north. These new towns were arranged around a market-place in building plots of a standard shape and size, with designated spaces for religious buildings. The place-names Kingston, Newtown, Newmarket or Newport sometimes indicate their origins, including failed plantations such as Newport (Isle of Wight). On the Sussex coast, the plan of New Winchelsea, which was founded in the 1280s after Old Winchelsea had disappeared under the sea, is preserved perfectly because its founder's hopes of

expansion were disappointed. Elsewhere, old settlements such as Stratford-upon-Avon had a new grid of streets and a market-place grafted on to them, and the most successful towns had new units added when economic opportunities arose.

This period of urban expansion came to an end in the aftermath of the Black Death. The population of Grimsby, for example, had approached 2,000 in 1348, but it shrank to about 1,500 by 1377 and to less than 900 in the early sixteenth century. Comparisons

A bird's eye view of Norwich, 1541, showing the castle, churches, market cross, city walls and gates, and domestic buildings. It was made to show the areas of sanctuary within the city.

of tax returns from 1377 and 1524–5 show that Boston, Lincoln, King's Lynn and York had lost half their inhabitants and that Beverley and Leicester had shrunk considerably. Winchester had 10–12,000 people in 1300, but fewer than 8,000 in 1417 and only about 4,000 in 1524–5. Many places were affected so badly that they could no longer be considered as towns. In Wales a dozen boroughs ceased to function as urban centres and at least nine others withered away completely.

Not all towns fared as badly as these. Judging by the tax records of the 1520s, about 20 per cent of the English population lived in towns, though of course the national level of population was far lower than it had been two centuries earlier. By far the most successful city was London, despite the regular visitation of plague. London had about 50,000 inhabitants in 1377, compared with the 80,000 or so at the beginning of the century, but by the 1520s the population had risen to about 60,000 in the City, with another 3,000 in Westminster, 8–9,000 across the river in Southwark, and an indeterminate number in other extramural suburbs. London was a great centre of trade and manufacture, with numerous 'livery companies' that controlled each craft. Whereas a provincial town would normally have only a single goldsmith, the London Goldsmiths' Company had 210 freemen by 1506. The capital city was the only place in England that attracted immigrants from all parts of the kingdom and the continent of Europe. The poor went there in search of casual employment in unskilled jobs and for the food doles provided by the numerous religious institutions and wealthy private households. Large crowds of paupers gathered at the funerals of merchants in expectation of a generous dole.

In all towns, the merchants ran the government and dominated the craft guilds and religious fraternities. In the late Middle Ages many a town specialized in a particular craft. The poll tax return of 1379 for Thaxted records 249 males, of whom 79 were cutlers, 4 were sheathers, 11 were smiths and 2 were goldsmiths. This specialization was especially noticeable in the clothing trades. At Lavenham, a muster roll of 1522 names 157 heads of households, of whom a third were specifically concerned with the manufacture of cloth, as clothmakers, weavers, fullers, dyers and shearmen, while numerous others worked in associated trades. It is likely that over half the men in Lavenham were dependent upon clothmaking. At the same time, Coventry had 83 cappers and hatters, and two years later Northampton had 50 shoemakers, 15 tanners and 13 glovers. Halifax was another town that became a wonder of the age through the success of its cloth manufacture. Yet all these towns were tiny when compared with those of the modern age.

IN BRIEF

- ☞ Many new towns were founded between the Norman Conquest in 1066 and the Black Death in 1348.
- ☞ Medieval town plans can often be traced on the ground and with the help of street names.
- ☞ In the later Middle Ages many towns shrunk considerably, and their trade withered.
- ☞ In Henry VIII's reign about 20 per cent of the English population lived in towns.

Stability and mobility

Map of Chertsey, Surrey, from the fifteenth-century Cartulary of Chertsey Abbey, showing the monastic church, water mill, meadows and pastures.

The old idea that peasants were tied to their manors and could do little about it has been proved to be wrong. Practice differed from the strict interpretation of the law. Studies of Norfolk manors where a lord had the right to a 'chevage' payment if a serf wished to move away have revealed very high rates of mobility, and similar conclusions have been drawn from the records of some Cornish manors and the Somerset estates of Glastonbury Abbey.

These conclusions are supported by the evidence of surnames derived from place-names. Up to half or more of the people who were recorded in thirteenth- and

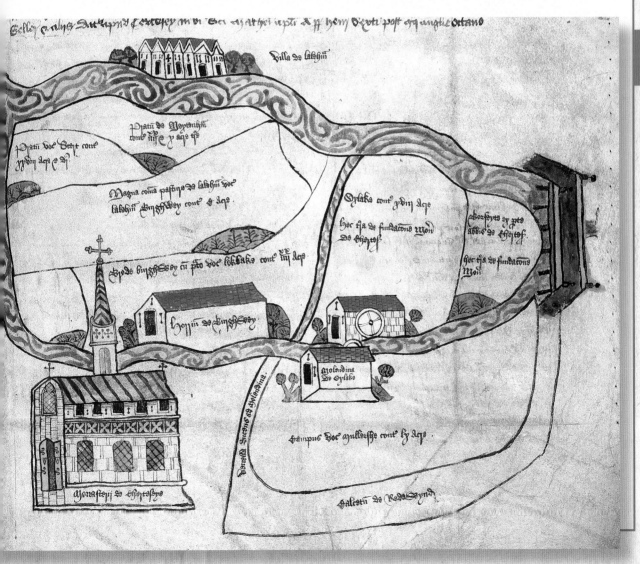

fourteenth-century manor court records and national taxation returns took their surnames from the names of settlements beyond the manor. These lists were made at a time when many names had not become hereditary, so they are useful indicators of recent migration. Although they are not totally reliable, they provide a rough-and-ready picture. The chief difficulty is that only about 40 per cent of

medieval English towns and villages were uniquely named, so more than half of the 'locative' surnames in medieval documents may have alternative explanations. No-one can be expected to know the names of all the minor settlements in England, including the ones that have disappeared, let alone the medieval forms of their names, and only detailed research will prove, for example, which Butterworth, Crawshaw or Hawkesworth was the one that produced the surname.

Even so, it is clear that medieval people had the same broad migration patterns as their successors in Tudor and Stuart times. Studies of movement into manors in Cambridgeshire, Huntingdonshire, Warwickshire and Wiltshire show that most migrants travelled only short distances, though examples can always be found of others who came from far away. Marriage partners were usually chosen from within a radius of 10 or 12 miles. A rigorous examination of locative by-names and surnames as evidence of rural immigration in medieval Nottinghamshire revealed that most journeys started no more than three parishes away. Between 36 and 40 per cent of these names were derived from places up to five miles away, about 60 per cent up to 10 miles away, and about 75 per cent up to 20 miles away. In other words, although people moved about, most of them remained within the mental horizons of their 'country', as men and women did in later periods. At village level the population was constantly changing, so that by the end of the Middle Ages families were usually in a different place from where their ancestors

The surviving section of a panoramic view of London, made about 1559. This view across the Thames shows the late-medieval city packed tightly within its walls. The Tower of London dominates the eastern edge of the city. Moorfields and Spitalfields stretch beyond the northern wall.

had been before the Black Death. Nevertheless, a high proportion of them was still found within a few miles of their ancestral homes.

Those who forsook the countryside to test their fortunes in an urban environment headed mostly for the nearest market towns, perhaps one of the new ones that had been laid out carefully and made attractive to immigrants. The provincial cities, such as Bristol, Norwich or York, attracted migrants from further afield, particularly after the Black Death, and London was as great a magnet in the Middle Ages as it was in later times. Although locative surnames do not provide proof of recent migration, they point to the places where migrant families had originated over the previous generation or two. The primary catchment areas of towns in the early fourteenth century ranged from a 10-miles radius for Leicester, 10–15 miles for Nottingham, 15–20 miles for Norwich and 20 miles for York to over 40 miles for London, with many people walking to the capital from much longer distances. Leicester and Nottingham were then small towns with rival attractions that could be reached within a day's journey, the bigger towns of York and Norwich

dominated much wider areas, but London's attractiveness to migrants was of an entirely different order. People of every walk of life went to London in large numbers.

The long-distance migrants were young people in search of adventure. Some eventually returned home and most left other members of their family behind. The composition of the various 'countries' of England and Wales was not seriously affected by migration. The great majority of local people was descended from families that were rooted within the neighbourhood. The poll tax returns of 1377–81 indicate the local origins of families whose locative surnames were found only within the 'countries' where they were formed. The High Peak region of Derbyshire had its Bagshaws and Heathcotes, north Staffordshire its Eardleys and Swinnertons, and Calderdale its Ackroyds, Barracloughs and Greenwoods. A list of families living in the archdeaconry of Stafford in 1532–3, which names about 51,000 people with 2,055 different surnames, has many examples of family names that were coined locally. It also has an interesting collection of surnames derived from places within other counties, which demonstrates the mobility of a small minority of the late-medieval population. Most of these migrants entered north Staffordshire from Cheshire, Derbyshire and Lancashire. The 38 locative surnames from Lancashire, such as Latham, Lummas and Nadin, accounted for 99 of the family names in the list. We do not know when they arrived, but as the only name from this group to be taxed in Staffordshire in 1377 was that of John of Lancaster, the general drift southwards seems to have occurred late in the Middle Ages.

The origins
of surnames

Finding the source of a family name back in the Middle Ages is the ultimate quest for the family historian. Whilst it is unlikely that we will place all our thirteenth- or fourteenth-century ancestors on a family tree, by proving each link, we can often show where a distinctive name originated. Sometimes we can point to a small settlement, perhaps even a particular farmstead, as the home of our surname. Even people named Smith, Turner or Wright might be able to find the 'country' where their family were living in the Middle Ages before parish registers began.

At the time of the Norman Conquest, English people did not have hereditary surnames. Instead, they were known by a wide range of Old English, Old Danish or Old Norse personal names. A few of the Norman barons had acquired surnames, many of them derived from the place-name of their chief residence, but most baronial families did not possess surnames until long after the Conquest. We often hear people say that their ancestor fought at Hastings, but the truth of the matter is that only those who are descended from William Malet can prove it in the male line. Some of the best-known baronial families had not

arrived in England when the Domesday Book was compiled in 1086. In the next two centuries genealogical information is hard to come by, so it is usually impossible to find certain proof of descent from those who were named in the Domesday Book. Where descents can be proved, they are either from female lines or from younger branches. The baronial families of Norman times have not survived.

The knightly families that were first recorded as the smaller tenants-in-chief in the Domesday Book are even more difficult to trace in the first two or three generations,

---

IN BRIEF

- Surnames were introduced by some of the Norman barons. The practice spread slowly down the social scale.

- Most English people had surnames by 1400, but new names continued to be formed in later centuries.

- The great majority of the population rarely appear in documents before 1200. Often, we cannot prove a family's descent for long afterwards.

- The Welsh had their own naming system and did not use English-style surnames until after the Act of Union of 1536.

for the documentary evidence in the eleventh and twelfth centuries is very thin. Proving descent is made more difficult by the slow adoption of hereditary surnames. Few of the names borne by knights in 1086 had become hereditary, and many families of this rank did not assume proper surnames until well into the thirteenth century. Another complication is that unfamiliar Norman names were later twisted into forms that the English could understand. The change from Bohun to Boone or Bown or from Beauchamp to Beecham is readily understood, but others, such as Scotney from Etocquiny, are hardly recognizable. Nor must we assume that all people with the same surnames as the barons and knights were related to them. Many people from much humbler backgrounds emigrated from Normandy later in the Middle Ages, bearing surnames derived from the same places as those of the aristocrats.

The great majority of the population rarely appear in documents before 1200 and where they do the information is sparse. Their family histories cannot be reconstructed before they had hereditary surnames and often we cannot prove descent for long afterwards. Why people began to acquire surnames is a question that cannot be answered satisfactorily. It is clear that under the Normans the large numbers of personal names that had been used fell dramatically, so that by the fourteenth century over 80 per cent of males were called either John, William, Thomas, Richard or Robert. These men had to be distinguished from each other by another name – a by-name derived from a father's name, a nickname, an occupation

or a place of residence – but this does not explain why these by-names became hereditary. Fourteenth-century manor court rolls, local deeds and charters, and taxation lists show that clerks were well able to identify someone who did not possess a surname. Fashion no doubt played a part in spreading the custom down the social scale and across the country, but perhaps it suited tenants to adopt hereditary surnames that would help prove a right of inheritance to property in a manor court. By-names originated in local communities long before they were written down, but the rise of hereditary surnames does coincide with the change from an oral to a written culture in manor courts and elsewhere. This change occurred slowly and it is common to find people who were recorded in medieval documents by more than one name. We cannot always be sure that someone in the thirteenth century who was known by a by-name, such as the name of his farm or his trade, was the ancestor of a person who used the same farm or occupational name as a hereditary surname in later times. It is unusual to identify the person who first took a surname that became fixed and hereditary. Nor can we tell why someone preferred a locative name while others accepted names from the other categories.

The process was long drawn out. Some London merchant families had surnames by the second half of the twelfth century, a generation or two before the wealthiest merchants of the leading provincial cities, but by 1300 many substantial burgesses were still known by non-hereditary by-names. The fashion spread during the first half of

A marginal illustration from the Luttrell Psalter, c. 1325–35. A mounted knight, caparisoned in the royal arms of England, unseats a Saracen from his horse with a lance.

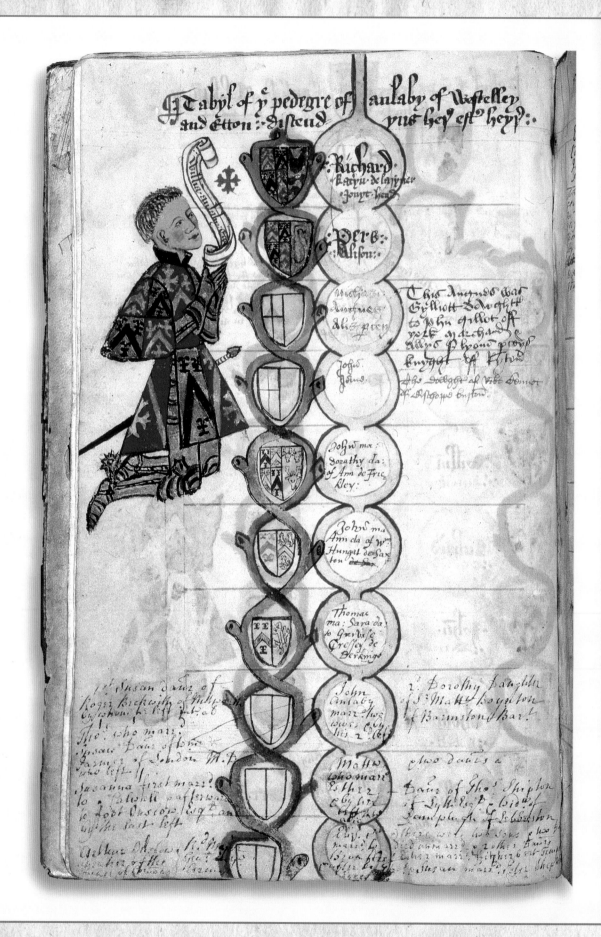

the fourteenth century, so that by 1377–81 very few urban families who paid the poll tax were without a surname, though of course some of the exempted poor may have managed without. In rural England the fashion was accepted more slowly. It first took hold in southern counties and East Anglia, amongst both freeholders and serfs, from about the middle of the thirteenth century. Halfway through the following century over half the rural families in these parts had acquired firm surnames. In the west and the north of England surnames took longer to become accepted and many families were without one when they were recorded as tax payers in 1377–81. The Welsh had their own naming system and began to use English-style surnames only after the Act of Union of 1536. The change was not completed until long after the medieval period.

The pedigree of the Anlaby family of West Ella and Etton, Yorkshire, showing William Anlaby as a kneeling knight, from the Anlaby Cartulary, 1450.

Even after they had become hereditary, many surnames were subject to change over the centuries, sometimes in a minor way but often to a form that was almost unrecognizable. We can determine the origin of a family name only if we trace it back, step by step, by genealogical methods, to the spellings that were recorded in the Middle Ages. Guessing the etymology of a name from its present form may bring us to a mistaken conclusion. Few of us can see immediately that Shimwell was originally spelt Shemyld, that the Elvidges were once named Helwys, and that the Beardsmores were once known as Bearman or Boardman.

Searching for the origin of a family name is hampered by the shortage of documentary sources during the centuries when surnames were formed. Several counties do not even have a poll tax return, and the lay subsidies of the late thirteenth and early fourteenth centuries record only the better-off. Even when we find an early reference, the family that bore the surname might not have any connection with a later family of the same name. Thousands of family names that were recorded before the Black Death did not survive the pestilence. While P. H. Reaney and R. M. Wilson, *A Dictionary of English Surnames*, the standard work of reference, is still a valuable source, it misleads us in providing early examples of names which are unconnected with modern families. Time after time, the authors provide thirteenth-century examples of names in counties where they are unrecorded in later centuries and many of these references are to by-names that never became hereditary surnames. In searching for the home and meaning of a family name, we should use genealogical methods to trace a family's history and map the distribution of the name at various points of time, working backwards from modern telephone directories, the 1881 census and the hearth tax returns of the 1660s and 1670s, before we turn to the medieval records.

The dictionaries offer explanations of the etymology of names, based on the earliest recordings, but they have little to say about the single-family origins of numerous family names of all kinds. Yet this is a matter of great importance for family and local historians. The major class of surnames known as patronymics, that is those derived from a father's personal name, include not only common surnames based on personal names that were brought into this country by the Normans and which are therefore widespread, but rarer ones, such as Eustace, whose later distribution is so restricted to a group of neighbouring parishes in the south Midlands that we must assume that all the present-day bearers of

Weighing and measuring, a Swedish engraving of 1555. In England the man in charge of a weighing machine was called a poyser. The surname Poyser is still concentrated near the Staffordshire/Derbyshire border and seems to be of single-family origin.

the name share a common medieval ancestor. This is certainly true of some of the Anglo-Saxon and Viking personal names that became surnames, names such as Cobbold or Oddy. Some surnames in this category arose independently in different parts of the country, but often family lines withered until just one was left. Other names of this type, such as Auty, may have two or three separate origins. An exciting new development in the science of genetics is helping to determine whether a surname has a single source or multiple origins, for

the DNA structure of the Y-chromosome is passed down from father or son, just like a surname. Genetic tests have proved, for example, that nearly all the Dysons are descended from John Dyson, the son of Dionysia, who lived in Linthwaite, to the west of Huddersfield, in the fourteenth century; the rest of those who were tested are probably descended from illegitimate or adopted children. The medieval documentary evidence and the later distribution patterns of the Dysons had suggested that this was how the name had started; now the genetic evidence has confirmed it.

The stock of patronymic surnames was increased greatly by the use of pet and shortened forms of first names. These were rarely recorded in medieval documents, which normally noted first names in Latin translation, so it is hard to pinpoint their earliest use as surnames. Their often tight distribution in modern times suggests that some were adopted as single-family surnames. The Jeffcocks of Sheffield, for example, seem to stem from John and William Jeffcock, who were recorded in the manor court rolls of neighbouring Eckington in the second half of the fourteenth century.

Nicknames, too, have produced distinctive surnames at all levels of society. The Dafts of Nottinghamshire, the Nices of Essex, and the Rounds of the Black Country each seem to have a single-family origin. Some of the rarer occupational names were also used as surnames by just one man. The Frobishers of the West Riding of Yorkshire, the Rimmers of south Lancashire, and the Trinders of Oxfordshire are good examples. By the time of the poll tax returns of 1377–81, many men with craft surnames no longer followed the trade of their ancestors. When we find coincidences of surname and occupation, we cannot be certain that the family name has just become fixed. The poll tax returns for Rugeley (Staffordshire) in 1381, for instance, record at least one Bower, Cooper, Fisher, Grinder, Piper, Stringer, Tailor and Thatcher, whose craft matched their surname.

The names that were derived from towns, villages, hamlets, farmsteads, or features of the landscape are the easiest to identify, though as we have seen similar place-names might confuse us and the forms of both surname and place-name might have changed over the centuries. Surnames that were derived from towns and villages were commonly given to migrants from those places, but those derived from farmsteads and topographical features became distinctive local names. If the distribution of such a name is confined to a particular 'country' and it can be traced back to the Middle Ages, we often find that the poll tax returns list only one or two examples and that earlier taxation records and manor court rolls will point to just one source for the name. In south Yorkshire, for example, we can be certain in our identification of the original homes of the Broomheads, the Micklethwaites or the Staniforths, and in Derbyshire we can be equally sure about the origins of the Greatorexes, Heathcotes and Padleys.

We cannot assume that everyone with the same surname shares a common ancestor. Clearly, this is not the case with the common names, but even with rare ones we have to use genealogical methods to prove links as far as possible before we search the earliest records that are available to us in the hope of discovering where our medieval ancestors were living. Often, the best we can do is to show that a family name was found in a certain locality in the thirteenth or fourteenth century. The great majority of us are unlikely to get back any further.

Manor court records

The records of manor courts are collectively the most important source for the study of family and local history in the two or three centuries before parish registers began. Where they survive, they provide detailed information about the everyday lives of our medieval ancestors, and in many parts of the country, where manors long remained flourishing institutions, their importance continues long after the Middle Ages. The first court rolls date from the 1230s, and by the 1260s they were replacing the former reliance on oral memories. Manor courts were a peculiarly English institution, whose records follow a remarkably consistent pattern.

- The busiest courts met every three weeks for both administrative and judicial purposes, to record the transfers of land, resolve disputes between tenants, prosecute those who had not complied with local rules and regulations, levy whatever was due to the lord, elect officers, and make decisions about local farming practices.

- All the unfree tenants of the manor were expected to attend meetings and even the free tenants had to turn up occasionally.

- The lord's steward or bailiff presided over the court, but the jurors, or 'homagers', who made the decisions were elected by the tenants. They in turn appointed the officers, such as the constable, the pinder and the ale-taster.

The best introductions are M. Bailey, *The English Manor, c.1200–c.1500* (Manchester, 2002), M. Ellis, *Using Manorial Records* (Public Record Office, 1997) and P. D. A. Harvey, *Manorial Records* (British Records Society, 2nd edition, 2000).

Thousands of manorial documents have survived from the middle decades of the thirteenth century onwards. Many courts continued to flourish during the sixteenth and seventeenth centuries and some met at regular intervals even into the nineteenth or early twentieth century. The manor court of Laxton (Nottinghamshire) still regulates the ways in which the village's open fields are farmed. Manorial records are sometimes difficult to locate because the owners of the records have moved well away from the district and a few collections, notably those of the Duke of Rutland's estate, are in private hands and are not available for study. The relevant county record office is usually the best place to try first. The card index of the *Manorial Documents Register* at the National Archives lists the known

accompt: archaic form of 'account'

affeerers: the officers appointed by a manorial court to fix the amount of the fines for offences

boon work: a manorial duty to do such seasonal work as ploughing and harvesting

bylawman: alternative name for a constable

chevage: a payment made to a lord by a villein who wished to move from one manor to another

compotus rolls: accounts of royal and seigneurial estates

custumal: a record of the customs of a manor, drawn up by the manorial jury

escheat: property that reverted to the lord when a tenant was guilty of a felony or when he died without adult heirs

essoin: an acceptable excuse for absence from the court

estover: the right to take timber, brushwood, bracken, etc. from commons for use in building, repairing fences, or as fuel, etc.

extent: a detailed survey and valuation

firebote: the right to remove wood from the commons as fuel

frankpledge: by the end of the Middle Ages the term was synonymous with court leet

grave, greave, reeve: a person chosen by the tenants of a manor to act as their representative in dealings with the lord

gressom: a fine paid to a feudal lord upon entering a property

heriot: a payment (to the lord, often of the best beast) upon the death of a tenant

homagers: the twelve jurors of a manor court

infangentheof: the right of a manorial or borough court to try and punish a thief arrested within its jurisdiction

leywrite: a fine payable by a medieval villein to the lord of the manor upon his unmarried daughter becoming pregnant

merchet: a payment from a villein to his lord upon the marriage of the villein's son or daughter

outfangtheof: the right of a manorial lord to arrest a thief beyond the manorial estate and to hold the trial at his own court

pannage: the right to graze pigs on the commons

tithing: the medieval system whereby groups of ten households were responsible to the manorial court leet for the good conduct of each member

whereabouts of manorial records in numerous record offices throughout England and Wales.

☞ The numerous manors which belonged to the Crown or the Duchy of Lancaster are kept in the National Archives.

☞ Those for the Duchy of Cornwall are mostly housed at the Duchy's estate office in Buckingham Gate, London.

☞ Other manorial records are kept in the British Library Department of Manuscripts and in university libraries, particularly those of the colleges of Cambridge and Oxford.

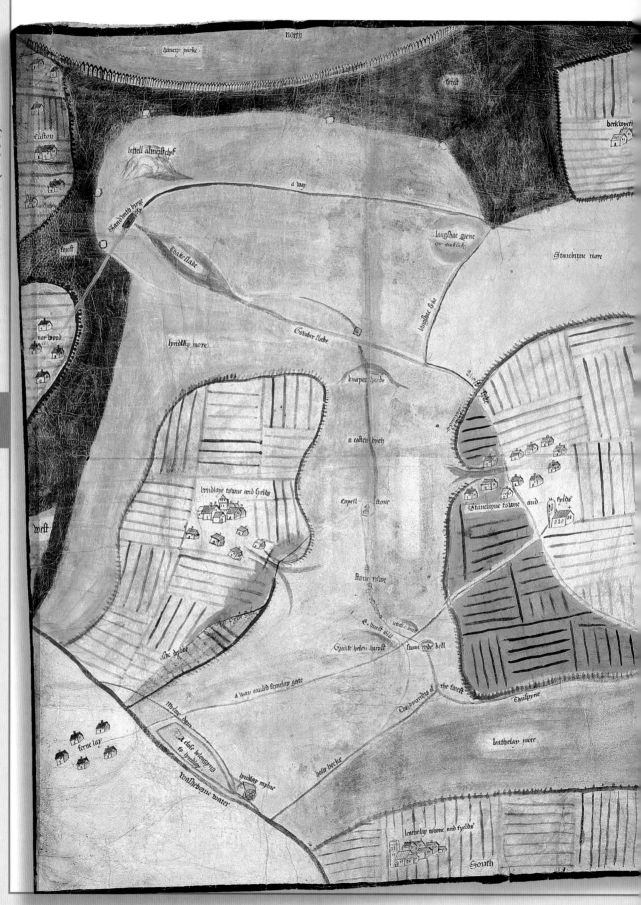

North

haney parke

forest

eliston

beckwyth

lettell almestclyf

a way

Sandwath bryge

langlhae grene or beck lake

Stanebrune more

thake flade

langlhae lake

nor wood

Cowber flade

knapes thaide

lyndlky more

lyndlaye towne and fyelds

a casten dyech

castell stone

Stanehope towne and fyelds

stone rawe

e. hurst gill lewell... hurst

the dybbe

Greate helen hurst

swan rode hill

a way caaled lemelay gate

The boundre of the tweft

Thuslyne

Mylne dam

ferne lay

a close belonginge to lyndlay

leathelay more

lyndlay mylne

holle brecke

wathebone water

leathelay towne and fyelds

South

☞ Archivists at county record offices can advise on the whereabouts of the records of local manors and the Access to Archives website at <www.nationalarchives.gov.uk> is informative.

The chances of finding an ancestor in manorial records, where they survive, are increased if the manor was a large and important one that continued to function long after the Middle Ages. The manor of Wakefield, which stretched across the Pennines to the Lancashire border, is a famous example, whose court rolls start in 1274 and continue into the twentieth century; 16 volumes have been published so far. Manor court records were generally written in Latin until 1733, so it is a great benefit to have them transcribed, translated and published.

What was a manor?

Map of the manor of Leathley, Yorkshire, 1596, showing the well-defined arable fields around each settlement in lower Wharfedale, the moors belonging to each township, the pale of Haverah deer park and the boundaries of the forests of Knaresborough and Wharfedale.

A 'manor' is difficult to define precisely. It sometimes covered the same area as a parish, but very often the boundaries overlapped, so that some parishes contained two or three manors. Conversely, a huge lordship (known perhaps as a barony, honour, or liberty) extended over many parishes. From time to time we find that some strips in a village's open fields lay within one manor, but neighbouring strips belonged to another. Manors commonly had detached portions, which might have been a considerable distance away. Some manors were just a few hundred acres in size, others were many thousands of acres in extent. The larger ones were often reduced by the creation of sub-manors for favoured retainers. They

were not necessarily static institutions but could change over time. The form, size and composition of manors varied considerably from one part of the country to another, and often within different regions of the same county. For example, the gentry families of the Kentish downlands kept a firm grip on their tenants, whereas in the Weald manors were weak; this basic division between neighbouring districts continued long after the Middle Ages.

In the Middle Ages, many manors included large freehold farms, others consisted of the lord's demesne and the smallholdings of the servile peasantry (the villeins). The demesne was either worked as a 'home farm' that provided food for the lord's household and a surplus for sale or it was leased to a tenant for an annual rent. The lord's possessions might also include a deer park, rabbit warren, fishpond and dovecote. He normally had a mill at which his tenants were compelled to grind their corn, he owned the mineral rights, and he appointed the rector of the church that his ancestors had built. The peasants were bound to the manor and its lord by a range of customary and legal ties and obligations. The services that they rendered to the lord varied from manor to manor, according to the customs that were agreed upon in the manor court. On the whole, peasants faced lighter demands on manors owned by the Crown or lay lords than on those held by bishops and monasteries. Manors were not just rural institutions, of course. Some corporations acquired the manorial rights and in many other towns the burgesses were not fully independent, for the lord still controlled many of their activities through his manor court.

Court baron and court leet

The functions of the manor court were divided between the court baron, where transfers of land were registered, and the court leet, which dealt with personal disputes, nuisances, petty crime, and the smooth running of communal farming. The records of the court baron are the more useful to the family historian, for they record the inheritance or sale of farms or cottages. The information that is recorded may allow us to deduce the date of death of the previous owner and to discover his relationship to the person who succeeded him. It is often possible to trace the descent of a property from well before the beginning of parish registers. For example, the Hallamshire court rolls show that the Bullas family had moved from Bullhouse, just to the north of the manor, during the fourteenth century. There are too many gaps in the evidence to connect the generations in the early years, but in 1440–41 Robert de Bulhous was the only person of this name in a long list of tenants. From 1478 we are on firm ground, for the rolls enable us to trace the family tree over seven generations from the time when Thomas Bullus inherited a farm from his father, John, until 1617, when the farm passed to his direct descendant George Bullas. By that time, the family's history can be traced from the parish register and other sources.

- It is often far from clear whether the transactions that are recorded in the court rolls of a manor are straightforward transfers to an incoming tenant or whether they represent sales, mortgages, or inheritance through entails, endowments, or trusts.

- The names of any sub-tenants who may have actually farmed the land are not recorded.

- Each manor followed its own customs. By the late Middle Ages many lands that had been inherited simply by custom had become 'copyhold tenure', whereby a tenant held a copy of the entry in the manorial court rolls which recorded the terms by which he possessed his holding. Depositions on manorial customs are listed in E 134 at the National Archives.

- From the middle of the sixteenth century onwards copyhold tenure began to be replaced by leaseholding; by the seventeenth century the business of a court baron was often confined to recording leaseholds and copyholds. Remaining copyhold tenures were abolished in 1922 by the Property Act, which was extended in 1936 to any surviving manorial customs.

Finding an ancestor in the records of the court leet is a more chancy business. We might come across someone who served on the manorial jury or one who was charged with an offence. A list of those who formed the jury, or 'homage', of the manor was normally recorded as the first item of business. This might be followed by the names of the freeholders, many of whom were absentee owners. After electing various officers, the jurymen passed the by-laws, which were known as 'paines' from the penalties that were payable by those who broke them, and fined those who had offended since the last court. During the

An extract from the manor court rolls of William Swanland, Harefield, Middlesex, 1422–3. It starts by listing the names of the jurors, the principal tenants of the manor.

sixteenth and seventeenth centuries many of the cases of law and order that had once been handled by the court leet were transferred to the petty and quarter sessions or to ecclesiastical courts. Nevertheless, court leets remained busy with the scouring of ditches, the removal of nuisances, the muzzling of dogs, encroachments and enclosures, and numerous other matters concerning social harmony and the smooth running of the local economy.

Manorial surveys, rentals and leases

☞ Surveys provide a 'snapshot' of a manor at a particular point in time.

They note the terms and conditions under which land was held; the rents, customs, services and obligations.

☞ Surveys measure farms carefully in acres, roods and perches, either in statute acres or in the customary acres of the district, which were often much larger. The Cheshire acre, for instance, was twice the size of a statute acre.

☞ The surveys that have a map of the manor are usually from the post-medieval period, often from when a new lord took over, for he was keen to know precisely what he had bought or inherited, and whether the manorial customs would allow him to raise the entry fines and rents.

☞ The fullest surveys name every tenant, describe farmhouses and outbuildings, measure and name the fields and crofts, and note the terms by which the land was held, but they do not mention the landless and have little to say about household or family structures.

☛ We must bear in mind that a farmer might also have had land beyond the manor or that he might have leased some fields to sub-tenants, but in most cases the picture will be an accurate

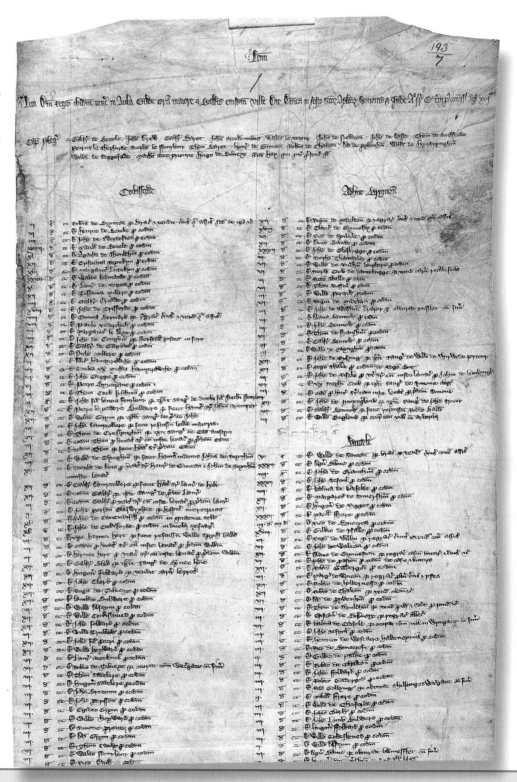

An extract from the court leet records for Cockisforde, Norfolk, 1348, showing a long list of names.

reflection of how much land an ancestor farmed.

- ➤ Rentals simply record the names of the tenants and the rents that were due each year, usually at Lady Day and Michaelmas, but sometimes at Christmas and Midsummer.

- ➤ In the post-medieval period the terms of leases were recorded by the court baron, and sometimes wills were copied into the rolls so as to prevent disputes over inheritance.

- ➤ In the western half of England, and on some estates elsewhere, leases were granted for three lives, determinable upon 99 years. The lives that were entered in the manorial records could be anyone's, but they were usually those of the parents and the eldest son. Such leases could be renewed with new names upon payment of another entry fine. Manors with a good run of leases help the family historian to trace the descent of property and to determine relationships.

A medieval villein held his land 'at the will of the lord' and could defend his inheritance only in the manor court. As long as he fulfilled his obligations, he was secure in his property, though in the inflationary age of Queen Elizabeth's reign he was often faced with demands for increased entry fines and rents. Manor court rolls reveal an active market in land and the clearing of 'assarts', 'stubbings' or 'intakes', which were formally surrendered to the lord and carefully recorded in the court rolls. The amount of freehold land within a medieval manor varied considerably. Freeholders paid nominal rents and held their property 'in

socage', usually in the form of military service when this obligation was demanded of them. The lord's permission was not needed to sell, grant or inherit a freehold property.

The manor was the most important local institution in the medieval period. It affected the lives of common people constantly. In many places it flourished as a unit of estate management long after the close of the Middle Ages. In later centuries, court records were no longer kept in rolls but entered into bound volumes or onto sheets of paper. They are often found in the catalogues of local record offices under the heading 'estate papers'.

Extract from a rental made as part of a survey of the manor of Manorbier and Penally, Pembrokeshire, 1618. The tenants held arable, pasture, furze and heath, and rocky land.

Subsidies and poll taxes

Medieval taxes fell into two categories: the lay and clerical subsidies, and the poll taxes of 1377–81 which were levied on heads, or 'polls'. The lists of names that are recorded in these returns are less complete than those of the hearth tax in the late seventeenth century. Their reliability and the number of people who evaded tax or who were exempt from payment on the grounds of poverty have been much debated. They are nevertheless useful to family historians when they show that a surname had become established in a particular place by the time that a tax was levied. In many cases, they provide the earliest references to family names.

The lay subsidies of 1290 to 1334 (which excluded the clergy) are sometimes known as tenths and fifteenths because the tax amounted to one-tenth of the value of the movable property of those who lived within a city, borough, or royal demesne and one-fifteenth of those who lived elsewhere. The returns are kept in the Exchequer division of the National Archives and so catalogue references can be found online under E 179. A number of county record societies have published their fullest returns. Each county is arranged by hundred or wapentake, and then by vill (or township) and borough. The names of taxpayers and the amount that they paid are recorded. The Suffolk lay subsidy of 1327, for instance, records a number of family names that are still concentrated in the county, names such as Aldous, Brundish, Cobbold, Greengrass, Ling and Sallowes.

All the different types of surname can be found, at the very time when they were first becoming hereditary. Surnames recorded in the Staffordshire lay subsidies of 1327 and 1332, for example, include such distinctive names as Blore, Bott, Eardley, Mynors, Salt, Sneyd, Tunstall and Wedgwood. The Adam de Fernihaleugh (the 'ferny hollow') who was taxed at Endon in the parish of Leek in 1327 was probably the ancestor of all the Fernihoughs, for the name is still concentrated in and around Staffordshire. When Elizabeth Fernihough of Fernihough made her will in 1649 she was said to be of

The online catalogue of the National Archives can be accessed on <www.nationalarchives.gov.uk>. To find subsidy records, click on E 179. You will not be able to see images of the original documents, but will be able to use a catalogue of all the central taxation records dating from 1198 to 1688. The names of people are not on the database, but individual documents can be located by place-name, date, the type of tax, and the type of document. They may be seen at the National Archives or photocopies may be ordered straight from the catalogue. Information leaflets are provided for each set.

Extract from the Suffolk lay subsidy of 1327, listing the taxpayers.

the parish of Leek. Shortly afterwards, 12 of the 15 householders with that name in the county's hearth tax returns of 1666 were living in Totmanslow hundred, which covered the Staffordshire Moorlands district around Leek. The farm that gave rise to the surname no longer exists, but a map of Endon in 1816 marks it on the eastern boundary of the township. The lay subsidy return of 1327 had pointed unerringly to the home of this family name.

From 1334 lay subsidy returns ceased to record the names of the taxpayers and in 1377 this method of taxation was replaced by the poll tax. Not until the reign of Henry VIII was the old method revived. The family historian will find many references in the E 179 online catalogue to lay subsidies levied in the 1520s, 1530s and 1540s. Many

people were exempt and others avoided payment, but family historians may well find the names of their ancestors amongst the taxpayers in the decades before parish registration began. The lay subsidy of 1523 seems to be the fullest for the south and east of England, but those of the 1540s are best for northern parts and for Wales. Some counties have published their fullest returns. Rutland, for example, has an indexed volume that includes a muster book of 1522 and the lay subsidy rolls of 1524–5.

Poll tax returns

In 1377 the Crown decided upon a new method of taxation; a poll tax was levied on everyone over the age of 14. Two years later, the tax was levied again on those who

281

had reached their sixteenth birthday, with payments graded according to wealth, starting at the basic rate of a groat (4d.). In 1381 everyone over the age of 15 was taxed, but that year the national rising, known somewhat misleadingly as the Peasants' Revolt, persuaded the government that this method of taxation should be abandoned. The returns are kept in the National Archives under E 179 and have been published as C.C. Fenwick, ed., *The Poll Taxes of 1377, 1379 and 1381* (2 vols., Oxford: The British Academy, 1997 and 2001, with a final volume forthcoming).

Although large numbers of people were exempt from the tax on the grounds of poverty and others managed to avoid payment, the poll tax returns list far more people than do the lay subsidies. Unfortunately, some counties, such as Cheshire and Nottinghamshire, do not have any surviving returns and some other counties have them only for a limited number of hundreds. First names are recorded in their Latin forms, e.g. Ricardus for Richard or Petrus for Peter, but surnames are in English, in a variety of spellings. Latin phrases such as *uxor ejus* for 'his wife', *filia* for 'daughter', or *ancilla* for servant, and the use of Roman numerals do not cause too much difficulty.

Poll tax returns are a prime source for

The Peasants' Revolt, 1381, from a fifteenth-century Flemish manuscript of Jean Froissart's Chroniques de France et d'Angleterre. *John Ball (on horseback) preaches to the rebels at Blackheath on the text, 'When Adam delved and Eve span/ Who was then the gentleman?' Wat Tyler listens (bottom left).*

identifying surnames at a time when most English people had acquired one. In the Blackburn wapentake of Lancashire in 1379 we can quickly spot such distinctive local surnames as Anderton, Chippingdale, Clegg, Dewhirst, Duckworth, Hargreaves, Hesketh, Kenyon, Leyland, Sharples, Sowerbutts, Tarlton, Turton, Whitworth, Wolfenden and many more. In Shropshire in 1381 we can readily identify numerous Welsh first names, such as Evan, Griffin and Howel and the use of the Welsh form of *ap* names. They were particularly numerous, as we might expect, near the Welsh border, in such townships as Wollaston, to the west of Shrewsbury.

The returns reinforce the belief that very many surnames are of single-family origin. Mingay is known to have been a Breton personal name that became adopted as a surname in East Anglia. In the hearth tax returns of 1664 and 1674 the name was concentrated along the Norfolk–Suffolk border, with eleven households on the Norfolk side and seven in Suffolk. This clue prompted a search of the poll tax returns for these two counties and the discovery that the Thomas Menggy and William Mengy who paid tax in the south Norfolk township of Busthorpe were the only taxpayers of that name. Likewise, the surname Daft or Dafte – a nickname whose meaning in the Middle Ages was 'meek' – is still an East Midlands name. In the Nottinghamshire hearth tax returns of 1664, 10 of the 45 householders of the township of Hickling were named Dafte, yet the surname did not appear in any other part of the county. This marked concentration suggested a common medieval ancestor, but the Nottinghamshire poll tax returns do not survive, except for a

brief list of constables in 1377. Fortunately, one of them was William Dafte, the constable of Upper Broughton, the township immediately to the south of Hickling. The name has not spread far from its origins.

The violence of the Peasants' Revolt convinced the Crown that no more personal taxes should be levied. This means that the family historian has no comparable records to search between 1381 and the 1520s. The fifteenth century is a notoriously difficult period for such inquiries. Lay subsidies were revived as a method of taxation by Henry VII, desperate to finance his wars with France, but the poll tax was dropped until the seventeenth century. It was revived in 1641 and levied seven times between 1660 and 1697. Some of the lists of taxpayers that survive in county record offices amongst the papers of lord-lieutenants, or sometimes in the National Archives, are very full and are as valuable as the contemporary hearth tax returns.

Medieval-type subsidies continued in the Elizabethan age. This tax assessment for the parish of St Helen, Bishopgate, in 1598 records William Shakespeare on the third line from the bottom.

Other medieval records in print

Medieval history has been far better served than the study of later periods by the publication of full transcripts or calendars of documents in translation from the original Latin or Norman French. These editions have usually been published by national or county record societies. They are of genealogical interest only for the barons and knights, but they are very usefulin noting what are often the first recordings of the surnames of ordinary families. For example, A. Hopkinson, ed., *The Rolls of the 1281 Derbyshire Eyre* (Derbyshire Record Society, XXVII, 2000) provides the earliest references to the local surnames Wildgoose and Drabble: Roger Wildegos (Foston), William Wyldegos (killed at Somersale) and Matthew Drabel (charged with selling wine against the assize at an unspecified place). The same is true of the cartularies of abbeys and priories. These are careful records of the grants of land and other property that had been made by aristocratic families, but they name people from lower down the social scale who appear as witnesses and as neighbouring landowners.

The earliest deeds and charters date from the twelfth century, but they record

ordinary people only from the thirteenth century onwards. They were undated before the reign of Edward I, then by regnal year and saints' days; for these, see C. Webb, *Dates and Calendars for the Genealogist* (Society of Genealogists, 1998). Many deeds and charters survive in the vast collections of the National Archives, particularly in the courts of Chancery and Exchequer or in the British Library, especially as 'Additional Charters'. Thousands of deeds are also kept in local record offices, deposited there by landowners and solicitors. Although numerous calendars have been produced, the great bulk has not been published. Specialist training is needed to read those which are not in print. Deeds and charters often provide the names of the owners of neighbouring plots of land, as well as those engaged in the transaction and the witnesses.

Feet of fines are judgements concerning titles to land. From the late twelfth century until 1834 the record of title that was made upon a purchase was written out three times on a single sheet of parchment. The three copies were then cut apart along wavy lines so as to prevent forgery. Two parts were given to the parties involved, and the copy at the foot of the fine was filed among the rolls of the Court of Common Pleas. These are now kept at the National Archives under CP 25 and 27. Until 1688 the rolls were arranged under counties, which has enabled county record societies to publish editions.

The better-off members of society might appear in the printed calendars of other major series held at the National Archives, chiefly the Patent Rolls, Close Rolls, Fine Rolls, Charter Rolls and Inquisitions Post Mortem. They are available at the National Archives and in good local reference libraries and university libraries.

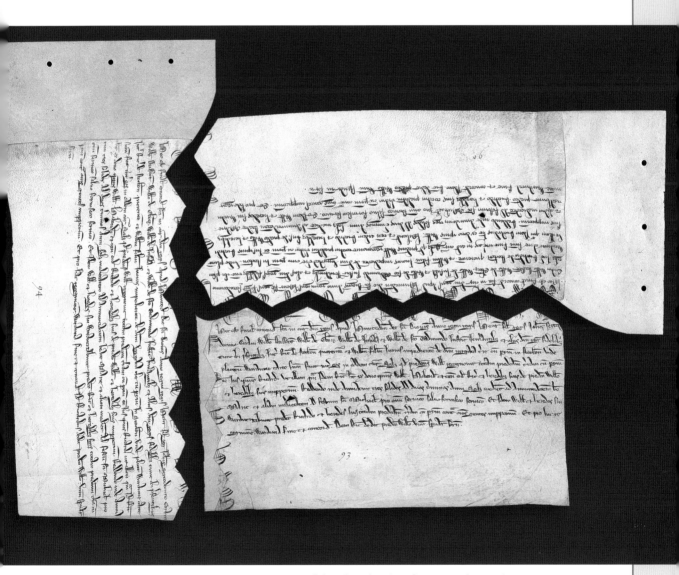

Feet of fines from the reign of Henry III (1216–72), showing how such documents were cut into three matching parts to prevent forgery.

Heraldry

The earliest documentary evidence for the use of heraldry comes from the knighting of Geoffrey Plantagenet, Count of Anjou, in 1127. The practice soon spread amongst barons and knights in different parts of western Europe as part of the pageantry of tournaments. The simple patterns that were used became more complex during the thirteenth century and by the early 1400s anyone who did not have a coat of arms that dated from time immemorial had to apply to the heralds appointed by the Crown. Originally part of the Royal Household, the heralds were incorporated as a College of Arms by Richard III in 1484. Their investigations of the claims to the right to bear arms, conducted at county level, began in 1530 and continued intermittently until 1686. Known as heralds' visitations, the most important ones were made in c. 1580, 1620, and 1666. The records of their decisions on these occasions, and the pedigrees that they accepted, have been published in various volumes of the Harleian Society or by county record societies.

The right to bear arms is confined to the eldest male successor and then to the senior female line. Only one person at a time is entitled to use a particular coat of arms. If you discover one in your family, you do not necessarily have a right to use it. Nor should you be misled by commercial organizations into thinking that all people with the same surname (or, worse still, approximations to it) are entitled to the same coat of arms. As it is based on inheritance, heraldry can be useful in elucidating the pedigrees of armigerous families. A knowledge of its conventions is indispensable when studying funerary monuments, stained glass

Grant of arms to Richard Pace, King's secretary, by Thomas Wryothesley, Garter, and Thomas Benolt, Clarencieux, 12 February 1517/18.

windows, and roof bosses in churches and cathedrals. The best introduction is T. Woodcock and J. M. Robinson, *The Oxford Guide to Heraldry* (1988).

The College of Arms at Queen Victoria Street, London EC4V 4BT has registers of grants of coats of arms made or confirmed to English and Welsh families from the fifteenth century to the present day. Charges are made for services. The Institute of Heraldic and Genealogical Studies, 79–82 Northgate, Canterbury, Kent CT1 1BA has a library with a large collection of original documents and many indexes, which is open to visitors for a small fee. The institute also runs courses on heraldry and all aspects of family history.

Resource Bank

Useful addresses and websites   290

Further reading   297

Useful addresses and websites

An up-to-the-minute list of archive providers is available on the website <www.hmc.gov.uk/archon/archon.htm>

Record offices, libraries and registries

Anglesey County Record Office, Shire Hall, Glanhwfa Road, Llangefni LL77 7TW; tel. 01248 752080; internet: <www.anglesey.gov.uk/english/library/archives/archives.htm>

Archive Office of the Chief Rabbi, 735 High Road, Finchley, London N12 0US

Bath and North East Somerset Record Office, Guildhall, High Street, Bath BA1 5AW; tel. 01225 477421; internet: <www.bath.archives.co.uk>

Bath Central Library, 19 The Podium, Northgate Street, Bath BA1 5AN; tel. 01225 787400; internet: <www.foursite.somerset.gov.uk>

Bedford Central Library, Local Studies Library, Harpur Street, Bedford MK40 1PG; tel. 01234 350931

Bedfordshire and Luton Archives and Record Service, County Hall, Cauldwell Street, Bedford MK42 9AP; tel. 01234 228833 ext 2833; internet: <www.bedfordshire.gov.uk>

Berkshire Record Office, 9 Coley Avenue, Reading, RG1 6AF; tel. 0118 901 5132; internet: <www.berkshirerecordoffice.org.uk>

Berwick-upon-Tweed Record Office, Council Offices, Wallace Green, Berwick-upon-Tweed, Northumberland TD15 1ED; tel. 01289 330044, ext. 230; internet: <www.northumberland.gov.uk>

Birmingham City Archives, Central Library, Chamberlain Square, Birmingham B3 3HQ; tel. 0121 303 4217; internet: <www.birmingham.gov.uk>

Black Cultural Archives, 378 Coldharbour Lane, London SW9 8LF; tel. 020 7738 4591

Bodleian Library, Broad Street, Oxford, OX1 3BG; tel. 01865 277180; internet: <www.bodley.ox.ac.uk>

Bolton Archives and Local Studies Service, Central Library, Civic Centre, Le Mans Crescent, Bolton BL1 1SE; tel. 01204 332185; internet: <http://bold.bolton.gov.uk/library>

Borthwick Institute of Historical Research, St Anthony's Hall, Peasholme Green, York YO1 7PW; tel. 01904 642315; internet: <www.york.ac.uk/inst/bihr>

Bristol Record Office, 'B' Bond Warehouse, Smeaton Road, Bristol BS1 6XN; tel. 0117 922 4224; internet: <www.bristol-city.gov.uk/record office>

British Library, 96 Euston Road, London NW1 2DB; tel. 020 7412 7677; internet: <www.bl.uk>

British Library Newspaper Library, Colindale Avenue, London NW9 5HE; tel. 020 7412 7353; internet: <www.bl.uk/catalogues/newspapers.html>

British Library, Oriental and India Office Collections, 96 Euston Rd, London NW1 2DB; tel. 020 7412 7873; internet: <www.bl.uk/collections/orientalandindian.html>

British Red Cross, Museum and Archives, 9 Grosvenor Crescent, London SW1X 7EJ; tel. 020 7201 5153; internet: <www.redcross.org.uk>

British Telecom Archives, Holborn Telephone Exchange, 268–270 High Holborn, London WC1V 7EE; tel. 020 7492 8792; internet: <www.btplc.com/corporateinformation/btarchives>

Centre for Buckinghamshire Studies, County Hall, Walton Street, Aylesbury HP20 1UU; tel. 01296 382587; internet: <www.buckscc.gov.uk/archives>

Bury Archive Service, 1st Floor, Derby Hall Annexe, Edwin Street, Bury BL9 0AS; tel. 0161 797 6697; internet: <www.bury.gov.uk>

Business Archives Council, tel. 020 7247 0024; internet: <www.archives.gla.ac.uk/bac/>

Cambridgeshire County Record Office, Shire Hall, Castle Hill, Cambridge CB3 0AP; tel. 01223 717281; internet: <http://edweb.camcnty.gov.uk>

Carmarthenshire Archive Service, Parc Myrddin, Carmarthen SA31 1DS; tel. 01267 228232; internet: <www.carmarthenshire.gov.uk>

Catholic Central Library, Lancing Street, London NW1 1ND; tel. 020 7383 4333; internet: <www.catholic-library.org.uk>

Centre for Kentish Studies, County Hall, Maidstone ME14 1XQ; tel. 01622 694363; internet: <www.kent.gov.uk/e&d/artslib/archives/home.html>

Ceredigion Archives, Marine Terrace, Aberystwyth, Swyddfa's Sir SY23 2DE; tel. 01970 633697/8; internet: <http://archifdy-ceredigion.org.uk>

Cheshire and Chester Archives and Local Studies Service, Duke Street, Chester CH1 1RL; tel. 01244 602574; internet: <www.cheshire.gov.uk/recoff/>

City of London Police Record Office, 26 Old Jewry, London EC2R 8DJ; tel. 020 7601 2297; internet: <www.cityoflondon.gov.uk>

Cornwall Record Office, Old County Hall, Truro, Cornwall TR1 3AY; tel. 01872 323129; internet: <www.cornwall.gov.uk/cro>

Corporation of London Records Office, PO Box 270, Guildhall, London EC2P 2EJ; tel. 020 7332 1251; internet: <www.cityoflondon.gov.uk/leisure_heritage>

Coventry Archives, Mandela House, Bayley Lane, Coventry CV1 5RG; tel. 024 7683 2418; internet: <www.coventry-city.co.uk/archives/home.htm>

Cumbria Record Office, The Castle, Carlisle CA3 8UR; tel. 01228 60728/5; internet: <www.cumbria.gov.uk/archives>

Cumbria Record Office, County Offices, Kendal LA9 4RQ; tel. 01539 773540; internet: <www.cumbria.gov.uk/archives>

Cumbria Record Office and Local Studies Library, 140 Duke Street, Barrow-in-Furness LA14 1XW; tel. 01229 894363; internet: <www.cumbria.gov.uk/archives>

Cumbria Record Office and Local Studies Library, Scotch Street, Whitehaven CA28 7BJ; tel. 01946 852920; internet: <www.cumbria.gov.uk/archives>

Denbighshire Record Office, 46 Clwyd Street, Ruthin LL15 1HP; tel. 01824 708250; internet: <www.denbighshire.gov.uk>

Derby Local Studies Library, 25B Irongate, Derby DE1 3GL; tel. 01332 255393; internet: <www.derby.gov.uk>

Derbyshire Record Office, New Street, Matlock DE4 3AG; tel. 01629 585347; internet: <www.derbyshire.gov.uk/recordoffice/>

Devon Record Office, Castle Street, Exeter EX4 3PU; tel. 01392 384253; internet: <www.devon.gov.uk/dro>

North Devon Library and Record Office, Tuly Street, Barnstaple EX31 1EL; tel. 01271 38860; internet: <www.devon.gov.uk/dro>

Dorset Record Office, Bridport Road, Dorchester, Dorset DT1 1RP; tel. 01305 250550; internet: <www.dorsetcc.gov.uk>

Dr Williams's Library, 14 Gordon Square, London, WC1H 0AR; tel. 020 7387 3727

Durham County Record Office, County Hall, Durham DH1 5UL; tel. 0191 383 3253; internet: <www.durham.gov.uk>

East Riding of Yorkshire Archives and Records Service, County Hall, Beverley HU17 9BA; tel. 01482 392790; internet: <www.eastriding.gov.uk/libraries/archives>

Essex Record Office, Wharf Road, Chelmsford CM2 6YT; tel. 01245 244644; internet: <www.essexcc.gov.uk/ero>

Family Records Centre, 1 Myddelton Street, London EC1R 1UW; tel. 020 8392 5300; internet: <www.familyrecords.gov.uk/frc.htm>

Flintshire Record Office, The Old Rectory, Hawarden, Deeside CH5 3NR; tel. 01244 532364; internet: <www.llgc.org.uk/cac/cac0032.htm>

Friends House Library, 173 Euston Road, London NW1 2BJ; tel. 020 7663 1135; internet: <www.quaker.org.uk/library>

Glamorgan Record Office, The Glamorgan Building, King Edward VII Avenue, Cathays Park, Cardiff CF10 3NE; tel. 029 2078 0282; internet: <www.glamro.gov.uk>

West Glamorgan Archive Service, County Hall, Oystermouth Road, Swansea SA1 3SN; tel. 01792 636589; internet: <www.swansea.gov.uk/archives>

Gloucestershire Record Office, Clarence Row, Alvin Street, Gloucester, GL1 3DW; tel. 01452 5295; internet: <www.gloucestershire.gov.uk/archives>

States of Guernsey Island Archives Service, 29 Victoria Road, St Peter Port, Guernsey GY1 1HU; tel. 01481 724512

Guildhall Library, Aldermanbury, London EC2P 2EJ; tel. 020 7332 1863; internet: <www.ihr.sas.ac.uk/gh/>

Gwent Record Office, County Hall, Cwmbran NP44 2XH; tel. 01633 644886; internet: <www.llgc.org.uk/cac/cac0004.htm>

Gwynedd Archives, Caernarfon Record Office, County Offices, Shirehall Street, Caernarfon LL55 1SH; tel. 01286 679095/679088; internet: <www.gwynedd.gov.uk/archives>

Hampshire Record Office, Sussex Street, Winchester SO23 8TH; tel. 01962 846154; internet: <www.hants.gov.uk/record-office/index.html>

Herefordshire Record Office, The Old Barracks, Harold Street, Hereford HR1 2QX; tel. 01432 260750; internet: <www.recordoffice.herefordshire.gov.uk>

Hertfordshire Archives and Local Studies, County Hall, Pegs Lane, Hertford SG13 8DE; tel. 01438 737333; internet: <www.hertsdirect.org/contact>

House of Lords Record Office, London SW1A 0PW; tel Palace of Westminster. 020 7219 3074; internet: <www.parliament.the-stationery-office.co.uk/pa/genlinfo.htm>

Huguenot Library, University College, Gower Street, London WC1E 6BT; tel. 020 7679 7094; internet: <www.ucl.ac.uk/library/huguenot.htm>

Huntingdonshire County Record Office *see* Cambridgeshire Archives Service, CRO Huntington, Grammar School Walk, Huntingdon, Cambridgeshire PE29 6LF; tel. 01480 375842; internet: <htpp://camcnty.gov.uk>

Isle of Man Public Record Office, Unit 3, Spring Valley Industrial Estate, Braddan, Douglas, Isle of Man IM2 2QR; tel. 01624 613383; internet: <www.gov.im/deptindex/reginfo.html>

Isle of Wight Record Office, 26 Hillside, Newport, Isle of Wight PO30 2EB; tel. 01983 823820/1; internet: <www.iwight.com/library/record_office>

Jersey Archive, St Helier, Clarence Road, Jersey JE2 4JY; tel. 01534 833333; internet: <www.jerseyheritagetrust.org>

Lambeth Palace Library, Lambeth Palace Road, London SE1 7JU; tel. 020 7898 1400; internet: <www.lambethpalacelibrary.org>

Lancashire Record Office, Bow Lane, Preston, Lancashire PR1 2RE; tel. 01772 533039; internet: <www.lancashire.gov.uk/education>

Land Registry, Lincoln's Inn Fields, London WC2A 3PH; tel. 020 7917 8888; internet: <www.landreg.gov.uk>

Law Society Archives, Ipsley Court, Berrington Close, Redditch, Worcestershire B98 0TD; tel. 020 7242 1222; internet: <www.library.lawsociety.org.uk>

The Record Office for Leicestershire, Leicester and Rutland, Long Street, Wigston Magna, Leicester LE18 2AH; tel. 0116 257 1080; internet: <www.leics.gov.uk>

Lichfield Record Office, Staffordshire and Stoke-on-Trent Archive Service, Lichfield Library, The Friary, Lichfield WS13 6QG; tel. 01543 510720; internet: <www.staffordshire.gov.uk/archives>

Lincoln's Inn Library, Lincoln's Inn, London WC2A 3TN; tel. 020 7242 4371; internet: <www.lincolnsinn.org.uk>

Lincolnshire Archives, St Rumbold Street, Lincoln LN2 5AB; tel. 01522 526204; internet: <www.lincolnshire.gov.uk/archives>

North East Lincolnshire Archives, Town Hall, Town Hall Square, Grimsby DN31 1HX; tel. 01472 323585; internet: <www.nelincs.gov.uk/leisure/archives>

Liverpool Record Office, Central Library, William Brown Street, Liverpool L3 8EW; tel. 0151 233 5817; internet: <www.liverpool.gov.uk>

London boroughs

Barking and Dagenham, Archives and Local Studies Centre, Valence House Museum, Becontree Avenue, Dagenham, Essex RM8 3HT; tel. 020 8270 6896; internet: <www.barking-dagenham.gov.uk>

Barnet, Local Studies and Archives Service, Daws Lane, Mill Hill, London; tel. 020 8203 0130; internet: <www.barnet.gov.uk/cultural_services>

Bexley, Local Studies and Archive Centre, Central Library, Townley Road, Bexleyheath, Kent DA6 7HJ; tel. 020 8301 1545; internet: <www.bexley.gov.uk>

Brent, Brent Archive, Cricklewood Library, 152 Olive Road, London NW2 6UY; tel. 020 8937 3541; internet: <www.brent.gov.uk/archive>

Bromley, Local Studies and Archive Section, Central Library, High Street, Bromley, Kent BR1 1EX; tel. 020 8461 7170, ext. 261; internet: <www.bromley.gov.uk>

Camden, Camden Local Studies and Archives Centre, Holborn Library, 32–38 Theobalds Road, London WC1X 8PA; tel. 020 7974 6342; internet: <www.camden.gov.uk/localstudies>

Croydon, Croydon Local Studies Library and Archives Service, Central Library, Croydon Clocktower, Katharine Street, Croydon, Surrey CR9 1ET; tel. 020 8760 5400, ext. 1112; internet: <www.croydon.gov.uk/ledept/localstudies>

Ealing, Local History Centre, 103 Ealing Broadway Centre, The Broadway, London W5 5JY; tel. 020 8825 8194; internet: <www.ealing.gov.uk/services/libraries/>

Enfield, Local History Unit, Southgate Town Hall, Green Lanes, Palmers Green, London N13 4XD; tel. 020 8379 2724; internet: <www.enfield.gov.uk>

Greenwich, Heritage Centre, Artillery Square, Royal Arsenal, Woolwich, London SE3 7SE; tel. 020 8854 2452; internet: <www.greenwich.gov.uk/council>

Hackney, Archives Department, 43 De Beauvoir Road, London N1 5SQ; tel. 020 7241 2886; internet: <www.hackney.gov.uk/history>

Hammersmith and Fulham, Archives and Local History Centre, The Lilla Huset, 191 Talgarth Road, London W6 8BJ; tel. 020 8741 5159; internet: <www.lbhf.gov.uk/>

Haringey, Archive Service, Bruce Castle Museum, Lordship Lane, London N17 8NU; tel. 020 8808 8772; internet: <www.haringey.gov.uk>

Harrow, Reference Library, Civic Centre, Station Road, Harrow HA1 2UU; tel. 020 8424 1056; internet: <www.harrow.gov.uk>

Havering, Reference and Information Library, St Edward's Way, Romford, Essex RM1 3AR; tel. 01708 432394

Hillingdon, Local Studies and Museums Service, Central Library, 14–15 High Street, Uxbridge, Middlesex UB8 1HD; tel. 01895 250702; internet: <http://hillingdon.gov.uk/education/library/heritage>

Hounslow, Chiswick Reference Library, Dukes Avenue, Chiswick, London W4 2AB; tel. 020 8994 1008; internet: <www.cip.org.uk>

Hounslow, Hounslow Reference Library, 24 Treaty Centre, High Street, Hounslow, Middlesex TW3 1ES; tel. 020 8570 0622; internet: <www.cip.org.uk>

Islington, Islington History Collection, Central Library, 2 Fieldway Crescent, London N5 1PF; tel. 020 7527 6900; internet: <www.islington.gov.uk/learning>

Islington, Local History Centre, Finsbury Library, 245 St John Street, London, EC1V 4NB; tel. 020 7527 7988; internet: <www.islington.gov.uk/learning>

Kensington & Chelsea, Local Studies Section, Kensington Central Library, Phillimore Walk, London W8 7RX; tel. 020 7361 3038; internet: <www.rbkc.gov.uk>

Kingston upon Thames, Local History Room, North Kingston Centre, Richmond Road, Surrey KT2 5PE; tel. 020 8547 6738; internet: <www.kingston.gov.uk/leisure/museums. htm>

Lambeth, Archives Department, Minet Library, 52 Knatchbull Road, London SE5 9QY; tel. 020 7926 6076; internet: <www.lambeth.gov.uk>

Lewisham, Local Studies Centre, Lewisham Library, 199–201 Lewisham High Street, London SE13 6LG; tel. 020 8297 0682; internet: <www.lewisham.gov.uk>

Merton, Local Studies Centre, Merton Civic Centre, London Road, Morden, Surrey SM4 5DX; tel. 020 8545 3239; internet: <www.merton.gov.uk>

Newham, Archives and Local Studies Library, Stratford Library, 3 The Grove, Stratford, London E15 1EL; tel. 020 8430 6881; internet: <www.newham.gov.uk>

Richmond upon Thames, Local Studies Library, Old Town Hall, Whittaker Avenue, Richmond TW9 1TP; tel. 020 8332 6820; internet: <www.richmond.gov.uk>

Southwark, Local Studies Library, 211 Borough High Street, London SE1 1JA; tel. 020 7403 3507; internet: <www.southwark.gov.uk>

Sutton, Archives and Local Studies Search Room, Sutton Central Library, Sutton, Surrey SM1 1EA; tel. 020 8770 4747; internet: <www.sutton.gov.uk/lfl/heritage>

Tower Hamlets, Local History Library and Archives, Bancroft Library, 277 Bancroft Road, London E1 4DQ; tel. 020 7364 1289/90; internet: <www.towerhamlets.gov.uk>

Waltham Forest, Archives and Local Studies Library, Vestry Road, Walthamstow, London E17 9NH; tel. 020 8509 1917; internet: <www.lbwf.gov.uk>

Wandsworth, Local History Service Library, Battersea Library, 265 Lavender Hill, London SW11 1JB; tel. 020 8871 7753; internet: <www.wandsworth.gov.uk>

Westminster, Archives Centre, 10 St Ann's Street, London SW1P 2DE; tel. 020 7641 5180; internet: <www.westminster.gov.uk/libraries/archives>

London Metropolitan Archives, 40 Northampton Road, London EC1R 0HB; tel. 020 7332 3820; internet: <www.cityoflondon.gov.uk/leisure_heritage>

London Metropolitan Police Archives, Room 517, Wellington House, 67–73 Buckingham Gate, London, SW1E 6BE; tel. 020 7230 7186/6940

Greater Manchester County Record Office, 56 Marshall Street, New Cross, Manchester M4 5FU; tel. 0161 832 5284; internet: <www.gmcro.co.uk>

Manorial Documents Register, The National Archives, Kew, Richmond, Surrey TW9 4DU; tel. 020 8876 3444; internet: <www.hmc.gov.uk/mdr>

Maritime History Archive, Memorial University of Newfoundland, St John's, Newfoundland, Canada A1C 5S7; tel. 001 709 737 8428/9; internet: <www.mun.ca/mha>

Metropolitan Police Archives, New Scotland Yard, Victoria St, London SW1 0BG; internet: <www.met.police.uk/>

Merseyside Record Office, Central Library, William Brown Street, Liverpool L3 8EW; tel. 0151 233 5817; internet: <www.liverpool.gov.uk>

Middle Temple Library, Middle Temple Lane, London EC4Y 9BT; tel. 020 7427 4800; internet: <www.middletemple.org.uk>

Modern Records Centre, University of Warwick, University Library, Coventry CV4 7AL; tel. 024 7652 4219; internet: <warwick.ac.uk/services/library/mrc/mrc.html>

National Archives, Kew, Richmond, Surrey TW9 4DU; tel. 020 8876 3444; internet: <www.nationalarchives.gov.uk>

National Archives of Australia, PO Box 7425, Canberra Mail Centre, ACT Australia 2610; tel. (00) 61 2 6212 3600; internet: <www.naa.gov.au>

National Archives of Canada, 395 Wellington Street, Ottawa, Ontario K1A 0N3, Canada; tel. 00 1 613 995 5138; internet: <www.archives.ca>

National Archives of Ireland, Bishop Street, Dublin 8, Ireland; tel. 00 35 31 407 2300; internet: <www.nationalarchives.ie>

National Archives of New Zealand, PO Box 12–050, Wellington, New Zealand; tel. 0064 4499 5595; internet: <www.archives.govt.nz>

National Archives of Scotland, HM General Register House, Edinburgh EH1 3YY; tel. 0131 535 1334; internet: <www.nas.gov.uk>

National Archives of South Africa, Private Bag X236, Pretoria 0001, South Africa; tel. 0027 012 323 5300; internet: <www.national.archives.gov.za>

National Library of Australia, Parkes Place, Canberra, ACT 2600, Australia; tel. 00 61 2 6262 1111; internet: <www.nla.gov.au>

National Library of Ireland, Kildare Street, Dublin 2; tel. 00 353 1 603 0200; internet: <www.nli.ie>

National Library of Scotland, George IV Bridge, Edinburgh EH1 1EW; tel. 0131 226 4531; internet: <www.nls.uk>

National Library of Wales, Aberystwyth, Ceredigion SY23 3BU; tel. 01970 632800; internet: <www.llgc.org.uk>

Norfolk Record Office, The Archive Centre, Martineau Lane, Norwich NR1 2DQ; tel. 01603 222599; internet: <http://archives.norfolk.gov.uk>

North Yorkshire County Record Office, Malpas Road, Northallerton DL7 8AF; tel. 01609 777585; internet: <www.northyorks.gov.uk/libraries/archives>

Northamptonshire Record Office, Wootton Hall Park, Northampton NN4 8BQ; tel. 01604 762129; internet: <www.northamptonshire.gov.uk>

Northumberland Record Office, Melton Park, North Gosforth, Newcastle upon Tyne NE3 5QX; tel. 0191 236 2680; internet: <www.swinhope.myby.co.uk/NRO/index.html>

Nottinghamshire Archives, County House, Castle Meadow Road, Nottingham NG2 1AG; tel. 0115 958 1634; internet: <www.nottscc.gov.uk>

Oxfordshire Record Office, St Luke's Church, Temple Rd, Cowley, Oxford OX4 2EX; tel. 01865 398200; internet: <www.oxfordshire.gov.uk>

Pembrokeshire Record Office, The Castle, Haverfordwest SA61 2EF; tel. 01437 763707; internet: <www.llgc.org.uk/cac/cac0002.htm>

Plymouth and West Devon Record Office, Unit 3, Clare Place, Coxside, Plymouth PL4 0JW; tel. 01752 305940; internet: <www.plymouth.gov.uk/archives>

Post Office Archives and Record Centre, Freeling House, Phoenix Place, London WC1X 0DL; tel. 020 7239 2570

Powys County Archives, County Hall, Llandrindod Wells LD1 5LG; tel. 01597 826088; internet: <http://archives.powys.gov.uk>

Principal Registry of the Family Division, Decree Absolute Section, First Avenue House, 42–49 High Holborn, London WC1V 6NP; 020 7947 7015

Principal Registry of the Family Division, Probate Searchroom, First Avenue House, 42–49 High Holborn, London WC1V 6NP; tel. 020 7947 6000

Public Record Office of Northern Ireland (PRONI), 66 Balmoral Avenue, Belfast BT9 6NY; tel. 028 9025 5905; internet: <www.proni.gov.uk>

Registry of Shipping and Seamen, Anchor House, Cheviot Close, Parc-Ty-Glas, Llanishen, Cardiff CF4 5JA; tel. 029 2074 7333

Religious Society of Friends (Quakers) – Library, Friends House, 175–177 Euston Road, London NW1 2BJ; tel. 020 7663 1135; internet: <www.quaker.org.uk/library>

Sheffield Archives, 52 Shoreham Street, Sheffield S1 4SP; tel. 0114 203 9395

Shropshire Archives, Castle Gates, Shrewsbury SY1 2AQ; tel. 01743 255350; internet: <www.shropshirearchives.co.uk>

Somerset Archive and Record Service, Obridge Road, Taunton, Somerset TA2 7PU; tel. 01823 278805/337600; internet: <www.somerset.gov.uk/archives>

Southampton Archive Service, South Block, Civic Centre, Southampton SO14 7LY; tel. 023 8083 2251; internet: <www.southampton.gov.uk>

Staffordshire and Stoke-on-Trent Archive Service, Staffordshire Record Office, County Buildings, Eastgate Street, Stafford ST16 2LZ; tel. 01785 278379; internet: <www.staffordshire.gov.uk/archives>

State Records New South Wales, PO Box 516, Kingswood NSW 2747, Australia; tel. 00 61 2 9673 1788; internet: <www.records.nsw.gov.au>

Suffolk Record Office, 77 Raingate Street, Bury St Edmunds IP33 2AR; tel. 01284 352352; internet: <www.suffolkcc.gov.uk/sro>

Suffolk Record Office, Gatacre Road, Ipswich IP1 2LQ; tel. 01473 584541; internet: <www.suffolkcc.gov.uk/sro>

Suffolk Record Office, Central Library, Clapham Road, Lowestoft NR32 1DR; tel. 01502 405358; internet: <www.suffolkcc.gov.uk/sro>

Surrey History Centre, 130 Goldsworth Road, Woking GU21 1ND; tel. 01483 594594; internet: <www.surreycc.gov.uk/surreyhistoryservice>

East Sussex Record Office, The Maltings, Castle Precincts, Lewes BN7 1YT; tel. 01273 482349; internet: <www.eastsussexcc.gov.uk/archives>

West Sussex Record Office, County Hall, Chichester PO19 1RN; tel. 01243 753600; internet: <www.westsussex.gov.uk/librariesandarchives/recordoffice>

Teesside Archives, Exchange House, 6 Marton Road, Middlesbrough TS1 1DB; tel. 01642 248321; internet: <www.middlesbrough.gov.uk>

Tyne and Wear Archives Service, Blandford House, Blandford Square, Newcastle upon Tyne NE1 4JA; tel. 0191 232 6789; internet: <www.thenortheast.com/archives/index.html>

Warwickshire County Record Office, Priory Park, Cape Road, Warwick CV34 4JS; tel. 01926 738959; internet: <www.warwickshire.gov.uk/countyrecordoffice>

West Country Studies Library, Devon Studies Centre, Castle Street, Exeter, Devon EX4 3PQ; tel. 01392 384216; internet: <www.devon.gov.uk/library/locstudywsl.html>

West Yorkshire Archive Service, Registry of Deeds, Newstead Road, Wakefield WF1 2DE; tel. 01924 305980; internet: <www.archives.wyjs.org.uk>

Wiltshire and Swindon Record Office, Libraries and Heritage HQ, Wiltshire County Council, Bythesea Road, Trowbridge BA14 8BS; tel. 01225 713709; internet: <www.wiltshire.gov.uk/heritage/html/wsro.html>

Worcestershire Record Office, County Hall, Spetchley Road, Worcester WR5 2NP; tel. 01905 766351; internet: <www.worcestershire.gov.uk/records>

York City Archives, Art Gallery Building, Exhibition Square, York YO1 7EW; internet: <www.york.gov.uk/learning/libraries/archives/index.html>

York Probate Sub-Registry, Postal Searches and Copies Department, Duncombe Place, York YO1 7EA; tel. 01904 624210; internet: <www.netprobate.com/resources/probateoffices>

Other useful addresses

Armed forces

Airforce

Airborne Forces Museum, Browning Barracks, Aldershot, Hampshire GU11 2BU; tel. 01252 349619; internet: <www.parachute-regiment.com/museum/index.htm>

Fleet Air Arm Museum, Records & Research Centre, Box D6, RNAS Yeovilton, Ilchester, Somerset BA22 8HT; tel. 01935 840565; internet: <www.fleetairarm.com>

Royal Air Force Museum Hendon, Department of Aviation Records (Archives), Grahame Park Way, London NW9 5LL; tel. 020 8205 2266; internet: <www.rafmuseum.org.uk>

Army

Army Personnel Centre, Historic Disclosures, Mailpoint 400, Kentigern House, 65 Brown Street, Glasgow G2 8EX tel. A-CLAD 0141 224 2743; CLAE-FE 0141 224 2826; FI-KE 0141 224 2544; KH-OL 0141 224 3515; OM-SHEQ 0141 224 2744; SHER-Z 0141 224 2335; email: apc_historical_disclosures@btconnect.com

Ministry of Defence, Army Medal Office, Government Buildings, Worcester Road, Droitwich Spa, Worcester WR10 8AU; tel. 01905 772323

National Army Museum, Department of Records, Royal Hospital Road, Chelsea, London SW3 4HT; tel. 020 7730 0717; internet: <www.national-army-museum.ac.uk>

Royal Hospital Chelsea, Museum Curator, Royal Hospital Road, London SW3 4SR; tel. 020 7881 5204; internet: <www.chelsea-pensioners.co.uk>

Royal Military Police, Roussillon Barracks, Chichester, Sussex PO19 4BN; tel. 01243 534237 ext. 237; internet: <www.army.mod.uk/rhqrmp>

Navy

Ministry of Defence, Directorate of Personnel Support (Navy), Bourne Avenue, Hayes, Middlesex UB3 1RF; tel. 020 8573 3831 ext. 323; email: navysearch.defencerecords2@gtnet.gov.uk

Naval Dockyards Society, c/o 44 Lindley Avenue, Southsea, Hampshire PO4 9NU; internet: <www.hants.gov.uk/navaldockyard>

Royal Marines, Historical Record Office, HMS Centurion, Grange Road, Gosport, Hampshire PO13 9XA; tel. 023 9282 2351; internet: <www.mod.uk> [For Marines enlisted or commissioned during or after 1930]

Royal Marines Museum, Eastney, Southsea, Hampshire PO4 9PX; tel. 023 9281 9385; internet: <www.royalmarinesmuseum.co.uk>

Royal Naval Museum, HM Naval Base, Portsmouth, Hampshire PO1 3NH; tel. 023 9272 7577; internet: <www.royalnavalmuseum.org>

Royal Naval Secretary, Medals Section, HMS Centurion, Grange Road, Gosport, Hampshire PO13 9XA

Association of Genealogists and Researchers in Archives, 29 Badgers Close, Horsham, West Sussex RH12 5RU; internet: <www.agra.org.uk>

Barnardo's (Head Office), Tanners Lane, Barkingside, Ilford, Essex, IG6 1QG; tel. 020 8550 8822; internet: <www.barnardos.org.uk>

The British Museum, Great Russell Street, London WC1B 3DG; tel. 020 7323 8000; internet: <www.thebritishmuseum.ac.uk>

Catholic Family History Society, 45 Gates Green Road, West Wickham, Kent BR4 9DE; internet: <www.catholic-history.org.uk>

College of Arms, Queen Victoria Street, London EC4V 4BT; tel. 020 7248 2762; internet: <www.college-of-arms.gov.uk>

Commonwealth War Graves Commission, Information Office, 2 Marlow Road, Maidenhead, Berks SL6 7DX; tel. 01628 34221; internet: <www.cwgc.org>

Federation of Family History Societies, Administrator, PO Box 2425, Coventry CV5 6YX; internet: <www.ffhs.org.uk>

Genealogical Office of the Republic of Ireland, 2 Kildare Street, Dublin 2; tel. 00 353 1 603 0200; internet: <www.heanet.ie>

Genealogical Society of Utah, 50 East North Temple, Salt Lake City, Utah 84150, USA; internet: <www.lds.org> <www.familysearch.org>

Genealogical Society of Utah, British Isles Family History Service Centre, 185 Penns Lane, Sutton Coldfield, West Midlands B76 8JU; tel. 08700 102051/0121 384 2028

General Register Office of England and Wales, PO Box 2, Southport, Merseyside PR8 2JD; (certicate enquiries) tel. 0151 471 4816 ; internet: <www.statistics.gov.uk/nsbase/registration/general_register.asp>

General Register Office for England and Wales, Traceline, PO Box 106, Southport PR8 2WA; tel. 0151 471 4811 (Mon–Fri 9:00–4:30)

General Register Office of Ireland, Joyce House, 8–11 Lombard Street, Dublin 2, Ireland; tel. 00 353 1635 4000; internet: <www.groireland.ie>

General Register Office of Northern Ireland, Oxford House, 49–55 Chichester Street, Belfast BT1 4HL; tel. 028 9025 2000; internet: <www.groni.gov.uk>

General Register Office for Scotland, New Register House, Edinburgh EH1 3YT; tel. 0131 334 0380; internet: <www.gro-scotland.gov.uk/>

General Registry (Isle of Man), Douglas, Isle of Man IM2 2QR; tel. 01624 673358; internet: <www.gov.im/infocentre/faqs/FAQ26.HTML>

Guild of One Name Studies, Box G, c/o 14 Charterhouse Buildings, Goswell Road, London EC1M 7BA; internet: <www.one-name.org>

Immigration and Nationality Department, Nationality Office, B4 Division, India Buildings, Water Street, Liverpool L2 0QN; tel. 0151 2375200; internet: <www.ind.homeoffice.gov.uk>

Imperial War Museum, Department of Documents, Lambeth Road, London SE1 6HZ; tel. 020 7416 5221; internet: <www.iwm.org.uk>

Imperial War Museum (Aviation Museum), Duxford, Cambridgeshire CB2 4QR; tel. 01223 835000; internet: <www.iwm.org.uk>

Institute of Heraldic and Genealogical Studies, 79–82 Northgate, Canterbury, Kent CT1 1BA; tel. 01227 768664; internet: <www.ihgs.ac.uk>

International Society for British Genealogy and Family History, PO Box 3115, Salt Lake City, Utah 84110–3115, USA

Irish Genealogical Research Society, c/o 18 Stratford Avenue, Rainham, Kent ME8 0EP; internet: <www.igrsoc.org>

Jewish Genealogical Society of Great Britain, PO Box 13288, London, N3 3WD; internet: <www.jgsgb.org.uk>

Jewish Museum, The Sternberg Centre, 80 East End Road, Finchley, London N3 2SY; tel. 020 8349 1143; internet: <www.jewishmuseum.org.uk>

Mormon [LDS] Church – see Genealogical Society of Utah

Museum of English Rural Life, University of Reading, PO Box 229, Whiteknights Park, Reading RG6 6AG; tel. 0118 378 8660; internet: <www.ruralhistory.org>

Museum of London, London Wall, London, EC2Y 5HN; tel. 020 7814 5588; internet: <www.museumoflondon.org.uk>

National Genealogical Society, 4527 17th Street North, Arlington, Virginia 22207–2399, USA; internet: <www.ngsgenealogy.org>

National Maritime Museum, Romney Road, Greenwich, London SE10 9NF; tel. 020 8312 6750; internet: <www.nmm.ac.uk>

National Monuments Record Centre, Kemble Drive, Swindon, Wiltshire SN2 2GZ; tel. 01793 414600; internet: <www.english-heritage.org.uk>

National Register of Archives, The National Archives, Kew, Richmond, Surrey TW9 4DU; tel. 020 8876 3444; internet: <www.nationalarchives.gov.uk>

Society of Australian Genealogists, Richmond Villa, 120 Kent Street, Sydney NSW 2000; tel. 00 61 2 9247 3953; internet: <www.sag.org.au>

Society of Genealogists, 14 Charterhouse Buildings, Goswell Road, London EC1M 7BA; tel. 020 7251 8799; internet: <www.sog.org.uk>

Theatre Museum, 1E Tavistock Street, London WC2 7PA; tel. 020 7943 4700; internet: <www.theatremuseum.vam.ac.uk>

Victoria and Albert Museum, Cromwell Road, South Kensington, London SW7 2RL; tel. 020 7942 2000; internet: <www.vam.ac.uk>

Further reading

N. W. Alcock, *Old Title Deeds: A Guide for Local and Family Historians* (Phillimore, 1986)

T. Arkell, N. Evans and N. Goose (eds), *When Death Do Us Part: Understanding and Interpreting the Probate Records of Early Modern England* (Leopard's Head Press, 2000)

A. Armstrong, *Farmworkers: A Social and Economic History, 1770–1980* (Batsford, 1988)

D. Ashurst, 'The Accuracy of the Parish Register', *Ancestors* 11 (Dec 2002/Jan 2003)

M. Bailey, *The English Manor, c.1200–c.1500* (Manchester University Press, 2002)

N. Barratt, *Tracing the History of Your House: A Guide to Sources* (Public Record Office, 2001)

J. V. Beckett, *The Aristocracy in England, 1660–1914* (Blackwell, 1988)

G. Beech, 'Maps and Plans at the PRO', *Ancestors* 4 (Oct/Nov 2001)

G. Beech and R. Mitchell, *Maps for Family and Local History* (The National Archives, 2004)

R. Bellingham, 'Dade Registers', *Ancestors* 15 (Aug/Sep 2003)

J. Benson, *The Working Class in Britain, 1850–1939* (Longman, 1989)

T. Benton, *Irregular Marriages in London before 1754* (Society of Genealogists, 1993)

M. W. Beresford, *Time and Place: Collected Essays* (Hambledon, 1984)

M. W. Beresford and J. K. St Joseph, *Medieval England: An Aerial Survey*, 2nd edn (Cambridge University Press, 1979)

A. Bevan, 'Wills before 1858: The Prerogative Court at Canterbury', *Ancestors* 1 (Apr/May 2001)

A. Bevan, 'Divorce, 1858 Onwards', *Ancestors* 10 (Oct/Nov 2002)

A. Bevan, *Tracing Your Ancestors in the Public Record Office*, 6th edn (Public Record Office, 2002)

G. Bourne (pseudonym of G. Sturt), *The Wheelwright's Shop* (Cambridge University Press, 1923)

S. Caunce, *Amongst Farm Horses: The Horselads of East Yorkshire* (Sutton, 1991)

S. Caunce, *Oral History and the Local Historian* (Longman, 1994)

P. Christian, *The Genealogist's Internet*, 2nd edn (The National Archives, 2003)

P. Clark and D. Souden (eds), *Migration and Society in Early Modern England* (Hutchinson, 1987)

R. Colls, *Identity of England* (Oxford University Press, 2002)

S. Colwell, *The Family Records Centre: A User's Guide* (Public Record Office, 2002)

S. Colwell, *The National Archives: An Introduction for Family Historians* (The National Archives, 2004)

M. J. Daunton, *House and Home in the Victorian City: Working Class Housing, 1850–1914* (Arnold, 1983)

C. Dyer, *Making a Living in the Middle Ages: The People of Britain, 850–1520* (Yale University Press, 2002)

M. Ellis, *Using Manorial Records* (Public Record Office, 1997)

G. E. Evans, *Spoken History* (Faber, 1987)

C. Fenwick (ed.), *The Poll Taxes of 1377, 1379 and 1381* (The British Academy, 2 vols, 1997–2001)

S. Fowler and W. Spencer, *Army Records for Family Historians* (Public Record Office, 1998)

P. Franks, *Yorkshire Fisherfolk: A Social History of the Yorkshire Inshore Fishing Community* (Phillimore, 2002)

M. Gandy, *Catholic Missions and Registers* (Catholic Record Society, 6 vols, 1993)

D. Gerhold, 'Searching for Justice: Chancery Records', *Ancestors* 13 (Apr/May 2003)

J. Gibson, *Bishops' Transcripts and Marriage Licences, Bonds and Allegations: A Guide to their Location and Indexes* (Federation of Family History Societies, 1997)

J. Gibson and A. Dell, *Tudor and Stuart Muster Rolls: A Directory of Holdings in the British Isles* (Federation of Family History Societies, 1991)

J. Gibson and A. Dell, *The Protestation Returns, 1641–2* (Federation of Family History Societies, 1995)

J. Gibson and B. Langston, *Probate Jurisdiction: Where to Look for Wills*, 5th edn (Federation of Family History Societies, 2002)

J. Gibson, B. Langston and B. W. Smith, *Local Newspapers, 1750–1920*, 2nd edn (Federation of Family History Societies, 2002)

J. Gibson and M. Medlycott, *Militia Lists and Musters, 1757–1876: A Directory of Holdings in the British Isles* (Federation of Family History Societies, 1994)

J. Gibson, M. Medlycott and D. Mills, *Land and Window Tax Assessments* (Federation of Family History Societies, 1993)

J. Gibson and C. Rogers, *Coroners' Records in England and Wales* (Federation of Family History Societies, 1992)

J. Gibson and F. A. Youngs, Jr, *Poor Law Union Records: 4. Gazetteer of England and Wales* (Federation of Family History Societies, 1993)

D. Ginter, *A Measure of Wealth: The English Land Tax in Historical Analysis* (Hambledon, 1992)

R. Gough, *The History of Myddle*, ed. D. Hey (Penguin, 1980)

K. Grannum and N. Taylor, *Wills and Other Probate Records* (The National Archives, 2004)

P. Hanks and F. Hodges, *The Oxford Dictionary of Surnames* (Oxford University Press, 1989)

A. Hanson, 'A Litigant in the Family', *Ancestors* 13 (Apr/May 2003)

P. D. A. Harvey, *Manorial Records*, 2nd edn (British Records Society, 2000)

D. T. Hawkings, *Criminal Ancestors: A Guide to Historical Criminal Records in England and Wales* (Sutton, 1992)

D. T. Hawkings, *Railway Ancestors: A Guide to the Staff Records of the Railway Companies of England and Wales, 1822–1947* (Sutton, 1995)

M. Herber, *Clandestine Marriages in the Chapel and Rules of the Fleet Prison, 1680–1754* (Boutle, 3 vols, 1998–2000)

M. D. Herber, *Ancestral Trails* (Sutton, 1997)

D. Hey, *The Oxford Companion to Local and Family History* (Oxford University Press, 1996)

D. Hey, *Family Names and Family History* (Hambledon & London, 2000)

D. Hey, *How Our Ancestors Lived: A History of Life a Hundred Years Ago* (Public Record Office, 2002)

D. Hey and G. Redmonds, *Yorkshire Surnames and the Hearth Tax Returns of 1672–73* (Borthwick Paper, 102, York University, 2002)

B. A. Holderness, 'Personal Mobility in Some Rural Parishes of Yorkshire, 1777–1822', *Yorkshire Archaeological Journal* 42 (1970)

C. Holmes, *John Bull's Island: Immigration and British Society, 1871–1971* (Macmillan, 1988)

P. Horn, *The Victorian Country Child* (Sutton, 1985)

H. Horwitz, *Chancery Equity Records and Proceedings, 1600–1800* (Public Record Office, 1995)

W. G. Hoskins, 'Leicestershire Yeoman Families and Their Pedigrees', *Transactions of the Leicestershire Archaeological Society*, XXIII, part 1 (1946)

C. R. Humphery-Smith (ed.), *The Phillimore Atlas and Index of Parish Registers*, 3rd edn (Phillimore, 2003)

P. Jenkins, *A History of Modern Wales, 1536–1990* (Longman, 1992)

E. C. Joslin, A. R. Litherland and B. T. Simpkin, *British Battles and Medals* (Spink, 1988)

R. J. P. Kain and R. R. Oliver, *Historic Parishes of England and Wales: An Electronic Map of Boundaries before 1850 with a Gazetteer and Metadata* (Historic Data Service, UK Data Archive, University of Essex, 2001)

R. J. P. Kain and H. C. Prince, *Tithe Surveys of England and Wales* (Cambridge University Press, 1995)

R. Kershaw and M. Pearsall, *Immigrants and Aliens* (Public Record Office, 2000)

A. J. Kettle (ed.), 'A List of Families in the Archdeaconry of Stafford', *Collections for a History of Staffordshire*, 4th series, 8 (1976)

B. Langston, *A Handbook to the Civil Registration Districts of England and Wales* (privately published, 2001)

R. E. Latham, *Revised Medieval Latin Word List* (British Academy, 1965)

J. Lawson, *Progress in Pudsey* (Caliban, 1978 reprint)

D. Levine and K. E. Wrightson, *The Making of an Industrial Society: Whickham, 1560–1765* (Oxford University Press, 1991)

N. Longmate, *The Workhouse: A Social History* (Pimlico, 2003)

S. Lumas, *Making Use of the Census*, 4th edn (Public Record Office, 2002)

P. McClure, 'Patterns of Migration in the Late Middle Ages: The Evidence of English Place-Name Surnames', *Economic History Review*, second series, 32 (1979)

R. McKinley, *A History of British Surnames* (Longman, 1990)

E. Miller and J. Hatcher, *Medieval England: Rural Society and Economic Change, 1086–1348* (Longman, 1978)

D. Mills and K. Schürer (eds), *Local Communities in the Victorian Census Enumerators' Books* (Leopard's Head Press, 1996)

D. R. Mills, *Rural Community History from Trade Directories* (Local Population Studies supplement, 2001)

G. E. Mingay (ed.), *The Victorian Countryside*, 2 vols (Routledge & Kegan Paul, 1981)

R. Mitchell, 'The National Farm Survey', *Ancestors* 7 (Apr/May 2002)

T. J. and P. Morgan, *Welsh Surnames* (University of Wales Press, 1985)

A. Morton, 'Assize Courts', *Ancestors* 1 (Apr/May 2001)

J. E. Norton, *Guide to the National and Provincial Directories of England and Wales, excluding London, Published before 1856* (Royal Historical Society, 1956)

B. Pappalardo, 'Indexing the Admiralty', *Ancestors* 15 (Aug/Sep 2003)

B. Pappalardo, *Tracing Your Naval Ancestors* (The National Archives, 2003)

R. Pols, *Family Photographs, 1860–1945* (Public Record Office, 2002)

C. Pooley and J. Turnbull, *Migration and Mobility in Britain since the Eighteenth Century* (UCL Press, 1998)

P. H. Reaney, *The Origins of English Surnames* (Routledge & Kegan Paul, 1967)

P. H. Reaney and R. M. Wilson, *A Dictionary of English Surnames* (Oxford University Press, 1997)

B. Reay, *Microhistories: Demography, Society and Culture in Rural England, 1800–1930* (Cambridge University Press, 1996)

G. Redmonds, *Surnames and Genealogy: A New Approach* (Federation of Family History Societies, 2002)

E. Roberts, *A Woman's Place: an Oral History of Working-Class Women, 1890–1940* (Blackwell, 1984)

J. and S. Rowlands, *The Surnames of Wales* (Federation of Family History Societies, 1996)

S. Rowntree, *Poverty: A Study of Town Life* (Macmillan, 1901)

K. Schürer and T. Arkell (eds), *Surveying the People* (Leopard's Head Press, 1992)

S. Scott and C. J. Duncan, *Biology of Plagues: Evidence from Historical Populations* (Cambridge University Press, 2001)

P. Seaman (ed.), *Norfolk Hearth Tax Exemption Certificates, 1670–74* (British Records Society, 2001)

G. Shaw and A. Tipper, *British Directories: A Bibliography and Guide to Directories Published in England and Wales (1850–1950) and Scotland (1773–1950)* (Leicester University Press, 1988)

B. Short, *The Geography of England and Wales in 1910: An Evaluation of Lloyd George's 'Domesday of Landownership'* (Cambridge University Press, 1989)

B. Short, *Land and Society in Edwardian Britain* (Cambridge University Press, 1997)

P. Slack, *The English Poor Law, 1531–1782* (Oxford University Press, 1990)

P. Slack, *The Impact of Plague in Tudor and Stuart England* (Oxford University Press, 1990)

K. D. M. Snell, *Annals of the Labouring Poor: Social Change in Agrarian England, 1660–1900* (Cambridge University Press, 1985)

W. Spencer, *Records of the Militia and Volunteer Forces, 1757–1945* (Public Record Office, 1997)

W. Spencer, *Air Force Records for Family Historians* (Public Record Office, 2000)

W. Spencer, *Army Service Records of the First World War*, 3rd edn (Public Record Office, 2001)

M. Spufford, *Contrasting Communities* (Cambridge University Press, 1974)

M. Spufford, *The Great Reclothing of Rural England: Petty Chapmen and their Wares in the Seventeenth Century* (Hambledon, 1984)

M. Spufford (ed.), *The World of Rural Dissenters, 1520–1725* (Cambridge University Press, 1995)

J. Thirsk (ed.), *Rural England: An Illustrated History of the Landscape* (Oxford University Press, 2002)

F. Thompson, *Lark Rise to Candleford* (Penguin, 1973)

F. M. L. Thompson, *The Rise of Respectable Society: A Social History of Victorian Britain, 1830–1900* (Fontana, 1988)

C. Webb, *Dates and Calendars for the Genealogist* (Society of Genealogists, 1998)

M. A. Williams, *Researching Local History: The Human Journey* (Longman, 1996)

T. Williamson, *The Transformation of Rural England; Farming and the Landscape, 1700–1870* (University of Exeter Press, 2002)

A. Wood, *The Politics of Social Conflict: The Peak Country, 1520–1770* (Cambridge University Press, 1999)

T. Woodcock and J. M. Robinson, *The Oxford Guide to Heraldry* (Oxford University Press, 1988)

K. Wrightson, *English Society, 1580–1680* (Hutchinson, 1982)

K. Wrightson, *Earthly Necessities: Economic Lives in Early Modern Britain* (Yale University Press, 2000)

F. A. Youngs, Jr, *Guide to the Local Administrative Units of England* (Royal Historical Society, 2 vols, 1980–91)

Picture sources

T = top, **B** = bottom, **L** = left, **R** = right
All document references are to holdings of the National Archives unless otherwise stated. Every effort has been made to trace copyright holders, but in some instances this has not been possible because of the antiquity of the images.

Jacket

Front Jane Parker **back** Ironbridge Gorge Museum, Telford, Shropshire, UK/www.bridgeman.co.uk; Robert Pols
left flap Mary Evans Picture Library **right flap** David Hey

Front matter

i COPY 1/130 **v** Jane Parker **vi** COPY 1/115(2)
vii © Yale Center for British Art, Paul Mellon Collection, USA/www.bridgeman.co.uk **viii** © The British Library, Royal 10 E. IV **xi** COPY 1/479

Introduction

1 Jane Parker **2** COPY 1/456 **3** COPY 1/453(1) **4** COPY 1/143(2) **7** Photograph by Keith Mitchell, Family Records Centre

1: Into Recent Memory (1900–)

Exploring your Past
12 COPY 1/260 **14** David Hey **15** Jane Parker **17** Jane Parker **18T** COPY 1/244 **18B** PRO 30/69/1663(73), James Ramsay MacDonald collection **19** Reproduced with kind permission of Unilever Plc from an original in Unilever Corporate Archives **20** HLG 47/323 **21** COPY 1/305 **22** COPY 1/515 **23** COPY 1/509 **24** COPY 1/143 **25** David Hey **27** COPY 1/419, photograph by F. M. Sutcliffe **29** PRO 30/69/1663(74), James Ramsay MacDonald collection **30** PRO 30/69/1663(61), James Ramsay MacDonald collection **32** COPY 1/265 **34T** RAIL 253/516 **34B** © Hulton-Deutsch Collection/CORBIS **35** © Ric Ergenbright/CORBIS

Finding your Ancestors
37 North West Kent Family History Society **39** © Rex Batten, reproduced by courtesy of the Friends of Nunhead Cemetery

41 Robert Pols **42** Jane Parker **44** COPY 1/555 **45** *Sheffield Daily Telegraph* **46** MAF 32/327(2) **47** MAF 73/49/273(15) **48** IR 58/29280 **49** WO 363 **50** WO 138/74 **51T/B** Deborah Pownall **53T** ADM 188/732 **53B** ZPER 34/149, *Illustrated London News*, 22 July 1916

2: Through the Nineteenth Century (1800–1900)

Exploring your Past
54 COPY 1/442(2) **56** COPY 1/78 **57** COPY 1/57 **58** COPY 1/416(2) **60, 61B** COPY 1/427 **61T** Norfolk Museums Service (Norwich Castle Museum) UK/www.bridgeman.co.uk **62** Blackburn Museum and Art Gallery, Lancashire, UK/www.bridgeman.co.uk, reproduced by courtesy of Felix Rosenstiel's Widow & Son Ltd, London **63** COPY 1/419(2), photograph by F. M. Sutcliffe **65** ZPER 34/90 **66** COPY 1/166 **68** COPY 1/416 **69** COPY 1/77 **70** Mallett & Son Antiques Ltd, London, UK/www.bridgeman.co.uk **71** COPY 1/443, photograph by John McMichael **72** COPY 1/115(2) **73** COPY 1/367 **74** COPY 1/428 **76** Mary Evans Picture Library **77** RAIL 410/1403 **78** COPY 1/169 **79** MH 12/7698 **80** From *The Jews in London* by C. Russell & H. S. Lewis, 1900 **82** COPY 1/149 **83** COPY 1/38 **84** Reproduced by permission of Birmingham Library Services **85** Mary Evans Picture Library **86** Photograph by Albert Jackson, from *Period House* by Albert Jackson and David Day (HarperCollins, 2002) **87** COPY 1/420, photograph by George Davison **89** COPY 1/78 **90** COPY 1/381, photograph by F. Broderick **91** COPY 1/115

Finding your Ancestors
93, 94 Photographs by Keith Mitchell, Family Records Centre **96, 98, 100** General Register Office **99** David Hey **103** COPY 1/29 **107** ZPER 34/98, *Illustrated London News*, 11 April 1891 **110** RG 13/1300 **111L** ZPER 34/56, *Illustrated London News*, 19 March 1870 **111R** HO 107/680 **113T** COPY 1/57 **113B** RG 11/855 **115** *The British 19th Century Surname Atlas*, Archer Software (www.archersoftware.co.uk) **117, 118, 119** The National Archives (library) **120** MFQ 107(1) **121T** The National Archives (library) **121B** MFQ 107(3) **122** WO 76/10 **123** WO 97/1797 **124** WO 12/7667 **126** COPY 1/168 **127** ADM 101/123/2

128 ADM 107/12 **130** BT 100/259 **131** COPY 1/498 **132** C 106/44(1) **133** IR 30/9/160 **135** IR 29/21/3 **136** IR 30/27/115 **139** HO 44/27/2 **141** MH 12/8208 **142** COPY 1/445 **143** MEPO 4/389 **144** PCOM 2/291/411 **145** HO 61/9 **146** RG 5/83 **147T** William Penn House, Buckinghamshire, UK/www.bridgeman.co.uk **147B** RG 6/690 **148** RG 4/3343 **151** House of Lords Record Office (Main Papers, 1767) **152** HO 334/4 **153** Guildhall Library, Corporation of London

3: Making Early Connections (1550–1800)

Exploring your Past

154 MPC 1/75 **156** David Hey **157** MPB 1/23(1) **158** Cheltenham Art Gallery & Museums, Gloucestershire, UK/www.bridgeman.co.uk **159** From *The Roxburghe Ballads* **160** Morden College, Corporation of London, UK/www.bridgeman.co.uk **162** © Yale Center for British Art, Paul Mellon Collection, USA/www.bridgeman.co.uk **163** From *The Roxburghe Ballads* **164** Guildhall Library, Corporation of London **165** SP 29/126 **166** MPC 1/251 **168** David Hey **169** Private collection/www.bridgeman.co.uk **171** Ironbridge Gorge Museum, Telford, Shropshire, UK/www.bridgeman.co.uk **172** Mary Evans Picture Library **174** MPC 1/85(2) **175, 176** David Hey **179** C 103/12/1 **180** Holburne Museum, Bath, UK/www.bridgeman.co.uk **181** Guildhall Library, Corporation of London **182** © Yale Center for British Art, Paul Mellon Collection, USA/ www.bridgeman.co.uk **184** SP 12/82 **185** C 73/13 **186** Ironbridge Gorge Museum, Telford, Shropshire, UK/ www.bridgeman.co.uk **189T** © The British Library, Add. 34856 **189B** © The British Library, Add. 34856

Finding your Ancestors

191 COPY 1/455 **192, 197** Courtesy of Cheshire and Chester Archives and Local Studies **198** Mary Evans Picture Library **199, 201** Courtesy of Cheshire and Chester Archives and Local Studies **202** Borthwick Institute of Historical Research, University of York **205** Guildhall Library, Corporation of London, UK/www.bridgeman.co.uk **207** Reproduced by permission of the Head of Leisure Services, Sheffield City Council (Sheffield Archives PR 3/12/1) **209** Surrey History

Service (Surrey County Archives P43/3/16) **210** Guildhall Library, Corporation of London **211T** COPY 1/42 **211B** National Probate Calendar, 1881 **213** PROB 11/46 **214T** © Bettman/CORBIS **214B** PROB 6/103 **216** PROB 12/218 **218** PROB 10 **220T** Reproduced by permission of Lichfield Diocesan Registrar (Lichfield Record Office B/C/11) **220B** David Hey **223** PRO 30/26/200 **224** From *The Pepys Ballads* **226** CHES 38/28/12 **227** IR 23/78 **228** IR 23/77 **230** E 179/335 **231T** Mary Evans Picture Library **231B** E 179/252/32 **233** E 179/256/31 **234** British Library, London, UK/www.bridgeman.co.uk **235** House of Lords Record Office (Main Papers, 1642: Protestations, Cornwall A) **236** E 101/59/21 **237** Guildhall Library, Corporation of London **238** Courtesy of the John Goodchild Collection **239** Guildhall Library, Corporation of London **241** The National Archives (library) **242** J 90/1711 **243** C 103/12/1

4: Back to the Middle Ages (–1550)

Exploring your Past

244 © The British Library, Add. 42130 **246** © The British Library, Royal 6 E. VII **249** E 163/22/2/60 **250** Private collection/www.bridgeman.co.uk **252** Osterreichische Nationalbibliothek, Vienna, Austria/www.bridgeman.co.uk **253** © The British Library, Royal 10 E. IV **255** INF 9/143, Dixon-Scott collection **256** © The British Library, Add. 42130 **259** MPI 1/221 **261** E 164/25 **262** MPEE 1/25 **266** © The British Library, Add. 42130 **268** Fitzwilliam Museum, University of Cambridge, UK/www.bridgeman.co.uk **270** Mary Evans Picture Library

Finding your Ancestors

274 MPC 1/238(1) **277** SC 2/19/2 **278** SC 2/193/13 **279** LR 2/206 **281** E 179/180/6 **282** © The British Library, Royal 18 E. I **283** E 179/146/369 **285** CP 25/1(92) **287** SP 9/1/2

Resource Bank

288 COPY 1/369

Index

abbreviations 5
absent voters, First World War 53
Access to Archives 10
Act of Settlement 1662 207
Additional Charters 284
Admiralty 127
   records (ADM) 52, 128–9
admons *see* letters of administration
adoption 103
agricultural labourers
   1550–1800 167, 180–81
   1800–1900 59–60, 63–4
agriculture
   –1550 250–51, 256–7
   1550–1800 167, 180–81, 185–8
   1800–1900 62–5, 133–7
   1900– 26–7
Air Ministry records (AIR) 52
aliases, parish registers 203
apprentices
   1550–1800 180–81, 183, 206–7, 222–5
   1800–1900 66
apprenticeship indentures 222–4
aristocracy
   1550–1800 169–70
   decline of 27
   family size 16
armed forces *see* Army; military records;
   Royal Flying Corps; Royal Marines;
   Royal Navy
Army
   First World War 49–52
   records 1800–1900 120, 121–7
Army Personnel Centre 53
assize records (ASSI) 144
attestation papers 51, 124–5
Australia 80, 184

Baines, Edward 67, 68
baptisms
   1550–1800 163–4, 190–203
   Nonconformist 146–9

Roman Catholic 150–51
Baptists 146, 149
Bell, Lady Florence 18
birth certificates 92, 95–7, 140
birth rate 73, 158–9
births
   civil registration 92, 95–7
   gravestones 36
   Jewish records 153
   Nonconformist 147–9
   overseas 101
   parish registers 197–8
   workhouses 140
Births and Deaths Act 1874 96
bishops' transcripts 190, 193, 196
Black Death 248–51, 258, 259–60, 269
Board of Trade records (BT) 130
Bodleian Library 45
Boer War 126–7
Booth, Charles 32
Borthwick Institute of Historical Research
   190, 212
Bourne, George 26
British Isles Vital Records Index 193–5
British Library, medieval records 284
British Record Society 230
burials
   1550–1800 165
   gravestones 36–40
   Jewish records 153
   Nonconformist 146, 148–9
   parish registers 203
   Roman Catholic 150–51

calendars 284–5
Cambridge University 132
cartes de visite 41
Catholic Central Library 150
Catholic Family History Society 150–51
Catholic Record Society 150
CD-ROMs, 1881 census 108
census returns 106–15

1801 56–7, 159
1881 108
1901 57, 108–9
   enumerators' books 106, 109–114
   naval personnel 129
   prisoners 145
   religion 149
   workhouses 141
certificates, copies 94–5
Chancery records (C) 102, 239–40
Charter Rolls 285
Chelsea Pensioners 125–6
children
   –1550 252–3
   1550–1800 163–4
   1800–1900 64, 66, 67, 72–4
   1900– 31
   census returns 114
Church of England
   Nonconformists 146–7
   parish registers 190–203
   wills and probate 212–21
Church of Jesus Christ of Latter-day
   Saints (LDS)
   census returns 106, 108
   Family History Centres 6, 193
   First World War records 50
   IGI 149, 193–5
   indexes of civil registration 101
   Nonconformists records 149
   Royal Navy records 129
   website 9
churchyards 36–40
civil registration 92–105
   census returns 113
   Nonconformists 149
   Roman Catholicism 151
   Royal Marines 129
Civil War 160, 197, 234–5
clandestine marriages 200–201
class
   1550–1800 169–72

1800–1900 83–7
family size 16
Close Rolls 102, 285
clothes 15
  dating photographs 43
coal-mining 15, 60–61, 68–9
The College of Arms 287
commercial directories 116–19
Commonwealth (1653–60) 197, 214
computer software 4
confirmation, Roman Catholicism 150
Congregationalists 146, 149
copyhold tenure 178–9, 276
Copyright Office, Stationers' Company
    records (COPY) 43
core families 177
coroners' courts 145
cotton mills 66–7
'country' 14
  –1550 263–4
  1550–1800 173–7
  1800–1900 76–7
  1900– 32–3
countryside
  see also agriculture
  –1550 256–7
  1550–1800 158–60
  1800–1900 57, 58–65
  1900– 20–21
county record offices
  criminal records 144–5
  estate papers 279
  manor court records 272–5
  parish registers 193
  Poor Law records 140
court baron 276–7
Court of Chancery 102, 133, 239–40, 284
Court of Common Pleas records (CP)
    285
Court of Exchequer 240, 284
  see also Exchequer records
court leet 276–7
Court of Requests 240
cremation 40
crime, 1900– 30–31
Crimean War 126–7
Cyndi's List 9

Dade Registers 176, 202
dates 196–7, 284
death certificates 92, 100–101
  First World War 53
  workhouses 140

death duty registers 221
death rate
  –1550 248–51
  1550–1800 158–9, 162, 164–5
  1800–1900 73–5
deaths
  civil registration 92, 100–101
  First World War 53
  gravestones 36–40
  London 1550–1800 182–3
  newspapers 44, 45
  Nonconformists 148–9
  overseas 101
  workhouses 140
Debt of Honour Register 53
deed poll, changing a name by 102
'deserving poor' 206–7
discharge papers 124–5
disease
  –1550 248–51
  1550–1800 164–5
  1800–1900 73–5
Dissenters 146–9
dissolution of the monasteries 170, 171
divorce 103
DNA 4, 270
Domesday Book 265–6
domestic service 24–5
  1550–1800 161, 180–81
  1800–1900 63, 71
Dr Barnardo's 103
Dr Williams' Library 147–8

education 31, 131–2
electoral rolls, First World War 53
emigration 30, 79–80, 183–4
enclosure 62–3, 133–4, 187
English, B. 133
estate duty registers 221
estate papers 279
Exchequer records (E) 230, 240, 280, 282

families
  –1550 252–3
  1550–1800 161–5, 176–9, 216–19
  1800–1900 72–5
  1900– 16–17
family history societies 5
  see also Federation of Family History
      Societies
  census returns 107
  gravestones 38
  parish registers 193

Family Records Centre 9
  Adopted Children's Registers 103
  census returns 106, 107, 110
  civil registration 92–105
  death or estate duty registers 221
  divorces 103
  First World War 53
  IGI 193
  Royal Navy records 129
  trade and commercial directories 116
  wills and probate 212, 214–15
family trees 4–5
farming see agriculture
Federation of Family History Societies 5,
    9, 108, 202
feet of fines 284–5
Finance Act 1910 48
Fine Rolls 285
First World War 34–5, 49–53
fishing 26
forenames, parish registers 203
France, immigration from 1550–1800
    183–4
FreeBMD 102
freemen 225–6
friendly societies records (FS) 143

General Register of Births for Dissenters
    147
GENUKI 8–9, 121
getting started 2–7
Gough, Richard 156, 163, 164, 204, 209
graves 36–40, 53, 148
Great Exhibition 1851 69
Guild of One-Name Studies 11
Guildhall Library 116, 130, 226, 241

Hardwicke's Act see Marriage Act 1753
Harrison, William 166, 167–8, 169,
    170–71
health 31, 73–5
  see also disease
hearth tax returns 176–7, 185–6, 229–33
Heath, Francis 20
heraldry 286–7
High Farming 64
holidays 78, 88
Home Office records (HO) 144
House of Lords, protestation returns
    234–5
houses
  –1550 254–5
  1550–1800 166–8

1800–1900 83–7, 90–91
1900– 18–21
Huguenots 184
husbandmen 170, 179, 185

IGI *see* International Genealogical Index
illegitimacy
1550–1800 163–4, 203, 210
1800–1900 73
birth certificates 95
marriage certificates 97
immigration
1550–1800 183–4
1800–1900 79, 81–2, 151
1900– 28–30
Imperial Yeomanry 127
Industrial Revolution 66–71, 160, 162,
188–9
industry 22–7, 60–61, 66–71, 170, 188–9
infant mortality 17, 73–5, 164
inheritance 178–9, 216–19
Inland Revenue
land and property surveys 1900–48
records (IR) 48, 135–7, 221, 222, 227
Inquisitions Post Mortem 285
Institute of Heraldic and Genealogical
Studies 93–4, 192, 287
International Genealogical Index (IGI)
149, 193–5
Internet 8–11, 102, 108–9
inventories 219–21
Ireland 81, 184

Supreme Court of Judicature records (J)
102–3
Jewish Genealogical Society of Great
Britain 153
Jews 28–30, 82, 152–3
journeymen 225
justices records (JUST) 144

Kelly, Francis 116

land surveys 46–8
land tax assessments 227–8
land title 284–5
Lawson, Joseph 88, 90
lay subsidy 280–81, 283
LDS *see* Church of Jesus Christ of Latter-
day Saints
lead mining 188–9
leases 178–9, 277–9
legal profession 1550–1800 241

letters of administration (admons) 211–12,
215
Lewis, Samuel 116–17, 229–30
libraries 5–6, 10–11
Library of the Religious Society of
Friends 148
life expectancy 17, 165
List and Index Society 149
Livery Companies, freemen 226
Lloyd's captains' registers 130
local newspapers 44–5, 52–3, 145
local record offices 5–6, 101
see also county record offices
employment records 142–3
land surveys 1900 48
websites 10–11
wills and probate 212
London
–1550 261, 264
1550–1800 159, 172, 182–3, 190
1800–1900 58, 71
1900– 21
census returns finding aids 110–111
freemen 225, 226
hearth tax returns 231
parishes 190
public cemeteries 40
wills and probate 212
London Metropolitan Archives 116, 143,
212
London Transport 143

manor court records 272–9
manorial surveys 277–9
maps 11, 137, 192, 195–6
marriage
–1550 252–3
1550–1800 161–3, 190–203
civil registration 92, 94, 97–8
Jewish records 153
Nonconformist 146, 147, 148–9
overseas 101
Roman Catholic 151
Marriage Act 1753 (Lord Hardwicke's Act)
147, 200–201
marriage certificates 92, 97–8
marriage portions 163
Medal Index Cards (MIC) 52
medals 52, 127
memorial cards 40
Merchant Navy 130
Methodists 148–9
microfilm, census returns 107

Middle Ages 244–87
middle class 83–4
migration
–1550 261–4
1550–1800 182–4
1800–1900 58–61, 76–8
military records
1550–1800 236–8
1800–1900 120–30
First World War 34–5
miscellaneous returns 101
militia lists 236–8
Ministry of Agriculture and Fisheries
records (MAF) 46
Ministry of Health records (MH) 141
miscellaneous returns 101
mobility
–1550 261–4
1550–1800 173–7, 182–4
1800–1900 76–8
1900– 32–3
Modern Records Centre, University of
Warwick Library 143
monumental inscriptions (MIs) 38
Moravians 148
Mormons *see* Church of Jesus Christ of
Latter-day Saints
motor car 21, 32
muster rolls 123–4, 125–6, 236

names
see also surnames
change of 102
parish registers 203
The National Archives
apprenticeship indentures 222–4
census returns 106, 108
death or estate duty 221
divorces 103
education records 131–2
employment records 142–3
hearth tax returns 229–30
indexes of civil registration 101
lay subsidy 280
legal profession 241
manor court records 272–5
medieval records 284
Merchant Navy 130
military records 49–52, 120, 121–9
National Farm Survey 46
Nonconformists 147–8, 149
prison records 144–5
Roman Catholic records 150

tithe awards 135–7
title deeds 242–3
website 9, 10
wills and probate 212, 214–15
workhouse records 140–41
National Burials Index 202
National Farm Survey 1941–43 46
national gazetteer 116–17
National Library of Wales
  census returns 106–7
  monumental inscriptions 38
  newspapers 45
  Nonconformists 149
  wills and probate 212
New Poor Law 138–41
Newspaper Library 45, 53
newspapers 44–5, 52–3, 145
Nonconformists 146–9, 198
North America 184

occupations
  1800–1900 116–19, 142–3
  1900– 22–7
  census returns 114
  surnames 266–7, 271
old age pensions 28
Old Bailey Proceedings 145
Old Dissenters 146–9
Old Poor Law 204–10
Ordnance Survey 11
Oxford University 132

Parish Register 197–8
parish registers 146–7, 158, 190–203
parishes
  1550–1800 190–93
  manors 275
  settlement disputes 207–9
  tithe awards 137
Patent Rolls 285
Pathways to the Past 120
pensions and National Insurance records
    (PIN) 51, 126
photographs 14–15, 25–6, 41–3, 123
picture postcards 43
plague 164–5, 182, 248–51
poll taxes 265, 280–83
Poor Law, 1550–1800 171–2, 204–210
Poor Law Amendment Act 1834 87,
    138–41, 204
Poor Law Unions 138–41
population 248–51
  1550–1800 158–60, 161–2

1800–1900 56–7, 72
Post Office 142
poverty
  1550–1800 171–2, 204–210
  1800–1900 87, 138–41
  1900– 28–31
Prerogative Court at Canterbury (PCC)
    215
Principal Registry of the Family Division
    103, 211–12
Prison Commission records (PCOM)
    144–5
probate 211–21
progress 88–91
proof 7
Protestant Nonconformists 146–9
protestation returns 234–5
public cemeteries 40

Quakers (Society of Friends) 146–9
quarries 69
quarter sessions 208–9

railways 76, 78, 143
record keeping 4
regiments 120, 121, 123–6
Registrar General records (RG) 148, 149,
    150, 201
registration districts 93–4, 106
Return of Owners of Land, 1873 48
Roman Catholicism 150–51
Rowlands, M.B. 150
Rowntree, Seebohm 28
Royal Flying Corps 52
Royal Marines 129
Royal Naval Air Service 52
Royal Navy 52, 120, 128–9
Russia, immigration from 28–30, 82,
    152–3

Salt, Titus 86
Salvation Army 149
Second World War 46, 53
settlement disputes 207–9
Society of Friends (Quakers) 146–9
Society of Genealogists 5
  apprenticeship indentures 222–4
  death or estate duty registers 221
  indexes of civil registration 101
  legal profession 241
  merchant seamen 130
  monumental inscriptions 38
  parish registers 193

universities 132
website 9
wills and probate 212
software 4
sport 89–90
stability
  –1550 261–4
  1550–1800 156, 173–7
  1800–1900 76–8
  1900– 32–3
Star Chamber 240
street indexes 110
surnames
  –1550 247, 261–4, 265–71, 280–81,
      282–3
  1550–1800 176–7, 184, 203, 229
  apprenticeship records 224–5
  census returns 114–15
  distributions 104–5
  getting started 3–4
  gravestones 38–9
  hearth tax 229, 232–3
  Jewish 153
  mobility 1900– 33
  origins 265–71
  parish registers 203
  poll taxes 280–81, 282–3
  protestation returns 235
surveys, manorial 277–9
synagogue records 153

taxation
  see also Inland Revenue
  –1550 264, 280–83
  1550–1800 227–33
  death or estate duty 221
  hearth tax returns 176–7, 185–6, 229–33
  land tax 227–8
  poll taxes 264, 280–83
  window tax 228
tenure 178–9, 276
Territorial Army 52
Thompson, Flora 64
tithe awards 134–7
title deeds 242–3
towns
  –1550 258–60
  1550–1800 158–60
  1800–1900 58–61
  1900– 18–20, 21
  public cemeteries 40
trade directories, 1800–1900 116–19
trade unions 143

transportation (penal) 144, 184

United States 79–81
universities 132
University of Surrey Roehampton 230
urbanization 57, 58–61, 77

visiting cards 41

wages 24–5
Wales
   see also National Library of Wales

surnames 247, 269
War Graves Commission, Debt of Honour
   Register 53
war memorials, First World War 53
War Office records (WO) 49–52, 122–7
wars 126–7
Wesleyan Methodists 148–9
wills 211–21
window tax 228
women
   census returns 114
   work 24–5, 26, 64, 67, 71

Women's Auxiliary Army Corps 51
woollen industry 67–8
work
   1550–1800 185–9
   1800–1900 59–71, 142–3
   1900– 22–7
workhouses 28, 91, 138–41, 210
working class 14–15, 83, 84–6

yeomen 170, 179, 185

Zulu War 127

THE LEICESTER AND HITC...